Can the School Build a New Social Order?

Can the School Build a New Social Order?

LOUIS EMMERIJ

Elsevier Scientific Publishing Company

Amsterdam · London · New York 1974

ELSEVIER SCIENTIFIC PUBLISHING COMPANY
335 JAN VAN GALENSTRAAT
P.O. BOX 211, AMSTERDAM, THE NETHERLANDS

AMERICAN ELSEVIER PUBLISHING COMPANY
52 VANDERBILT AVENUE
NEW YORK, NEW YORK 10017, U.S.A.

Library of Congress Card Number: 73-85221

ISBN 0-444-41153-4

Elsevier Scientific Publishing Company, Jan van Galenstraat 335, Amsterdam

Printed in The Netherlands

Educational Policy, Planning and Administration

Contents

Introduction

This book is primarily about the effect of education on people's life chances, and secondarily about educational policy and planning as a means to relate education more systematically and more flexibly to societal and individual needs as these are now emerging in the 1970's. In the process of looking at educational development patterns over the past fifteen years or so, we were quite naturally led to examine what economists, sociologists, psychologists and educators had to say about educational policy goals, educational growth, educational planning and, of course, about what happens in the classroom. It is disturbing, but unfortunately normal, to note that these various disciplines pursued their investigations and queries in parallel and that, not unexpectedly in these circumstances, they have come up with a series of results and findings which, once related to each other, are not necessarily consistent.

This book has no methodological or technical pretences and has, therefore, not sought to impress readers with scores of learned footnotes in order to display the encyclopedic knowledge that went into its elaboration. If the book has any pretences, they are educational policy oriented. Parts One and Two are retrospective and rather descriptive. Part Three is prospective and rather analytical. In Part One we review the major trends in educational development during the 1950s and 1960s, and present in passing a clinical case of incipient paranoia. We show that this period can be summarised, and certainly not in the field of education alone, by the four words "more of the same". Educational expansion and quantitative growth did not bring with them qualitative growth in education, nor any meaningful changes in methods, aims and structures of education, and therefore did not contribute in any way to solving pressing problems such as equal educational opportunity. The economists, celebrating the renaissance of the economics of education during this period, did not do or propose anything against this "more of the same" approach, on the contrary. In Part Two we take a look at the educational planning experience during the past ten to fifteen years. The one striking fact in that domain is the divorce between the decision-making world on the one hand and the educational planning world on the other. We try to show that this is not only a result of the partial (in the sense of incomplete) nature of the planners' work and of their crude analytical tools, but also, and in particular, of organisational, human and, thus, psychological factors.

In Part Three we take a forward-looking view and discuss educational policy goals and strategies for the 1970s as well as the desirable and necessary policy-planning framework. We go to some lengths to explain why the present expansion patterns taking place in a sequential educational structure cannot possibly continue indefinitely and we present an alternative educational strategy. It is our thesis that this alternative is unavoidable for various reasons, not the least important of which is to avoid rendering to the term "educational explosion" its literal meaning . . . .

The book is based on a variety of background material, some of which is mentioned in the references. A good proportion of this material is based on OECD studies and the geographical coverage is almost exclusively confined to the OECD area. In other words, we are mainly concerned with the retrospective and prospective trends of education in the industrialised countries and we only touch marginally on the problems of the developing world. Liberal use has been made of the background material that was prepared for the 1970 OECD Conference on Policies for Educational Growth for which we were responsible. The book was written after we had spent about seven years with the OECD on problems related to the economics of education, educational planning and educational policy. To a certain extent, the book can be considered our testament, prepared just before we left the educational and manpower planning world for another world which may very well turn out to be Purgatory!

Thus, the book is an outgrowth of the work of many people with whom I worked during these OECD years. I would like to express my gratitude to only a few of them, namely, Ron Gass, Gareth Williams and Jean-Pierre Jallade. I would also like to mention Rob Hollister who can never stay in the same place for a long time but who has always kept in touch and has always been ready to give ideas and share in new and unorthodox ventures. Obviously, I have betrayed in this book most of the ideas I got from these people and many others, but that is the privilege of the individual author.

Part One

The Decade of Lost Opportunity?

I

Expectations and Outcome: A Retrospective View

To begin we shall present, firstly, a sample of quantitative and qualitative expectations which we personally consider fairly typical for those held in the 1950s and early 1960s. Secondly, we shall attempt to compare those expectations with the actually observed development of education during the 1950s and 1960s.

1. The Expectations at the Beginning of the 1960s

The expectations quantified

One of the more interesting documents for our present purpose is a paper presented to the OECD Washington Conference on Economic Growth and Investment in Education, held in October 1961. The paper is called *Targets for Education in Europe in 1970* and was written by Ingvar Svennilson in association with Friedrich Edding and Lionel Elvin. It states right from the start that educational policy, within general national policy, has two main objects: to meet the demands of individuals for their own development, and to meet the needs of society for its general development. The authors go on to say that "free choice may have its advantages even if it leads to a situation where the number of students in a particular field exceeds the forecast of minimum demand, a forecast which can be made with a fair degree of accuracy." These quotations are interesting insofar as they put the emphasis on the so-called social demand for education (demands of individuals) and the manpower requirements (the needs of society). The debate around the social demand approach and the manpower approach to educational planning would run high during the 1960s. We will have more to say about this in Part Two. It is significant that the authors state these two — and only these two -- priority objectives in the way they do, significant for the tone of the decade to come (remember we are in 1961). However, it is heartening that the complementary relationship between these two approaches, based on the two mentioned objectives, is clearly stated and in this respect later years would do much to obscure the picture.

As to the rate-of-return approach, here too the authors have their opinion and a policy conclusion readily available: "All the indications are that private returns on investment in prolonged education are high. But they represent only a part of the additional social return. This is an important reason why society as a whole should contribute to investment in education." Somewhat later in their report we find a very important paragraph:

> Lastly, we must not forget that investment and productivity are after all not ends in themselves, but means to a better and fuller life. If education has not been too narrowly "economic," the generations educated and trained to meet the needs of a growing economy will have developed tastes and interests which will in due course be reflected in a further demand for education both for themselves and for their children. If our society is to offer a full and satisfying life, it is of the greatest importance that tastes and interests should be cultured and not solely concerned with "productivity." Ultimately, quality in education means quality in individual and social life. In the long run and from a broad viewpoint, there is no inherent reason why there should be a conflict between the concept of education as a means to a better and fuller life, and the concept that tests the value of education by its economic returns (page 35).

Having made their bow to what is now called the "quality of life" (one of the authors, Lionel Elvin, is an educator), the paper proceeds to deal with the "logistics of balanced (educational) expansion." It is worthwhile to summarise the author's presentation of this problem because they present under this heading the basic model which they use for their educational forecasts up to 1970. The interest of doing so is increased because much of the subsequent educational forecasting to be carried out during the 1960s has followed this basic model. The best way to present it is through the following three definition equations:

$$U = S \times C = P \times e \times C \qquad (1)$$

where U stands for total educational expenditure on an age group; S stands for students; C stands for cost per student; P stands for a specific age-group; and e stands for enrolment ratio.

$$C = t \times W \times (1 + k) \qquad (2)$$

where t stands for the ratio of teachers to students; W for the average annual salary per teacher; and $(1 + k)$ for the relation of total cost per pupil to teacher cost per pupil.

From the above two equations it follows that:

$$U = P \times e \times t \times W \times (1 + k) \qquad (3)$$

Thus, the Washington Educational Model (WEM) includes a demographic variable (P); evidence on the proportion of each age-group enrolled in the educational system (e); the teacher - student ratio (t) in order to deduce the number of teaching staff from the number of students ($P \times e$); evidence on teacher salaries (W); and evidence on other-than-teacher expenditures (k). After discussing each of these factors the authors present their "iron law of educational expenditure" which can be expressed in the following terms:

> It is reasonable to assume that, in the long run, teacher salaries will not lag behind the growth of national output per head; it is also reasonable to assume that costs other than teacher salaries will not diminish in relation to the teacher wage bill. If these two assumptions are granted, expenditure on education will rise faster than national output, as enrolment and teacher - pupil ratios have positive income elasticity. The "law" is modified by changes in the age-distribution of the population. It is valid *a fortiori* if the student age-groups rise faster than the total population (pages 43—44).

In working out their targets for the sixties the report states:

> To a large extent, however, national plans are incomplete or non-existent. Our projections had, therefore, to be based mostly on other considerations. The projection of education development in Europe presented here is thus a hybrid of forecasting and policy recommendations. It is in the nature of a model which comes as close to reality as our limited knowledge of educational systems in such a large number of countries allows. In working out these projections we have been guided by the line of thought running throughout this study. It is founded on the basic belief and assumption that more and better education for more people is desirable in itself and is at the same time one of the most important factors in economic growth. It is assumed that this belief will have an increasing influence on national policies in the decade ahead (page 82).

In fixing their targets, a low alternative as well as a high alternative is presented. The *low alternative* assumes no extraordinary effort, in fact, not much more effort than in the recent past. It assumes that current expenditure will on the whole increase *pari passu* with average real income, and that enrolment ratios in countries lagging behind other countries which are on a similar economic level will rise relatively more, while student - teacher ratios will remain the same as in the base year. The *high alternative* reflects what is regarded as a reasonable maximum effort. In this projection all countries, whether lagging behind or being in advance of others, will make an extraordinary effort, bearing in mind that there is an upper limit to what can be achieved in such a short period as a decade. The authors add: "It takes time to expand the number of teachers, to organise teaching institutions and to plan and to erect new buildings; the supply of teachers is often the most difficult bottleneck impeding the expansion of education. A deterioration in the quality of teachers may be too high a price to pay for a rapid increase in the number of students. The more ambitious national plans fall within the range of this high alternative."

The authors then proceed to a rather general discussion about each of the variables mentioned above. Thus they discuss the basis of their forecasts of population trends, enrolment ratios and student numbers, teachers and student - teacher ratios, and expenditure. We will not here reproduce the actual results of these forecasts. Some of them will be presented later in this chapter when we compare the expectations with the outcome. We will restrict ourselves to presenting some general conclusions of the forecasts. In the high alternative, total expenditure on education in the OEEC area in 1970 would reach 4% of GNP, as against 3.2% in the base year (1958). As for the supply of teachers, which in many countries was the real bottleneck, their number will have to increase, for the first age-group (5-14), by an average of 28%, except in the Mediterranean countries where the rise is assumed to be 40%. For the second age group (15-19), the high alternative assumes an average increase in teacher numbers in the OEEC area of 110% (the low alternative being 63%), with increases up to 150% in some countries. For the third age-group (20-24) the high alternative implies an increase in teaching staff of 88%, the low alternative being 45%. The report ends with the following statement: "It can thus be seen clearly that, viewed against the background of achievements in the recent past, the targets for 1970 do not appear unreasonable. Given the precondition of steady economic growth, the OEEC countries can undertake with confidence the expansion and improvement of their education systems in the coming decade" (page 97).

Expectations based on inferences from the economics and the sociology of education

The preceding discussion has concentrated on a specific attempt at the beginning of the 1960s to forecast alternative educational developments over the decade. This attempt was made in quantitative terms coming up with figures concerning the future development of students, teachers and expenditures. But over and beyond these concrete and quantified expectations, there are more general, qualitative expectations which the discussions of the past decade about the role of education in the economy and in society at large have aroused on the part of the general public. Several of these broad expectations are set out below.

There is first of all the expectation that a re-allocation of a country's investment leading to an increase in education will increase the rate of growth of the national product. This expectation might be based upon the results of (i) the rate-of-return approach which showed that rates of return on investment in education were higher than those obtainable on other (private and social) forms of investment; and (ii) the results of the residual approach which tended to give major credit to increasing levels of education in the explanation of economic growth rates. We shall have more to say about these various approaches in Chapter II.

The second broad expectation is that higher expenditures on education will be associated with less inequality in the distribution of income. The basis for this expectation is the belief that increased expenditure would provide educational opportunities to less privileged social groups, and that positive rates of return on education are reasonably uniform across social classes. There are indeed some strong assumptions here. One of them is that the expected educational expansion can bring equal educational opportunity with it automatically. In the words of sociologist Halsey, summarising a Conference held in June 1961, in his *Ability and Educational, Opportunity*: "As we have repeatedly noted, economic development has profoundly modified the context of social forces in which the educational process goes on and changing forms of social stratification are among the most obvious aspects of contemporary economic prosperity. One characteristic feature of these developments is that, as first primary and then secondary education has expanded, so social class wastage in the traditional form of lack of adequate educational opportunity has been, so to say, pushed further and further up into the higher stages of education" (page 32). Another assumption is that "educational expansion leads to a reduction of traditional income differentials and that just as educational opportunity influences the distribution of income so does the latter react to alter the social distribution of demand for education and indirectly the content of education: and so, through a complex interaction, educational policy is brought into the total process of allocating 'life chances' between individual members of society" (pages 22-23).

And finally, for positive rates of return on education to be reasonably uniform across social class, it must be assumed that "innate ability" is *not* highly correlated with social origins.

A third expectation which could be implied from the literature is that increased expenditure on the education of any given group will increase the amount of measured academic achievement of that group. This is, of course, the basic expectation which links educational expenditures with the results of the rate-of-return approach and with the second expectation. Additional financial outlays on education lead to educational expansion, which leads to equality of educational opportunity through higher academic achievements. The economic rewards of a higher academic achievement in turn are reflected in a higher earned income of the individual.

At this early stage in our discussion there is no need to argue how widespread these broad expectations are or were, or to set out the necessary qualifications to make them acceptable to research scholars in the field. However, we may already point out that the above expectations are those upon which most policymakers have operated and if they are misleadingly simple, then the policies which they reflect, and which we will review later, have also been too simplistic.

Concluding remarks on the expectations

The above selection of expectations implies a double risk. In the first place we may have been biased in the expression of the expectations simply because this is written in the beginning of the 1970s and not in 1960. We have tried to avoid this bias by sticking closely to existing texts written some ten to fifteen years ago. There is a second risk in the selection of the texts themselves. Our guiding principle has been, as already mentioned, to select those texts and those expectations that can be considered "typical", in the sense that they have turned out to be in the mainstream of attention of educational policy-makers and planners. Obviously there have been some other "sounds" — which according to our choice must logically be classified as "dissident views" — and it is fair to quote some of them. For example, in Halsey's review of the above-mentioned Conference we read: "Professor Dahrendorf pointed out that, though the structure of educational systems showed immense variety, wastage of talent was endemic, and he went on to conclude that the reduction of wastage *was to be sought more in social than in educational reform*" (page 38, italics ours). In a well-known article by C. Arnold Anderson, "A Skeptical Note on Education and Mobility", which appeared in 1961, the author concludes that

> education is but one of many factors influencing mobility and it may be far from a dominant factor. To say that its efficiency is low in this respect measured on an absolute scale, however, is not necessarily to say it "should be" higher. Education has multiple functions and preparation for a vocation is only one of these. In the three countries for which data exists, mobility independent of schooling occurs frequently. Because of the different classifications used in the three sets of data one cannot draw explicit comparisons, though one might infer that education has more influence in the United States. Even with more equal distribution of educational opportunities, the independent operation of "intelligence" will probably damp the impact of schooling upon individual careers (page 176).

2. Expectations and Outcome

We shall begin with a quantitative comparison of some forecasts, based on the Washington "model", with the observed development; this comparison of numbers will be followed by the, more important to our mind, evaluation of how the more policy oriented qualitative expectations have stood up to the evolution of events.

Quantitative comparisons of forecasts and outcome

From the series of definition equations presented earlier, it can be seen that the final objective of the Washington forecasting "model" was to estimate future educational expenditures. It did so through a "chain calculation" in which demographic forecasts, forecasts of enrolment ratios, pupil—teacher ratios and teachers' salaries entered. It is, therefore, interesting to start with the end of the chain and to examine how the forecasts of educational expenditures presented at the 1961 Washington Conference compare with the actual development observed during the 1950s and 1960s. The available evidence is presented in Table I-1. The figures bring out clearly that growth in educational expenditures was considerable in all countries under observation: rates of increase exceeded 10% per annum in half the countries, and only a few had rates below 7%. In passing, it must be noted, that the observed trends as shown in the table refer to public expenditure on education; however, additional evidence, not shown in the table, indica-

TABLE I-1
Observed Trends in Educational Expenditures Compared to Washington Forecasts — Average Annual Growth Rates

Country	Period	Total public education expenditure	Current public education expenditure	Forecast 1957—1970 of Washington Conference	
				Low hyp.	High hyp.
Germany, F.R.	1950—66	9.3	8.9	5.1	6.8
Austria	1950—54 1955—67	12.0 7.9	11.6 9.1	3.0	4.6
Belgium	1958—67	8.6	9.2	3.4	5.1
Denmark	1955—66	11.4	11.7	3.7	5.3
Spain	1950—68	12.8	10.3	6.0	9.2
Finland	1950—67	7.5	8.3	—	—
France	1952—67	11.0	10.7	5.4	7.0
Greece	1950—66	—	12.2	4.0	5.5
Ireland	1950—65	5.7	4.4	1.7	2.8
Italy	1950—65	13.2	12.1	5.9	7.3
Norway	1950—67	7.4	8.5	3.7	5.2
Netherlands	1950—68	11.4	11.5	3.4	5.1
Portugal	1950—65	6.5	5.9	3.3	5.4
England & Wales	1950—66	6.8	6.6	3.7	4.3
Sweden	1962—66	11.4	10.8	2.7	4.8
Switzerland	1955—64	7.9	7.5	3.3	5.1
Yugoslvaia	1952—67	17.5	17.9	7.8	10.4
United States	1955—67	8.2	8.8	4.5	5.6
Canada	1954—65	13.5	11.2	5.7	6.9
Japan	1950—65	10.2	9.7	4.6	5.8

Source: *Trends in Educational Expenditure in OECD Countries Since 1950*, OECD, Paris, 1971.

TABLE I-2

Enrolments (in millions)	1958	1970
Age-group 5—14	78.0	90.4—93.0
Age-group 15—19	13.6	22.3—25.0
Age-group 20—24	2.4	3.9— 4.9

tes that, if private expenditure were also included, this would *not* diminish the rate of increase, on the contrary.

This development has clearly surpassed the forecasts made at the Washington Conference. For purposes of comparison, the average annual growth rates for current expenditures on education between 1957 and 1970 were calculated in line with the low and high hypotheses of the Washington Conference Report. The growth rates corresponding to these forecasts are given in the last two columns of Table I-1. It can be seen that the highest assumed level has been exceeded by all countries. These are not small differences, but substantial ones, the more so if it is considered that this comparison is based on average *annual* rates of increase, and that the base year for most of the observed trends goes frequently back to the beginning of the 1950s. If we disregard errors in demographic forecasts, the reasons for this considerable underestimation of the "upper limit to what can be achieved in such a short period as a decade" should lie in (i) errors in the forecast of student numbers, and/or (ii) errors in the forecasts of pupil - teacher ratios, and/or (iii) errors in the estimate of real salary increases of teachers.

Taking the Washington forecast of enrolments first, Table I-2 presents the base year and target year (low and high alternatives) figures as presented in the report by Svennilson, Edding and Elvin.

The above figures include all OECD countries, except Japan and Finland. In terms of annual rates of increase these figures correspond to:

1.2 — 1.5% for the 5-14 age group;
4.2 — 5.2% for the 15-19 age group; and
4.1 — 6.0% for the 20-24 age group.

Comparing these forecasts with what actually happened is a haphazard exercise because of the clumsy categories selected by the authors: the three-age-groups distinguished quite clearly do not exactly correspond to the primary, secondary and tertiary education levels. Between 1958 and the end of the 1960s, primary education in the OECD countries has grown at a rate of 1.1% per year, secondary education at a rate of 4.6% per year, and higher education has grown at an annual rate of 8.0%. This would mean that it has only been for higher education enrolments that the forecast has underestimated the actual development. Using data by level of education and by age-group — available for several countries — it has been possible to confirm that on the whole the observed developments of enrolments within the first two age groups have been within the range set by the low and high alternatives of the Washington forecast, but that the expansion of higher education has gone beyond the high alternative.

All in all, the errors in the forecasts of student numbers are not such as to explain, by themselves, the wide divergences noted in Table I-1. To the extent that the forecasts of numbers of pupils were nearer to reality than the financial forecasts, it would appear that the other factors pushing up expenditures were badly underestimated. Moving therefore to the second factor, the estimate of pupil - teacher ratios, the Svennilson report assumed for the high alternative (we will disregard the low alternative for obvious reasons) that the pupil - teacher ratio for the first age-group would on average be reduced from 29.4 to 27.0; for the second age-group from 18.4 to 17.1, and that this ratio would hardly be changed for the third age-group: from 13.9 in the base year to 14.0 in 1970. These assumptions are not in contradiction with the paragraph we shall devote to developments in teaching staff in Chapter III. It will be emphasised there that, particularly in higher education, deteriorations in student - staff ratios could only be avoided by downward shifts in the qualification structure of the teaching body. However, this phenomenon exercises a downward bias on educational expenditures and cannot, therefore, explain Table I-1.

We must logically conclude that the main responsibility of the discrepancy lies in the last factor of the Washington "model" chain: the translation of real resources into monetary resources, which poses the problem of real wage increases of the teaching and administrative staff. The Washington Report assumed that "in real terms, teachers' salaries and other instructional expenditure will rise *pari passu* with GNP *per capita* (page 91). As will be shown in Chapter III, teachers' salaries have increased faster than was frequently believed and we probably hold here the key to the observed discrepancies in Table I-1.

There are several reasons why we have somewhat insisted on the Washington forecast. Firstly, it is a relatively complete forecast in the sense that it does not only deal with student numbers, but also with teaching staff and expenditures. Secondly, it is one of the few forecasts which has not been too far off the mark with respect to the estimated number of pupils and students. This fact, in turn, has thrown a clear light on the sensitivity of the final result of the forecast to the estimates of pupil - teacher ratios and real salary increases. How much worse would these final results have been had the enrolment estimates also been very much in error. Thirdly, since real wage increases and, in particular, the pupil - teacher ratio are instrument variables, i.e., they are to a large extent under the control of the policy-makers, the forecast is also a good illustration of how important it is to make the decision-making process explicit. Fourthly, the forecast also illustrates that, when popular pressure is combined with political will, much more is possible than one expects "in such a short time period as a decade."

In Table I-3 a number of *national* forecasts (of student numbers only) are presented, most of which were made at around 1960. It shows very clearly how persistently the so-called social demand forecasts have underestimated the actual development during the 1960s, underestimates which are often quite considerable and which frequently occur already a few years after the forecasts were made. In the few cases where the table shows that the forecasts have overestimated the actually observed number of students, this is either the result of manpower forecasts (Spain), or caused by wishful thinking with respect to the scientific and technological subjects (France).

The table is sufficiently clear and "one-sided" so that, rather than commenting on the situation in each individual country, the general question must be asked why "social demand" forecasts have so consistently underestimated the growth in enrolments. Gareth Williams, in his paper "Educational Policies, Plans and Forecasts During the Nineteen-Sixties and -Seventies," begins to give an answer to this question. He argues that the reasoning behind the use of trend projections of enrolment ratios is based on the assumption that at any point in time a certain proportion of each age group of boys and girls have the "propensity" to be in school. This propensity is a combination of ability to pursue courses at the level of education in question and desire to do so. Since enrolment ratios have increased for several decades, this propensity to be in school is assumed to increase with time. However, it is not at all clear that the enrolment ratio of any age-group measured at any particular point in time is a very good measure of the propensity to be in school or the "social demand" for educa-

TABLE I-3

Comparison of Enrolment and Graduates, Forecasts and Actual Outcome: OECD Countries

Country	Sources of forecast	Year forecast made	What forecast	Projection year	No. of years after forecast	Projected figure	Actual figures	% over-estimate or under-estimate
Belgium	"Prévision des populations scolaires, Nouvelles projections jusqu'en 1970-71"	1959	Enrolments in general secondary schools (lower level)	1965/66	6	175,238	197,270	—13%
	idem	1959	*idem* (upper level)	1965/66	6	75,000	85,349	—14%
	idem	1960	Enrolments in technical and vocational secondary schools (lower level)	1965/66	5	205,393	244,488	—19%
	idem	1960	*idem* (upper level)	1965/66	5	49,459	71,279	—44%
	idem	1960	Grads. of general secondary (upper level)	1963/64	3	16,053	20,834	—30%
	idem	1960	Grads. of technical and vocational schools (upper level)	1962/63	2	13,181	11,890	+10%
Britain	Robbins Report	1962	Enrolments in H.E.	1967	5	328,000	376,000	—15%
	Robbins Report	1962	Enrolments in universities	1967	5	197,000	200,000	— 2%
	Robbins Report	1961	Qualified school-leavers (2 or more 'A' levels)	1967	5	63,000	79,000	—25%
France	IV Plan	1960/61	Enrolments, university faculties	1964/65	4	291,000	341,000	—16%
	IV Plan	1960/61	Science faculties, enrolments	1964/65	4	117,000	106,000	+ 9%
	V Plan	1964/65	Enrolments, university faculties	1967/68	3	525,000	499,000	+5%
Germany	Academic Council	1959	Recommended enrolments in technical universities	1966	7	51,200	54,300	— 6%
	Academic Council	1959	Recommended enrolments in science and technology	1966	7	103,000	139,000	—35%
	Academic Council	1959	Recommended enrolments in economics and social science	1966	7	22,000	44,000	—100%

	Standing Conference of Ministers of Education of Länder	1961	Enrolments in non-academic secondary education (excludes secondary level classes in Volkschule)	1967	6	744,000	830,000	−12%
	idem	1961	Enrolments in Gymnasia	1967	6	911,000	1,124,000	−23%
	idem	1962	Enrolments in Realschule	1967	6	557,000	640,000	−12%
	Academic Council	1959	German students in universities	1966	7	225,000	241,000	− 7%
	Academic Council	1959	Recommended enrolments in existing universities	1966	7	193,000	263,000	−34%
Italy	Relazione della Commissione di Indagine sullo Stata e sullo Sviluppo della Pubblica Istruzione	1961	Graduates of higher schools	1965/66	4	43,015	42,310	+ 2%
		1961	Graduates of technical institutes	1965/66	4	70,975	73,004	− 3%
		1961	Graduates of teacher training institutes	1965/66	4	29,600	31,358	− 6%
Japan	"Educational Planning in relation to Economic Planning in Japan"	1960	Enrolments in lower secondary schools	1964/65	4	6,489,000	6,475,693	+0.2%
		1960	Enrolments in upper secondary schools	1965/66	5	4,580,000	5,073,882	−11%
		1963	Graduates of upper secondary schools	1965/66	2	1,160,000	1,160,075	0
Portugal	OECD (MRP)	1960	Enrolments in general, technical and teacher training secondary schools	1964/65	4	296,700	297,252	−0.2%
Spain	OECD (MRP)	1961	Enrolments in general secondary schools (lower, upper and pre-university)	1966/67	5	868,300	929,589	− 7%
	idem	1961	Enrolments in higher education	1966/67	5	92,300	105,370	−14%
	idem	1961	Graduates of general secondary schools (upper courses)	1966/67	5	49,000	35,702	+27%
	idem	1961	Graduates of higher education	1966/67	5	8,900	6,924	+22%
Turkey	OECD (MRP)	1963	Enrolments in higher education	1965/66	2	93,900	98,684	− 5%
Yugoslavia	5-year plan, 1966-70	1965	Enrolments in higher education	1967	5	328,000	376,000	−15%

Source: *The Development of Educational Planning*, OECD, Paris, 1971.

tion by persons in that age-group at that point in time. This is so for two reasons: (i) there is an interdependency between the number of places available at a given place and at a particular point in time, and the number of people asking entry and being admitted. This is simply another illustration of the inter-relationship between supply and demand; (ii) moreover, and going further, many children and adolescents do not even attempt to apply because they estimate their chances of success *a priori* as nil.

This begins to give us some insight into the question why "social demand" projections have so consistently underestimated the growth in enrolments. There was during the 1950s an increase in the desire to take advantage of educational opportunities. This meant that there was constant pressure on the number of places available. This pressure for places coincided both with the view of looking at education as an investment for economic growth, and with a growing political and social belief in equality of educational opportunities which it was assumed expansion would bring about. Accordingly, attempts were made to provide sufficient places to satisfy the demand. A variety of more or less sophisticated methods of time-series analysis has been used to estimate the extent of this growing demand, which in all essence amount to the forecast of enrolment ratios as in the first step of the Washington model. However, this in effect simply meant a forecast of the number of places that happened to have been available during the preceding few years.

Thus the forecasts were made, and were often acted upon in the sense that extra resources were provided. The effect was rather like removing the cork from a champagne bottle. As more places became available more children realised that it was worth their while trying to reach the upper levels of secondary and higher education. The doctrine of promoting educational opportunity meant that more pupils were squeezed into available places. The more places that were created to alleviate the new overcrowding, the more this stimulated further increases in demand, which in turn caused further overcrowding. The problem shows analogies with the one urban traffic planners have. The more roads that are built, the more people prefer to use private cars instead of public transport for their journeys to the city centres. As in educational planning, they are plagued by the problem that the more roads they build the more traffic jams they have. As far as education is concerned, the general lesson is that much more explicit account needs to be taken of the interaction of demand for places and the number of places available, and of the effect of time-lags in constructing forecasting models.

The above evidence and considerations do not mean that the education forecasts have had no effect. The least one can say is that they have prepared public opinion and policy-makers to expect considerable quantitative enrolment growth. What it does mean is that nobody ten or fifteen years ago expected the increase in scale to be what it has turned out to be. In 1961, a meeting took place in the Abbaye de Royaumont organised by the French committee working on Frank Bowles' study on "Access to University Education". Those present were educators, economists, education and manpower planners. With a lot of courage some of those present advanced the possibility that in 1970 there would be 500,000 students in French universities. The assumption was received with awe and disbelief. But, at the end of 1970, there were about 700,000 students crushing the universities of France!

The evidence in relation to the "qualitative" expectations

The basic idea implicit in the human capital theory developed over the past decade is that expenditure on education produces an output in the form of human capital. There may, of course, be other outputs such as discoveries or inventions, that constitute physical capital, but here we concentrate on the student as the recipient of the investment. In this context, the "technology" of the educational system is expressed as the relationship between such inputs as teachers and school characteristics, and the "educational output" in the form of recipients of education. One of the obvious problems is measuring the "educational output" in terms that do not simply count the number of years of school attendance. One approach is to measure the "output" of human capital in value terms, through a calculation of the present value of the money earnings from that asset (the additional years of schooling) over the life time of the owner. Studies using this type of approach are the so-called rate of return calculations. Another approach to measuring "educational output" relies on test scores of academic or school achievement — an approach rather analogous to measuring output in terms of physical units, such as horsepower.

One would expect to find a roughly positive relationship between school and teacher characteristics (as inputs) and the two types of measure of "educational output." The rates of return studies — based on cross-section evidence on age, education and personal income — indicate that investment in education yields a substantial positive rate of return. A large number of cases lend support to the broad expectations that more money spent on education would increase the growth rate of GNP. However, as already indicated, these studies compare additional years of schooling with additional earnings. They do not, therefore, include characteristics of the schools in which the individuals were trained. In contrast, those studies which set out to measure the independent effect of the school and teacher variables on the "educational output" have used the "internal" measure of output, namely test scores. These two types of study have been designed by different people, with different backgrounds and interests, and asking different questions. In the first case, economists asked the question what the contribution of education to economic growth was. Thus, they had to adopt an "external" measure of educational output and they opted for the differential life-stream earnings attached to groups of people with different levels of educational attainment. In the other case, sociologists, psychologists and educators were interested in the impact of differences in school and teacher inputs on school achievement of pupils and students. They were not asking the further question what impact differences in school achievement had on "life chances" and thus, among others, on the economy, via the individual's occupational career. These two approaches, coming up each with their own sets of evidence, have lived an independent life and have never really been confronted and subjected to a consistency analysis.

What do these second type of studies show us? It may be said, though admittedly we generalise here, that these studies indicate that when non-school variables (such as social background or, more generally, the characteristics which children have acquired before entering school) have been controlled for, virtually no relationship can be found between achievement and those school characteristics which have traditionally been thought to be significant, such as expenditures, pupil-teacher ratios, classroom size, etc. Of the many studies available on the subject, one of the best known is the so-called Coleman Report, *Equality of Educational Opportunity*. Its conclusion of the section concerned with the relation of school factors to achievement deserves to be quoted in full, because it sums up neatly what most other studies take longer to say, although they say it nevertheless:

Of the many implications of this study of school effects on achievement, one appears to be of over-riding importance. This is the implication that stems from the following results taken together:

(1) The great importance of family background for achievement.

(2) The fact that the relation of family background to achievement does not diminish over the years of school.

(3) The relatively small amount of school-to-school variation that is not accounted for by differences in family background, indicating the small independent effect of variations in school facilities, curriculum and staff upon achievement.

(4) The small amount of variance in achievement explicitly accounted for by variations in facilities and curriculum.

(5) Given the fact that no school factors account for much variation in achievement, teachers' characteristics account for more than any other.

(6) The fact that the social composition of the student body is more highly related to achievement, independently of the student's own social background, than is any school factor.

(7) The fact that attitudes such as a sense of control of the environment, or a belief in the responsiveness of the environment, are extremely highly related to achievement, but appear to be little influenced by variations in school characteristics.

Taking all these results together, one implication stands out above all: That schools bring little influence to bear on a child's achievement that is independent of his background and general social context; and that this very lack of an independent effect means that the inequalities imposed on children by their home, neighbourhood, and peer environment are carried along to become the inequalities with which they confront adult life at the end of school. For equality of educational opportunity through the schools must imply a strong effect of schools that is independent of the child's immediate social environment, and that strong independent effect is not present in American schools (page 325).

This is a basic and extremely important result, but several qualifications must be made at this point. The above conclusions obviously do not mean that the school does not bring anything to the individual over and above his characteristics acquired before the school period, and which continue to exercise their influence during his school career. However, they do mean that gaps in educational achievement observed at the beginning of the school period, and caused by differences in family and social environment characteristics, do not narrow as the individuals advance in their school career; on the contrary, in many cases the achievement gap between pupils from different social backgrounds may even increase. It is in this sense that the independent effect of the school and teacher variables (in short, of the school) is very small in relation to social background variables and the influence of the peer group. Furthermore, there are many theoretical, conceptual and analytical difficulties which arise when one attempts to explore the relationships between school characteristics and school achievement. Most of these studies, and in particular the Coleman Report, have come under heavy professional attack for this reason.

It will be clear that the translation of educational theories into quantifiable relationships is extremely difficult. An *operational* theory of the educational process does not yet exist. Not only do we not have an adequate theory of feasible pedagogical alternatives, but neither do we have a theory of administrative choice by which alternatives are selected or by which we might infer the normative significance of observed allocations of educational resources. In more simple language, the main problems appear to lie in finding, or measuring accurately, many of the theoretical variables, particularly in terms of the time sequence in which they enter the model. Thus, the models used in the Coleman type studies appear, in retrospect, to be too crudely specified to isolate adequately the relationships between school characteristics and school achievement. However, these rather simple models have been the basis for most large-scale studies of the educational system. These studies do reasonably reflect beliefs of policy-makers about the characteristics of schools which affect achievement; policy-makers formulate and discuss educational policy as though the variables selected in these studies were those which determine "educational output." To this extent, these studies do constitute a test of assumptions upon which most policy-makers have operated; if the relationships tested are misleadingly simple, then the policies which they reflect have also been too simplistic.

The finding that current educational systems do not exercise strong enough an independent effect to compensate for initial gaps in school achievement caused by differences in family and social environment factors explains to a large extent another finding, namely that the tremendous expansion in enrolments has caused very little change in social disparities in educational participation. Although everyone is getting more in absolute terms, in relative terms the situation is very much the same as before. On the basis of an OECD statistical survey which reviews evidence from nineteen member countries (Nam, 1971), the situation may be summed up as follows:

(i) Considerable social selection takes place below the university level, especially at the secondary level. It favours the upper and middle classes, and thus creates a social differential in eligibility for higher education. Time trends show no tendency for this selection to lessen, except in countries where participation rates in primary and secondary education are exceptionally high.

(ii) Young people from upper classes are highly over-represented in a statistical sense in higher education — over-represented that is, in relation to the proportion of the same classes in the total labour force.

(iii) Young people from the middle classes are also over-represented among students, though less so than those from the upper classes; and young people from the lower classes are under-represented in the student body.

(iv) Educational disparities, as measured by the index of dissimilarity[1], are slightly narrowing in the majority of countries, but only very slightly.

(v) An increase in the participation rate per 1000 active males of the age-group 45-54[2] was observed for all social classes, but the gain for the lowest class was appreciably smaller than that for the highest class — which suggests that disparities have been widening in the recent past. This conclusion is based on the evidence of a few countries only.

(vi) Differences in participation in particular academic disciplines by socio-economic category, though exhibiting a rather broad selection of academic fields by students of all classes, show a definite tendency by students to choose a field closely related to their social background.

The limited scope of data on educational participation by social category does not allow for precise comparisons of social disparities between countries and over time, but the phenomenon is clearly universal. In almost every country reviewed, the opportunities for education are very great for children from the upper classes, good for those from the middle classes, and distinctly poor for those from the lower classes or with an agricultural background. The differences may be greater in some countries than in others, but in most cases, the similarities are more marked than the dissimilarities. In short, social differences in education participation seem to be a pervasive and constant characteristic of educational structures in all countries. What change has taken place has been gradual and has not so far appreciably altered the above picture.

---

1 This index represents the total percentage of students or of the labour force which would have to shift to another socio-economic category to allow for equality of the two distributions.

2 Whereas the number of students from a given social group is normally known, the total age-group of the same social group is rarely available. That is why we have chosen the age-group 45—54 as giving a reasonably close approximation for a comparison of students with *all* young people of the same age-group, because persons in this age bracket are most likely to have children of university age.

All this brings us to the problem of the effect of increased education on the distribution of income. In our earlier statement of initial expectations, it was assumed that less inequality of educational opportunity would imply less inequality in the distribution of income. Meade (1964) and Reder (1969) have pointed out that this is by no means certain. The outcome would depend on the relative importance of talent and training. As Reder observes: "The marginal return imputable to native talent, relative to that imputable to training, will surely vary as investment in training becomes greater and more widespread. As appropriately trained persons become more abundant, jobs which have paid well heretofore because of the great training required, but which require little native talent, will decline in earning power relative to those requiring greater degrees of talent." In simpler terms, Meade and Reder refer to the replacement of an "aristocracy" by a "meritocracy", the net effect of the income distribution being unclear. Moreover, Meade states "... in the past the spread of public elementary education in the developed countries has almost certainly been an important equalising factor. It has in essence been an investment with a high return, financed out of general taxation for the benefit of every citizen ... ." He goes on to point out that publicly supported higher education may have just the opposite effect. In a recent book, *Benefits, Costs and Finance of Public Higher Education*, W.L. Hansen and B.A. Weisbrod show that this possibility is in fact the case in the United States. What is most striking about their findings is that Meade's speculation holds for what had generally been supposed to be the most egalitarian system of public higher education in the world, that of the State of California. Thus, there is the distinct possibility that whereas public education at the early stages was an equalising force on the income distribution, at later stages of development, with extensive public higher education, it becomes just the reverse, costs of education being broadly shared by the taxpayers but benefits being captured primarily by the higher income groups.

These findings by Hansen and Weisbrod for the United States, which are corroborated by studies undertaken in European countries, suggest that indexes of educational inequality based solely on years of education may be misleading. It might be more relevant to utilise an index based upon the distribution of educational resources. Clearly, years of higher education cost more and, thus, although years of education may become less unequally distributed across the population, educational resources may well become

TABLE I-4
Index of Inequality in the Distribution of Educational Resources in the Labour Force in the United States

Year	Gini coefficients of distribution of educational resources *
1950	.789
1960	.806

* Years of education in the U.S. Labour Force were weighted by the 1949 costs of education (both direct and foregone earnings) drawn from Tables 1 and 2 of W.L. Hansen, "Total and Private Rates of Return to Investment in Schooling," *Journal of Political Economy*, 1963.

more unequally distributed. In order to check on this possibility, Table I-4 presents Gini coefficients for education in which the educational level attained is weighted by the cost of that education. Whereas Gini coefficients calculated on the distribution by educational years alone show a slight decline between 1950 and 1960, the data in the table indicate that, when account is taken of the differences in educational costs, the inequality in the distribution of educational resources in the labour force seems to have increased in the United States during the 1960s. The above considerations may go some way to explain the seemingly weak relationships between changes in the distribution of education in the population and in the labour force, and changes in the distribution of income, as shown by several empirical studies.

3. Concluding Remarks

These remarks will concentrate on the "qualitative" expectations rather than on the "expectations quantified". Indeed, the conclusions with respect to the latter are clear and straightforward: During the past ten to fifteen years the scale of education, particularly at its higher levels, has increased at a pace which nobody had expected or foreseen, let alone quantified and planned. We have advanced a hypothetical "model" to explain why most of the "scale forecasts" of the 1950s and 1960s have underestimated actual developments in enrolments.

As to the former, we propose the following tentative conclusions. Rates of return on investments in education have generally been found to be positive and greater than, or equal to, opportunity costs. This would seem to lend support to the expectations with respect to the effect of education on economic growth rates. The great expansion in enrolments, combined with the positive rate of return on education, led to the expectation of a lesser inequality in the distribution of income. The evidence on this point is not conclusive. Firstly, educational expansion has *not* led to significant changes in group disparities in educational participation, particularly at the higher levels. Secondly, even if one could obtain equal participation rates in education, this would be consistent with unequal occupational chances. We have shown elsewhere — in a study on "Occupational and Educational Structures of the Labour Force and Levels of Economic Development" (1970) — that "as more university graduates become available, the more they can be found in *all* occupational categories. As more people with complete secondary education become available, the more they go into the "lower" occupational categories." We will come back to these points in Part Three. Thirdly, because of the above points alone, it should not come as a surprise that there is a lack of a strong relationship between educational changes and income changes.

It is with respect to the third broad expectation — that increased expenditure on the education of any given group will increase the amount of measured school achievement of that group — that the available evidence is most ambiguous. School achievement seems to be much more determined by family and social background factors and the social composition of the student body, rather than by school and teacher factors. The criticisms raised with respect to the studies measuring relationships between school characteristics and school achievement should certainly make one cautious about interpreting their results. However, the failure of even the simpler studies thus far carried out to find such relationships is a fact which must give rise to scepticism with regard to conclusions based upon studies on the rate of return.

During the past period of educational growth a number of studies have been carried out concerning the various aspects of the educational system in the economic and social context: cost - benefit or rate-of-return studies; educational participation analysed by social groups; studies of occupation - education relationships as observed in the labour force; school characteristics - achievement studies of the type mentioned above; studies of levels of expenditure and sources of finance, etc. It is time to try to put these pieces into some sort of order so as to establish what it is one knows and does not know about the relationship of educational processes to the level and distribution of income, and to other social and economic features of a country. Are there not, for example, some necessary relationships between the rate-of-return findings, the distribution of income, and the shifts in the educational distribution of the population and the labour force? This whole aspect will be taken up in Part Three, but let us first turn to possible explanations of this mismatch between expectations and outcome.

II

A Case of Paranoia: The Strange Relationship Between Economists and Educators

1. The Renaissance of the Economics of Education

The proposition that the knowledge and skills embodied in the labour force have something to do with its productivity and consequently with economic growth is neither revolutionary nor profound. Economists such as Marshall and, particularly, Irving Fisher in his classic work on capital and income, had already drawn explicit attention to the link between physical and human capital. However, the inter-war period was characterised as far as economics is concerned, by a concentration on business cycle and short-term full-employment theory. When, after World War II, attention swung back to longer-term problems of economic development, the importance of the "human factor" was not immediately recognised.

Assistance to what were then called underdeveloped countries was conceived mainly in terms of investment in physical capital which resulted some years later in lengthy discussions about the so-called "absorptive capacity" of these countries. At the same time, it could be observed that the German Federal Republic with a seriously destroyed capital-stock was able to recover extremely rapidly, a recovery which to no small extent was a result of the skills and know-how of its population. It gradually began to dawn upon certain more imaginative economists, and others who still had time to read some of the classic authors, that the early post-war emphasis on investment in material capital in the methodology of economic planning might be mistaken and that more emphasis had to be given to the "quality" of labour inputs.

It was not until the end of the 1950s that a systematic effort began to attempt to establish a quantitative relationship between education and economic growth and that the economics of education was rediscovered. Looking back over the last decade one can distinguish several paths along which economists have undertaken their explorations. Some of them immediately chose a familiar path and addressed themselves to the question how much was being spent on education, how this total amount was distributed over the various levels and branches of education, and how educational expenditures and their allocation pattern within the educational sector had developed over time. Here the focus was, therefore, entirely on the cost side, or better and more restricted, on the expenditure side. Another group followed a direction which led further than the preceding one and investigated the costs as well as the benefits of education. This is the so-called rate-of-return to investments-in-education approach. Again another group stumbled on the economics of education via the bottleneck called "shortages of highly qualified personnel". These real or alleged shortages — particularly with respect to scientists, engineers and technicians — came to be considered as serious barriers on the road towards economic and technological progress particularly during the post-Sputnik era. The estimates of such future "shortages" or "needs" have led over the years to an ever more comprehensive methodological approach and to more complete and complex forecasts of the occupational and educational structures of the total and active population, an approach which ended up embracing the educational system at all its levels and branches. This came to be called the "manpower approach" to educational planning and policy problems. While these three groups cut their way uneasily through conceptual smoke screens and tumbled every once in a while into technical and statistical ditches, another small group walked majestically along the *voie royal* laid out for them by what some have called, an enthusiastic neoclassical vanguard. We refer, of course, to the work by economists to refine production function estimates through identification and quantification of additional causal components. This has been labelled the "residual approach."

Although, as mentioned in the Introduction, this book has no "technical" or "methodological" pretences, a few words need to be said about such issues from time to time for the comprehension of our conclusions. We will therefore say a little more about the above four groups.

The "residual approach" is based on the discovery that changes over time in capital and labour inputs alone did not entirely explain the changes observed in economic output. There was a "third" or "residual" factor which had to be held responsible for this unexpected difference which, it was thought, could not possibly fall from the blue sky. Thus, our economists set out to explain this residual, called immediately by one of them "a measure of our ignorance", by introducing additional causal variables, one of which reflects the changes in educational attainment embodied in the labour force. The residual includes, therefore, more than education alone (it also comprises management, technology, shifts from low to high productivity sectors, etc.). But even if it were possible to isolate the educational component, as has been attempted by E.F. Denison (1962) for example, this would not be of much operational value to serve as a guideline for educational policy given the aggregate character of the education variable in the production function. The bulk of this work has been carried out at the macro-economic level, and is of great interest to come to judgements as to global investment aspects of educational outlays, but it is not detailed and specific enough for educational policy purposes.

To give educational policy guidelines is precisely the aim of the manpower and the rate of return approaches. Let us say first a few words about the manpower approach. Given economic growth targets and their sectoral distribution, shifts in the occupational structure of the labour force at some future date are estimated: so many engineers, jurists, managers, technicians, skilled workers, etc., etc. The future occupational distribution thus estimated must be translated into educational equivalents and this, in turn, into annual educational expansion requirements for each level and branch of education. In this way, conceptually at least, minimum education expansion targets can be set, minimum with respect to economic and technological growth and development objectives. This approach is bedevilled with difficulties. To name just a few: manpower forecasts have not paid sufficient attention to the monetary and non-monetary incentives existing on the labour market and in society at large. The forecasts are based on technical coefficients, and questions about whether all the people can be absorbed at current remuneration levels or whether the individual pupils and students will actually choose the "required" educational branches and disciplines are not explicitly dealt with. This set of problems is narrowly related to a second complicating factor: substitution possibilities between different occupations and particularly between people holding different levels of educational attainment within the same occupational category. To give an example: Suppose we find that the technology in use in the manufacturing sector is such that there exists a fixed relationship (and thus complementarity) between a unit of output and, say, the number of engineers required. No substitution possibilities between, for example, engineers and technicians exist at this level. But there may exist several education and training paths which make people eligible for engineering occupations in manufacturing. There is thus a substitution possibility at this second level. The relationship between output in manufacturing and the educational system would, therefore, still be variable in spite of the fixed occupational coefficients. If these latter are also variable the picture would be further complicated. The conclusion must be that: (i) the single-valued occupational forecasts so widespread during the 1960s have to be taken with a grain of salt; and (ii) not sufficient attention has been paid to the problem of how to get from the present educational and occupational structure of the labour force to the required one. The only indication presented in these studies, in the most favourable of cases, refers to the expansion of the various levels and branches of education necessary to reach the occupational and educational targets. However, very little attention is being given to the functioning of the labour market in general and to the salary and wage structure in particular. This is obviously an absurd position because it could and will degenerate into a situation in which the manpower-educational planner would forecast time and time again, say, more technical school graduates, where the bulk of the youngsters keep preferring to opt for the general secondary schools. Why? Because the incentive schemes, the salary structure, the social status attached to certain jobs, bottlenecks in the educational sector itself, etc. push them in that direction.

Cost - benefit analysis of educational investment, or rate of return analysis, is supposed to provide (i) an *ex post* check on the efficiency of investment now embodied in different kinds of educational facilities; and (ii) a signal for the desired direction of change in the educational system. The essence of the technique is the *assumption* that lifetime earnings differentials between more or less educated individuals are close approximations to the differences in their contributions to national income, coupled with the *empirical assertion* that differences in earnings can be largely attributed to differences in educational attainment, rather than to differences in native ability and family background. So far for the benefit side of additional schooling. By "costs" is meant not only the out-of-pocket costs of students in the form of fees, books and travel, as well as the costs of teachers, buildings and equipment that students may not pay for, but also the earnings foregone by students for being at school rather than at work. When all resource costs are taken into account and earnings are taken before tax, we speak of the "social rate of return." When the costs are confined to out-of-pocket costs and when the earnings are taken after tax, we speak of the "private rate of return." This rate of return approach is being objected to as putting all its eggs in the wage basket and as saying ultimately that each person or group of persons will earn the salary it deserves. Moreover, because one examines present salary differentials, one can only expect short-term signals from which no long-term conclusions can be drawn. This is obviously a serious drawback in the field of educational policy and planning, since it simply is not feasible to change directions every year unless one is in the presence of a perfectly flexible educational system.

The question of how much is spent on education was one of the first questions to which economists turned their attention. The measure of expenditure on education is primarily an exercise in classification, and secondarily an exercise in sorting through complex accounts to fit the figures into the classification. Expenditures on education have risen very quickly indeed during the past 15 years or so. It is this rapidly rising trend which is drawing much public attention, and it is becoming widely believed that this rise in public expenditure will become increasingly difficult to maintain. Related to this problem of educational expenditures and finance, one notes a growing apprehension about the "productivity" of the educational sector, or its internal efficiency as it is sometimes called. An important aspect of this has to do with the early leaving (drop-out) rates, repeating of grades and duration of studies. Having arrived at these issues it is opportune to turn to the reaction of the educators in the face of the mounting interest of the economists in the affairs of the school.

2. The Reaction of the Educators

Looking back at the spate of reports and books published during the 1960s by representatives of each of the four groups distinguished above, it becomes quite clear that. almost without exception, economists have been during that decade very strong advocates in favour of educational expansion. This is true to such an overwhelming extent that without too much exaggeration one can speak of an "economic lobby" which has been quite helpful in obtaining the additional outlays from finance ministers in the face of the tremendous expansion in enrolments. Indeed what economists showed and even quantified was that education — through the skill structure of the labour force — is an important explanatory factor in the economic growth process and that, therefore, if you wanted more of the latter you were well advised to secure more of the former. They also showed that the social and private rates of return on money invested in education were remarkably high, in many instances substantially higher than the return on investment in physical capital. Moreover, the vast majority of the manpower forecasts indicated rapidly expanding future needs for all kinds of highly qualified and middle level personnel and consequently pleaded in favour of an accelerated educational expansion. In short, the economists' answer to any questions about education could be summed up in one single word, "more." They certainly had preferences for some levels and branches of education rather than for others, but all in all the generalisation holds.

Given this idyllic picture, what made many educators behave like bulls each time the economist entered the educational arena? We think that two reasons can be advanced for this behaviour. The first relates to a certain confusion between two areas which, although interdependent, gain by being discussed separately. We refer to "economics *in* education" on the one hand, and "economics *of* education" on the other. The second reason has to do with certain doubts about the "more of the same" implications of the economics of education.

Many educators have a long-standing aversion toward what one author has called the "cult of efficiency" in education. This is so mainly because they frequently have the impression that what is being sought is not the "finest product at the lowest cost", but that the emphasis has been on the "lowest cost" and not at all on "producing the finest product." Clearly, when economists became again interested in education they also started to examine what happened inside the educational sector and to evaluate what the "internal efficiency" of the educational system was as opposed to its "external efficiency." They did so by concentrating on relatively easily quantifiable indicators such as pupil - teacher ratios, cost per pupil (also called "unit costs"), drop-out and repetition rates, etc. Some went further and related output to input trends to show that the "productivity" of the education system was declining. There is, of course, nothing new in these types of calculations. Victor Cousin in 1837 produced one of the more elegant international comparisons, summing up in one table certain quantitative differences in primary, secondary and university education between Holland and Prussia, ending up with how much the State spent for each pupil. In 1909, Leonard Ayres proposed an "Index of Efficiency" which was determined by comparing the theoretical distribution and number of students with the actual distribution and number of students. In modern parlance this index compares a theoretical system without any drop-outs and repeaters with the actual progression of pupils through the system. And here is how Raymond E. Callahan (1962) in *Education and the Cult of Efficiency* presents a more recent article in this area:

> Adminstrators are also under pressure as they were in the efficiency era to apply business and industrial values and practices to education. One of the most prominent manifestations of this pressure was an article which appeared in *Fortune* in October 1958, entitled "The Low Productivity of the Education Industry." The author conceded that it was more difficult "to put a firm figure on the value of the output" in education than it was in industry but he said there was "still something to be learned from the cold figures on quality." "For the schools," he said "no less than the automobile industry, have an inescapable production problem." The schools were no different from General Motors for their job was to "optimise the number of students and to minimise the input of man-hours and capital." The main point of the article was to show that whereas the productivity per worker had increased in the steel industry and others, the productivity of the education industry had declined. Like Spaulding, the author could reach no conclusion as to the difference in the quality of education (in this instance between 1929 and 1958) but the per-pupil costs were easily available so they were used as the "most relevant measure of productivity." For this unfortunate state of affairs the author had a happy solution — introduce new techniques such as television, audio-visual aids, teaching machines, teacher aids, and more efficient utilisation of buildings and classrooms — this latter incidentally was entitled "scientific programming," a label which somehow did not occur to school administrators in the age of efficiency. The author's crowning achievement, however, was his recommendation that schools could improve their efficiency by hiring management consultants — the modern term for efficiency experts. "The schools," said the author seriously, "have just begun to discover scientific management" (pages 256—257).

Thus, while the economists used such terms as production, efficiency, income streams, labour force, human capital or even worse "education as an industry," many educators did not so much appreciate the virtues of considering education as an investment as they bristled with rage, sensitive as they were to this terminology, when such cold-blooded terms as "efficiency," "waste" and "productivity" were applied to education. Rather than being happy with the economists' fresh arguments which proved useful for persuading reluctant finance ministers of the virtue of larger educational expenditures, the traditional educator chose to attack that part of the economists' contribution having to do with economics in education. Since much of the educators' argumentation hinges on the "quality of education," the economists in turn got very frustrated each time they tried to get educators to define just what "product" it is that they were trying to produce, in sufficiently specific terms to be able to determine whether in fact they are producing it, and if so how much. The more articulate educators' advocate would reply to this that one should not lose sight of the fact that "students go through two processes which are parallel but not particularly correlated. They are becoming educated, a process which probably defies definition and certainly defies comprehensive measurement, and they are simultaneously developing an ability to use or display certain facets of that education. This development is subject to some sort of relative if not to absolute measurement. Both of these processes are important, and so is recognition of the dichotomy. Those of us who are teachers have an obligation to make clear to our students and, equally important, to the community that part of what we are trying to do is measurable and part is not" (Ivey, 1968). If this is correct, it follows that educators are inclined to assess their output mainly by the inputs — things such as precisely the pupil - teacher ratio, expenditures per pupil, or the number of hours a student spends in a classroom — rather than by the output, the performance of the product. In such circumstances it is, of course, impossible to appraise the efficiency of resource use or compare the advantages of alternative systems of production. At the limit this is exactly what many educators mean without saying it: more per pupil expenditure means better quality education.

Whilst the sketched skirmish between economists and educators comes very close to problems of semantics and circular reasoning, more serious to our mind are the objections to be classified under the second reason given above. The mentality which aroused this second reaction may be summed up in the following quotation, which is as good as any other quotation one could find:

> Now there is one thing about education that I would like to stress because it explains the character of this Conference. To provide for education means that we have to look far ahead. If there is to be more education

in 1970 or 1980 we must now not only build schools and universities, but we must provide for training of teachers of all grades, and it takes many years to educate qualified experts for industry and agriculture, so much so that you must train the teachers who are later on to train the experts. We have for the moment a great shortage of teachers in the Western world. This is because we did not twenty or thirty years ago think enough of the future needs. This is what we have to do now. Therefore, one of the purposes of this Conference is to discuss the assessment of the needs of the future, in order to know how much we must invest in school buildings, and in the brains of teachers and so on (Kristensen, (1962), page 22).

Although it is nowhere said in so many words, the whole quotation smacks of the "more of the same" approach. This approach, implicitly, puts the bulk of the emphasis on the purely quantitative dimensions of educational development and thus on expanding the educational *status quo* into a substantially larger version of itself. Particularly in retrospect, many economists who pioneered in the educational arena would reject such an accusation with indignation. However, it remains a fact that many of them created the impression — by certain silences — of holding such a view. They did so by concentrating on the future manpower needs which the (existing) educational system should try to meet; by stressing the high rates-of-return on investments in additional years of (present) education; by quantifying how the increases in (past) education as embodied in the labour force had been a phenomenal factor in the economic growth records of countries, etc. When the economists did touch on what happened during the educational process they were concerned with such "superficial" indicators as mentioned above: more teachers, more school buildings, less "wastage," more financial outlays and so on. Rarely did they mention the needs for internal change and improvement in the deeper and fuller sense of these words as opposed to "mere" expansion: changes in structure, content and in educational technology in the wide sense of the teacher-learning process. Even if it were economically feasible to achieve a vast and rapid expansion of the educational *status quo*, this still would fail to meet today's and especially tomorrow's educational needs in this deeper and fuller sense.

It is, of course, not true that none of the economists have drawn explicit attention to this problem. John Vaizey, one of the pioneers in the economics of education, has always been very much aware of the danger of too one-sided an economic approach. The following quotation taken from one of his articles refers to developing countries and in the formulation of the problem may arouse strong disagreements. The important point, however, is the author's awareness of the danger of the "more of the same" line of thought:

> ... education, as such, has historically speaking probably been more opposed to growth than it has supported it. It is a necessary condition for growth, but not a sufficient one. My second point is this: that because of the adoption universally of the view that it is through scientific techniques and technological progress that the problems of the underdeveloped countries will be solved, we economists now are quite clear what the debate on the content of education throughout the world should be about. That is to say that apart from its cultural component (and possibly its religious component) its major task is the quite specific one of developing technological and scientific insights, whether these be in specifically technological and scientific fields or whether they be in the traditionally more humanistic subjects, such as those concerned eventually with administration. This is important because it means that the debate over the curriculum is a debate which is now not so much concerned with ultimate ends and human values (and therefore a debate which is likely, in many ways, to be sterile) but is a debate about the actual content of a curriculum which could lead to certain widely agreed ends, among which one of the most important is this "scientific" attitude. So far it has been easy to laugh off the cultural and economic "conflict" in educational thought, because while there is a shortage of education almost any question can be answered by the single word "more." Nevertheless, I must confess that 'more' education of a sterile "cultural" kind seems to me to be not only uneconomic but unwholesome (Vaizey, (1963) pages 41—42).

Finally, we would like to make two remarks concerning this debate. First, changes in the educational process are far easier to advocate than to attain. Not only are educational systems all over the world notoriously resistant to innovation, but education lacks sufficiently strong and creative internal institutional mechanisms to provide a continuing critical appraisal of its prevailing processes and products, and to invent and foster better ones. Second, although economists may have given the impression of being in favour of "more of the same," very few have been those who thought of being involved in more than one dimension of the educational planning and policy world. Most of them were convinced that other dimensions — sociological, cultural, psychological, pedagogical — were at least as important as theirs, but they also knew they were not qualified to tackle these questions. The pioneer educators who approach their work with a scientific spirit, who are not afraid of constructive criticism and new ideas, constantly complain of being frustrated by a deep-rooted and stubborn folklore. Educators are much to blame themselves for not coming up with appropriate ideas in their domain. This may partly explain their tendency to look around for others to blame and in that respect the economics of education upsurge came in handy!

3. Concluding Remarks

In this short chapter we have presented a brief survey of one of the more interesting developments in economics of the past fifteen years which unfortunately degenerated at one moment in a rather amazing game of shadow boxing between economists on the one hand and educators, psychologists, etc. on the other. We have given an overview of the different paths economists have followed in their attempts to integrate the education sector in the main stream of economic thinking. We have subsequently advanced two reasons which may explain why economists and educators have not always found themselves on the same wavelength, to say the least. We have *not* touched upon the somewhat masochistic relations between the different groups of economists following different paths, mainly because we have done that elsewhere. (See Emmerij, 1969.)

The two hypotheses we have put forward to explain the behaviour of educators in the face of the economists' pioneering efforts are (i) the reduction of the endeavours to quantify the relationship between education and economic development to the much more narrowly defined investigations into the "productivity" or "internal efficiency" of the "education industry"; and (ii) the interpretation that economists were irresponsibly forecasting the educational *status quo* on a bigger scale, or the "more of the same" approach.

It must be immediately said that these controversies were to no small extent a result of the extreme quantitative approach of the first economists' attempts and their influence on educational planning documents. It is equally true that many educators have had a purely reactive attitude and have not gone to great pains to look at the complementary relationship between their own responsibilities and those of the economists. We are here in the presence of again another example of reasoning in mutually exclusive terms: "Only we know what and where the truth is; all the others are in the wrong." And thus, in spite of the formidable aid which the economists suddenly extended to the educators in search for additional public funds, these latter behaved frequently in a manner which showed certain characteristics of incipient paranoia. But there is no smoke without fire. And in our opinion there is no doubt that the noise economists made around their new baby and the attention their work got, has in no small measure contributed to a diversion from fundamental, qualitative educational reform in favour of an obsession for "more." Since this phenomenon occurred at a moment of unprecedented individual and family pressure for more and longer education, this convergence in itself explains much of what some have called the "educational explosion." How this explosion, together with its corollaries, has railed and sailed will now be considered.

III

Educational Expansion in the Nineteen-Fifties and Nineteen-Sixties: An Overview

1. Quantitative Growth, Structural Change and Educational Opportunity

We start by sketching out the overall growth and structural changes of educational systems in the OECD area, and by presenting a general statement about change in educational opportunities. Between 1950 and the end of the 1960s, school and university enrolments in all OECD countries rose from 100 million to well over 160 million, i.e. a 60% increase. During the same period, the growth of the total population between 5 and 24 years of age was less than half: 27%. As a consequence, two-thirds of the population in this age-group was enrolled at the end of the period as against slightly more than half at the beginning. In terms of the total population, some 25% was at school or university at the end of the 1960s. There are, of course, wide differences between countries: The school population remained virtually stable in the Federal Republic of Germany while it was multiplied by 2.6 in Turkey. Differences in demographic trends and structures play a certain role in these discrepancies: The total population in the 5-24 age-group rose by 60% in Canada, by about 50% in the United States and Turkey; it diminished in Greece and Ireland and remained virtually stable in Italy and the Federal Republic of Germany. Quite clearly, large differences between the percentages enrolled in this age-group persisted among countries at the end of the period: 80% for Belgium, Canada and the United States, as against 35% and 40% for Turkey and Portugal, respectively. This remarkable expansion of the numbers enrolled is, of course, a result both of increasing *numbers* of young people (demographic trends) and increasing *proportions* of young people attending schools (increasing individual and family demand for education).

Along with, and partly under the pressure of, this quantitative growth, several traditional distinctions between educational levels and branches have been blurred by important structural reforms. The structural impact of educational expansion has been most purposefully felt at the lower rungs of the educational ladder, resulting in the merger of primary education, which thus loses its terminal character, with lower secondary education, which is characterised by a distinct move away from its former selective character. These two levels combined now correspond more or less to the period of extended compulsory schooling which most developed countries have come to adopt as policy following the *de facto* situation created as a result of increased voluntary participation. Even at the upper-secondary level, the traditional division between academic and non-academic streams has come under increasing pressure. At the higher levels of education, growth in enrolments is fostering the emergence of new types of institutions alongside traditional ones.

Pre-primary, primary and compulsory schooling

Enrolments in pre-primary and primary education increased from 73 to close to 100 million pupils between 1950 and the end of the 1960s in the OECD area: this represents approximately a one-third increase. In a few countries (Austria, Germany, Japan) a slight decrease in enrolments is observed, while others witness impressive increases: 60% in the United States, slightly more than 80% in Canada and 140% in Turkey. These differences, and at this educational level, are of course largely due to the demographic structures of the respective countries, although less so for relatively less developed Mediterranean countries like Turkey, where compulsory schooling was far from being effective at the beginning of the period. The rates of growth observed at this level are usually inferior to those observed for secondary and higher education, thus resulting in a narrowing of the base of the school pyramid. In 1950 there were only five countries in which enrolments in pre-primary and primary schooling represented less than two-thirds of the total enrolments at all levels; in the beginning of the 1970s, sixteen countries were in this position.

Enrolments rates, defined as the ratio between the number of pupils enrolled in pre-primary and primary education and the number of children between 5 and 14 years of age, give a poor picture of the progress made, since a fairly large part of those enrolled in pre-primary institutions are under 5 and a significant part of those beyond 11 or 12 is already enrolled in secondary schools. These rates have remained constant over the period, except in Turkey and Yugoslavia where they increased significantly. All this makes it clear that the two factors which explain the development at this level are the demographic situation and the *initial* level of enrolments rates.

The duration of compulsory schooling, which ranged between a minimum of three years and a maximum of ten years in 1950, is now comprised between eight and ten years in the overwhelming majority of OECD countries, thus matching the combined primary-plus-lower-secondary-education level. However, this lengthening of compulsory schooling is more formal than real in some countries where laws are more advanced than reality. A breakdown of the population by age, educational cycle and grade within this cycle is indispensable to establishing a clear idea of the progress made: When a child of 12 is said to be enrolled, it is important to know where — he may be an "old" repeater in the fourth grade of primary, or a bright child in lower secondary. Curiously enough, very few OECD countries are able to provide information on the matching between ages and grades at the primary level. However, the problem of repeaters and delays in general is still plaguing many countries, some of them among the most advanced.

All in all it can be said that, with the exception of Portugal and Turkey, universal compulsory schooling for longer periods of time has been achieved, and that the two mentioned countries are well under way to achieving this aim as well. In other words, disparities in educational participation have all but disappeared at this level. Sex, social class, regional origin, are no longer obstacles to school participation to the extent that the school attendance is enforced. In addition, primary education has always been an educational experience common to all children in terms of curricula, teaching techniques, and so on. It is, therfore, the egalitarian cycle *par excellence*. However, increasing attention was drawn during this period to the fact that in spite of the equality in participation of groups defined according to non-educational criteria (sex, race, social background, etc.), large inequalities persisted between those groups as far as educational achievement is concerned. A first and rather crude measure of achievement is given by the existing disparities between the legal and the effective duration of schooling. The existence of large numbers of repeaters, systematically higher in proportion in the lower social classes, is indicative of the fact that primary schools are far from being egalitarian with respect to the speed of learning. Slightly better measures of achievement, such as ranking in the final grade or ability test scores, yield analogous results, that is, far from eradicating initial inequalities in achievement caused by social and family background differences, primary eduction maintains or even reinforces them.

Secondary education

Time series since 1950 concerning enrolments in secondary education cannot, of course, take due account of the new educational structures alluded to above and which have started to emerge gradually in the 1960s. In other words, they refer in the main to a long secondary education cycle (the lower part of which is becoming the upper part of compulsory schooling) and to the short as well as technical and vocational cycles. In short, they include all branches of secondary as well as post-primary education where this still existed, and part-time education for Austria and Germany.

Thus defined, the number of pupils enrolled in secondary education in the OECD area rose from 25 million in 1950 to close to 50 million at the end of the 1960s — an increase of 100%. Enrolments doubled in North America and almost trebled in the Mediterranean countries. They increasd by 85% in Western Europe, 75% in Northern Europe and 55% in Japan. These rates of growth are superior to those observed for primary education in all countries, but in absolute terms enrolments rose more rapidly in secondary than in primary in only eleven countries. This expansion was more or less evenly spread out over the period, and no sign of slowdown can yet be observed.

No definite tendency can be observed with respect to the relative growth of enrolments in technical and general education. About half of the countries with which we are concerned have registered higher rates of growth in secondary general, and half in technical and vocational education. This expansion pattern is, broadly speaking, favouring general education in absolute terms, since initial enrolments in this branch are superior, sometimes to a great extent, to enrolments in technical and vocational education in all countries but five: Austria, Denmark, German Federal Republic, The Netherlands and Yugoslavia. Enrolments in primary teacher-training usually increased less rapidly than total enrolments in secondary education, but more rapidly than enrolments in primary education.

The growth of total enrolments in secondary education was more than 1.5 times higher than the growth of the corresponding age-group (10—19), thus reflecting an important progress in the overall enrolment rates. Broadly speaking, countries with low initial enrolment rates have registered more substantial increases: Disparities in educational development between countries may therefore have been reduced. However, these advances were greatly facilitated in countries whose 10—19 years age-group remained more or less stagnant during the period; this was the case for Italy, Portugal, Spain and Yugoslavia. Conversely, in countries like Canada, Finland, France, Norway and Turkey, big increases in enrolment rates were observed despite the demographic boom. Here again, overall enrolment rates fail to give a clear picture of the increase in actual educational opportunity available at each age of the demographic pyramid. From those countries that have enrolment rates available by individual age-groups it can be deduced that, at the end of the period, about one adolescent aged sixteen out of three is still enrolled in full-time education in the Mediterranean countries; one out of two in Western European countries, and approximately two out of three in Northern European countries.

This expansion of enrolments, and the resulting pressure of numbers, has been one of the major factors behind the structural reforms undertaken by some countries. When pupils were leaving school at different ages and undertaking different courses, parallel systems made some sense. Where this is no longer the situation, they make little educational sense. Allied to this practical point is a series of theoretical ones, all of which are related to the objectives of the system. Several are common to most systems — ensuring equality of opportunity, maximisation of the utilisation of human talent, enabling all youngsters to develop to the full their potentialities and capacities. These are objectives that most educational systems would applaud. The theoretical argument is that they can only be achieved in a common school system. Parallel systems imply choice and selection; if this is done early then talents cannot be assessed and potentialities realised. Early selection becomes rigid selection if it is followed, as it usually has been, by qualitatively different educational experiences. What secondary school reorganisation is trying to achieve is the postponement of the time when such decisions have to be made, ensuring that they do not result in different types of education and so become virtually irreversible. It is for these types of reasons that the introduction of common lower secondary schooling has become more widespread in recent years.

At the beginning of the fifties, the structure of secondary education still reflected its nineteenth century origin, with three important pillars: (i) the academic secondary branch through which a minority flirted its way to the university; (ii) the technical and vocational secondary cycles aiming at teaching the infantry of industrial society; and (iii) post-primary education permitting a period of compulsory schooling longer than the traditional primary cycle, but not integrated into the mainstream of secondary education. For the reasons given earlier, this differentiated organisation is tending to give way to a common educational structure. Obviously, the situations vary largely across countries in this respect: Sweden and Norway with nine years of common schooling have probably gone further than most other European countries; other countries, like Austria and Switzerland for instance, have not yet started to move towards comprehensive schools at the secondary level. Between these extremes one finds countries like Italy with its comprehensive "scuola media"; parts of the secondary education system in the United Kingdom and Germany; France with a new network of geographically integrated "collèges d'enseignement secondaire"; The Netherlands with the introduction of one common year ("brugjaar") at the beginning of the secondary cycle, etc. There is already some discussion in Scandinavian countries to postpone differentiation even further, i.e., to build also the upper-secondary cycle along comprehensive lines.

However, it appeared difficult to reorganise the external structure of schools without changing the internal organisation of the school as well. In view of the "theoretical" justifications given for the external reorganisation, it became quickly clear that simply having a common school without parallel changes in the classroom may not achieve the objectives of equality of educational opportunity or maximal utilisation of talent. It may merely mean the re-introduction of all inequalities in a disguised form as a result of the system of internal differentiation of the curriculum. A comprehensive school system that streams pupils into particular lines and subject groups at a relatively early age can be just as rigid as a parallel system of education. It is, therefore, worth looking at the various overlapping ways in which institutions can be, and have been, internally differentiated:

(i) Differentiation by ability: this is the division of a population according to intellectual ability and performance, dividing an intellectually heterogeneous population into its relatively homogeneous sub-groups.

(ii) Differentiation by types of subjects: this is a division into broad types of discipline: the academic, the general, the vocational; pupils in different classes taking different subjects and/or similar subjects at different speeds, to different levels or in different ways.

(iii) Differentiation by particular groups of subject: here the differentiation is into different subject grouping (arts or sciences, languages or social studies, technology or natural sciences) which can be taken as part of an academic, vocational or general course, to any particular level.

The question facing current and future educational policy is at what age will what type of differentation be introduced into the educational institutions, and to what extent can any decisions taken by an individual be later reversed by him? Further, on what types of information will these decisions be based, and who will make them?

In the light of the preceding review of quantitative growth and structual change in secondary education, what have been the implications with respect to changes in group disparities in educational participation? A first way to assess disparities is by using transition rates from primary to the various branches of secondary education by social background, regional origin, etc.; another and further way is to examine repeat and drop-out rates by social background as well as enrolments in the last form of secondary education. Frequently, the only statistic available consists of total enrolments in a branch of secondary education broken down by father's occupation, etc. Whatever the nature of the data base, the available evidence clearly indicates that a considerable social selection, favouring upper and middle social classes, takes place during the secondary educational level. In addition, time trends reveal no tendency for this socially biased selection to lessen, exept in countries having exceptionally high secondary school participation rates. In other words, it appears that the "saturation theory" — which maintains that group disparities will start to decrease only after the point at which the next higher social group has reached a near hundred percent enrolment rate — has so far given the better explanation of the evolution of social class disparities in time. This would mean that the only way to reduce these disparities is to realise universal enrolments. The OECD countries are still far from this goal at the secondary level. Towards the end of the 1960s, more than three-quarters of the relevant age-group successfully completed secondary school in the United States, half of the age-group did so in Japan and Finland; this proportion dropped sharply in a few "advanced" European countries to around 20% in Belgium, Norway and Sweden, and between 10 and 15% in France,The Netherlands and the United Kingdom.

At this level — the last grade of secondary education — sex disparities still exist in all OECD countries except five (France, Japan, Norway, Sweden and the United States). There are about two boys for one girl completing long secondary education successfully in Germany, Italy and the United Kingdom. The disparity is greater still in some Mediterranean countries. .

Tertiary education

Around 1970, there were 12 million students enrolled in all institutions of post-secondary education in the OECD area, as against less than 4 million in 1950. This represents an increase of 200% over the period. Dispersion around this average is small between groups of countries: the number of students enrolled was multiplied by more than 3 in Japan and Western European countries, by 2.7 in North America and North European countries and by 2.5 in the Mediterranean countries. The countries which witnessed the fastest expansion during the period were Canada, Sweden, Finland, Greece and Turkey. Italy, Ireland, Iceland, Spain, Norway and Switzerland were among the more slowly expanding countries. In 1950, no OECD country had more than 4% of its total school population enrolled in tertiary education, with the exception of 7.2% in the United States. In 1970, much more than half of the countries had gone beyond this 4% mark, the United States still leading with 12%. Moreover, the growth of enrolments in tertiary education accelerated at the end of the period in all countries except in Germany and Turkey.

In most countries, enrolments in science and technology, at the university level, have increased at the same rate or faster than enrolments in the other faculties or departments. As to the relative growth rates of post-secondary non-university and university education, the expansion of the former has been more rapid as compared to the latter. However, the importance of post-secondary non-university institutions varies largely among countries: they are virtually non-existent in Austria and enrol less than 10% of the total number of students at the tertiary level in Greece and Italy. At the other extreme we find countries like Belgium, Denmark, The Netherlands and the United Kingdom where this percentage exceeds 40%.

The total population in the 20-24 age-group increased by just about 3% during the entire period. In nine countries the number of persons in this age-group decreased, and in seven countries, an increase of more than 10% was observed. Enrolment rates, that is in this case the ratios between the number of students enrolled in tertiary education and the total population in the 20-24 age-group, rose by more than 60% between 1950 and 1970 in all countries except Switzerland. They more than doubled in ten countries; among them we find six out of the nine countries where demographic stagnation was observed: Belgium, France, Greece, Luxembourg, Portugal and Yugoslavia. These increases in enrolment rates were not inversely proportional to their initial level and there is, therefore, no tendency towards a reduction of differences between countries. At the end of the period, enrolment rates as defined reached over 40% in the United States, over 20% in Canada, while lying somewhere between 10 and 20% in France, Belgium, Denmark, The Netherlands, Yugoslavia , Sweden, the United Kingdom and Japan (in decreasing order). The remaining countries had not yet reached the 10% level.

International comparisons of enrolment rates suffer from a major bias since the numerator is clearly influenced by the effective length of studies which varies quite wildly between countries. It is, therefore, essential to complement the picture by presenting evidence concerning access to, and graduation from, higher education. Over 40% of the relevant age-group was enrolled in the first year of higher education in the United States, as against between 15 and 20% in Belgium, Denmark, Japan and Sweden, and between 10 and 15% in Italy, The Netherlands and the United Kingdom. These data refer to the end of the 1960s. However incomplete, they show that access to tertiary education is still restricted to a small minority in most European countries, despite the progress made over the last decade. Still for around 1970, well over one million first degrees were awarded by universities in the OECD area, as against 550,000 in 1955. In five countries, Canada, France, Sweden, Turkey and Yugoslavia, the annual number of first degrees more than doubled between 1958 and 1965; it increased by less than 50% in Denmark, Germany, Greece, Italy, The Netherlands, Portugal and Spain. The other countries fall within this range. Considering now the number of graduates as a percentage of the relevant age-group, the following picture emerges: the United States graduates 25% of each generation, Canada and Japan come next with 12 and 10% respectively, while between 5 and 6% graduate in the most advanced (in this respect) European countries, Belgium, France, Sweden and the United Kingdom.

To round off this review of numbers, two observations must be added. The number of advanced degrees granted by universities increased faster than the number of first degrees, although the situation is, of course, very different from country to country. The same holds for degrees granted by post-secondary non-university institutions. These are particularly numerous in Belgium, Germany, The Netherlands, Norway, the United Kingdom and Yugoslavia, thus increasing the score of these countries when it comes to enrolment and graduation rates.

Turning now to the structural reforms, it seems that whilst at the secondary level the general tendency is towards less differentiation between the various branches, the tendency in higher education is the reverse: Here, in many countries the pressure is to introduce greater differentiation into the system of higher education. This has been, and is, taking a variety of forms, of which three can be singled out as the more significant.

(i) Special courses or cycles, usually of shorter duration, are created or developed within the university leading to a terminal degree generally considered below the traditional university terminal degree level. Thus,for example, German-speaking universities in Switzerland, where so far the only terminal degree has been the doctorate, have introduced the "licence" as a first terminal degree. A similar differentiation has been introduced in Austria and Germany ("Magister") and is currently under discussion in Italy. In fact, this trend implies a greater differentiation between undergraduate and post-graduate studies.

(ii) New institutions are created and developed outside the existing universities. This is not the creation of new universities, but of para-university level institutions in addition to the traditional ones. Good examples are the French "Instituts Universitaires de Technologie" (IUT), and the Norwegian "District Colleges." In the United Kingdom after the Robbins Report, Colleges of Advanced Technology were transformed into universities and, since that time, polytechnics provide further examples of either the development or creation of new types of higher education institutions. In this context, it is interesting to draw attention to the distinction between attempts to develop special and high prestige institutions within a mass system (e.g. the Centre of Excellence), and attempts to achieve a mass system by developing a level of higher education carrying lower status than traditional universities (for example, junior colleges in the United States and new types of polytechnics in the United Kingdom).

(iii) Institutions which in the past have operated on the secondary level were upgraded, or are being upgraded, into institutions of higher education. One example stands out: the situation of teacher-training in most countries. Many systems are attempting to give teacher-training parity of prestige with higher education and recruit into it graduates of the academic secondary school system. Again the motivation is multiple. It is clearly a way of providing higher educational facilities for the swollen numbers of secondary school graduates; in turn, it may well be a way of both raising the status of the teacher and obtaining better qualified entrants to the system of teacher-training. Many other specialist institutions concerned with professional training, especially of engineers and technologists, are experiencing similar upgrading attempts.

These three broad types of strategies do not exhaust the possibilities and, more important, they tend to overlap. Perhaps the best illustration of this "blurring" is the American junior college system, which could certainly be considered as an example of the first two types of strategy, and was also designed to achieve some of the objectives of the third (i.e., give higher education to the increased and increasing proportion of the age-group, without immediately expanding universities). In addition, it serves as something of a "cautionary tale." It is designed to give a shorter, non-university type of education, with possibilities for some of its graduates to transfer to university. And there seems little doubt that a large proportion of entrants do aspire to higher education; but the drop-out rate in junior colleges is high — perhaps two-thirds of entrants. For half the remainder of entrants the education is terminal, and the other half enter universities.

As we did when discussing secondary education, the question must be asked what the implications with respect to group disparities have been of the quantitative growth and structural change in higher education. Taking due account of the reservations and qualifications that must be made in any international comparison in this domain, it can nevertheless be advanced that around 1960, the proportion of students of "working class" origin in university education was over 20% in four countries only: Belgium, Norway, the United States and the United Kingdom. The proportion was between 10 and 20% in five countries (Denmark, Greece, Italy, Sweden and Switzerland), and below 10% in all other countries. These figures must be seen in the light of the fact that the proportion of the total active population varies around 50%. Conversely, upper strata youth constituted a high proportion of the total student body and, statistically speaking, they are highly over-represented, based on the proportion of the male labour force from the same strata.

In those cases where time series are available, so that changes over time within a given country can be determined, the evidence shows that educational disparities are narrowing slightly in a majority of countries in relative terms, but not in absolute terms. In plain language, this means that upper and middle strata youth have benefited from recent educational opportunities to a greater extent than lower strata youth. With regard to socio-economic disparities in participation in a particular academic discipline, there is a definite tendency for students to study in a field that is closely related to their social background: Law and medical faculties show a higher social recruitment than arts and sciences, for example. The poor progress achieved to reduce social class disparities at the higher education level should not come as a surprise after what has been said about the considerable social selection process that takes place at the secondary level.

The preceding discussion has been concerned with educational *participation*, or what may be called *quantitative* equality of educational opportunity. But with a growing generalisation of a given level of education, through which quasi-equality of educational opportunity is reached in quantitative terms, qualitative differences in the educational opportunities provided become more and more conspicuous. For example, in the United States, more than 80% of the relevant age group completed successfully high school by the end of the 1960s. In other words, a long-standing objective of American educational policy — extending to everyone 12 years of education — is on the point of being reached. But this impressive performance could only be accomplished by introducing an important diversification in the qualitative domain, resulting in what one author has called the creation of "neighbourhood effects." In a recent study *Group Disparities in Educational Participation*, the author concludes: "It would seem, therefore, that disparities in educational participation are not as great as disparities in educational attainment and educational quality for populations in general, and that even were disparities in participation to narrow considerably or disappear, differences in kinds and quality of education received would create gaps in education equally important as those now observed with regard to participation." (Nam, (1971) p. 90).

Finally, a few words must be said about sex disparities. Finland is the only OECD country where full equality of male and female students has been achieved for some time. In France, Sweden and the United States, female students represent nearly 40% of total enrolments; in Austria, West Germany, Japan, The Netherlands and Spain, less than one student out of four is female. Other countries are to be found within this range. In all countries for which data are available, the proportion of females in new entrants is higher than their proportion in total enrolments. This points to the fact that sex disparities in drop-out and graduation rates are important. In addition, females are relatively more numerous in post-secondary non-university types of institutions than in university education proper. When the different kinds of disparities, by sex, by social background, by region, are combined, the educational opportunity gap between the most deprived category — females from the lower social classes in certain rural and sometimes predominant catholic areas — and the most advantaged one — sons of high-level professional and executive personnel — appears still very impressive at the end of the 1960s.

2. Financial and Real Resources for Education

In view of the important growth of and changes in educational systems, it is not too difficult to imagine how impressive the results have been in terms of increases in educational expenditures. As we saw in Chapter II, these increases were more readily acceptable by the national decision-makers as education appeared more and more not only as a socially desirable objective, but also as a prerequisite for rapid and sustained economic growth. This enthusiastic "mood of discovery" was clearly reflected in the 1961 Washington Policy Conference on Economic Growth and Investment in Education, which was referred to previously. The purpose of the present section is to review the available evidence on the evolution of educational expenditures in OECD countries between 1950 and the late 1960s. Moreover, it will deal briefly with what constituted one of the more important bottlenecks during the period under review: the supply of qualified teaching staff.

Educational Expenditures

It is necessary to start out this discussion with a critical note on the state of statistical sophistication — or rather the lack of it. However incredible it may appear when concerned with the more highly-developed countries of this planet *total* educational expenditures are known for only about half of the countries under review. Data on private sources of finance of the private sector of the education system are in too many cases non-existent. Information on public educational expenditures is generally available as far as the budget of the Ministries of Education is concerned, but a non-negligible part of public expenditure is supported by other ministries and/or by local authorities. In this latter case, the distinction between those funds which are transferred from the central to local authorities (subsidies) and those which are really additional funds, is too often made difficult by the ambiguities of public accountancy. Direct contributions from families or firms to educational expenditures, whether in the public or private education sectors, are frequently unknown. The bulk of the following analysis will, therefore, refer to *public educational expenditures* which are an acceptable proxy for total expenditures, as shown by the countries where both series are available.

The annual rate of increase in public educational expenditure during the period 1950—1970 (depending on country information) has been over 10% (in constant prices) in more than half of the developed countries. Only four countries show increases which are inferior to 7%. The data also show that capital expenditures increased faster than current expenditures in a majority of countries. Moreover, and as could be expected in the light of the educational expansion pattern reviewed earlier in this chapter, a significant switch in expenditures from primary and secondary education to higher education took place during the period; thus expenditures on higher education have increased faster than at other levels: the annual rate of increase has been over 12% in 15 countries out of 22.

Time series indicate that the rate of increase in public educational expenditures has been nearly twice as fast as the rate of increase of the national product, always during the period 1950—1969/70. In 1965, public educational expenditures represented more than 6% of GNP (at market prices) in two countries (Sweden and The Netherlands), between 5 and 6% in Belgium, Canada, Denmark, Finland, Italy and Norway, and less than 5% in all other countries. Ten years earlier, in 1955, only two countries (Finland and Japan) spent more than 4% of GNP on education. By contrast, in 1967 one country (Sweden) spent more than 7% and three (Denmark, Finland and The Netherlands) more than 6%. In the same way, the percentage of total public expenditure devoted to education increased impressively in many countries, although these increases are not so spectacular as those of the percentages of GNP spent on education, since total public expenditures have increased faster than GNP in the majority of OECD countries. It is interesting to note that in all these countries except two (German Federal Republic and Portugal), military expenditure as a proportion of total public expenditure has decreased, sometimes considerably, during the same period. The hypothesis can, therefore, be advanced that the more than proportional increase in educational expenditure observed over the period has been partly made possible because of the reduction in the rate of growth of military expenditure.

Attempts to explain the global differences in the above figures across countries is a haphazard exercise. Broadly speaking, if the level of educational expenditures is closely correlated with the levels of economic development, as measured by per capita income, the rate of increase of educational expenditures appears to be independent of both the rate of economic growth and the initial level of economic development. In other words, the level of educational expenditure is proportionate to the level of resources of each country, but the financial effort exerted during the past 15 to 20 years is not explained by economic factors. It would, of course, be valuable to investigate the non-economic factors which appear to have determined the rates of growth in educational expenditure in the various countries. The fact that they have grown so steadily during the period concerned suggests that long-term social factors are at work, apparently almost unaffected by the fluctuations of the economy or by educational policy decisions.

This leads us to say a few words about the components which enter the educational expenditure equation. Reduced to its most simple expression, the main factors of increase are: (i) the expansion of enrolments; and (ii) the rise in unit costs (expenditure per pupil and per year). Trying to determine which of these two factors was dominant during the period is not unimportant since it would give a clue as to which countries, faced with huge increases in enrolments, succeeded in also improving the quality of the existing educational services — assuming (but see Chapter II) that per-pupil expenditure is an acceptable proxy for "quality". Available data show very different situations from country to country and within countries. The expansion-of-enrolments-factor was more important than the unit-cost-factor in France and The Netherlands (secondary and higher education), the United States (higher education) and Yugoslavia (all institutions of higher learning). Conversely, the "quality" factor primed the expansion factor in France and The Netherlands (primary level), the United States (only very slightly at the primary and secondary level), and the United Kingdom (secondary and university education).

The unit-cost factor is itself an aggregate and its components are the current expenditure (on teaching and on administrative staff) and the capital expenditure dimensions (on equipment and buildings). Although available evidence on the last item is limited, it does not appear as the main factor of rising expenditures. The major factor at work has clearly been the increases in current (personnel) expenditure. Increased spending on teaching staff has been caused both by reductions in pupil - teacher ratios and by substantial increases in teachers' average salaries, at all levels of the educational system. The tendency towards more favourable pupil - teacher ratios is not universal: it is clear in France where the ratio fell at all levels except general secondary. Improvements can also be observed in The Netherlands except in post-secondary non-university education, in British secondary education, and in the American elementary and secondary school levels. In Yugoslavia the pupil - teacher ratio improved considerably in primary schools but deteriorated seriously in secondary and higher education.

On the contrary, the trend towards higher average real salaries for the teaching staff has been general and does account for a major part of the increase in total expenditure per pupil. When one examines the development of teachers' average salaries, one finds that they rise much faster than the cost of living, contrary to an opinion one often hears. This phenomenon reflects, of course, to a large extent the general increase in purchasing power observed in all OECD countries. But even when it is established that teachers' average salaries grow faster than other salaries, as seems most often to be the case, the various factors responsible for this still remain to be analysed. There are, first of all, the relative changes that have occurred between the different levels of education as reviewed earlier. In addition, there are many categories of teachers within each level and account must be taken of changes in the pattern of their distribution. Certain countries (United States, for example) have been able to raise appreciably the standard of their teachers' qualifications at the elementary and secondary levels, while at the same time coping with a phase of rapid increase in enrolment numbers. On the other hand, in other countries (France), it was possible to meet the need for intensive recruitment only at the expense of raising the proportion of under-qualified teachers or by promoting teachers wholesale from lower levels. As regards higher education, it seems that the proportion of titular professors, or of teachers holding a doctorate, has declined everywhere. Account should also be taken of changes in age structure, since teachers' salaries are, as a rule, closely linked to seniority. Changes in the breakdown by sex must also have a certain effect, insofar as women's salaries are often (*de jure* or *de facto*) below those of male teachers.

To measure the effects of the above changes on the structure of the teaching staff one would need accurate data for the numbers in each category (including changes in time) and their respective salaries, such as do not seem to be assembled systematically by national statistical departments, even for public education. However, for those countries where more complete evidence is available, it would appear that the oft-repeated claim that teachers' pay has dropped continuously relative to pay in other professions is not supported by the partial calculations made, which in many instances show a relative improvement. This improvement is perhaps a result of the state of the labour market, where demand for teachers has been stronger than for many other professions; but perhaps it has also been a case of "taking up the slack" after lagging behind, considering that, as compared with people holding equivalent degrees, teachers' salaries are even now lower than those in most other professions. It seems likely that the upward thrust of the level of salaries as a whole has had a more important influence on the trend of teachers' salaries than fluctuations of supply and demand on the labour market, especially as specific shortages in certain categories of teachers (science or mathematics teachers, for example) have hardly ever been reflected by differential pay rates, owing to the attitude of the trade union organisations and the strict codification and ranking of the teaching profession.

To sum up, the foregoing account has given us a strong impression of the importance of other factors besides the number of students in explaining growth in educational expenditure. Qualitative factors, such as the pupil - teacher ratio, play an important role. However, it has also become clear that the rise in the real wage per teacher has been one of the strongest factors behind the observed increases in educational outlays. If this is correct, it goes a long way in explaining a previously-noted finding, namely that the rate of increase of educational expenditures is independent of both the rate of economic growth and the initial level of economic development. This rate of increase will depend to a very large extent on the initial level of educational development and in particular on the number of teachers already in the system. This kind of "commitments of the previous year" will tend to determine in a quasi-automatic way the bulk of the increase in expenditures of "this year." Although this begs the question with respect to long-term educational policy options (about which we will have more to say in subsequent chapters), the importance and the almost lethargic weight of the noted short-term mechanism will be clear and cannot be underestimated.

Teaching staff

In reviewing the past twenty years with respect to one of the most strategic resources needed in the educational sector, namely teachers, two periods must be distinguished: During a first period, speaking very broadly, enrolments were outpacing the supply of qualified teachers — this period can be equated to the 1950s and early 1960s; during a second period the number of qualified teaching staff picked up to a point where in many cases the deteriorations in pupil - teacher ratios suffered during the first period were more than compensated. Thus, if we take the case of primary education, practically all industrialised countries trained at the end of the 1960s a number of teachers such that the increase in full-time primary school teachers was well above that of the numbers enrolled, resulting in improved pupil - teacher ratios. However, during the decade 1950 - 1960 many of those countries had known a reversed tendency, caused in some countries by the post-war baby boom. This has resulted in the recruitment of under-qualified primary school teachers who, between 1955 and 1960, constituted up to 25% of the total teaching staff in some countries.

As noted earlier, the increase in enrolments at the secondary education level has been much faster than at the primary level. It is, therefore, not surprising that secondary schools have had great difficulties recruiting qualified teaching personnel in sufficient numbers. Again, these difficulties were felt particularly during the 1950 - 1960 period but, contrary to what happened at the primary level, only less than half the countries had succeeded in reversing the trend during the 1960s and had obtained a rate of increase in their teaching personnel higher than the rate of increase in secondary school enrolments. Once more, the obvious short-term and stop-gap reaction has been to recruit under-qualified personnel. It is interesting to see that around 1965 the difficulties are much greater in those countries which had completely unified the first cycle of secondary education: Italy with 17% non-qualified teachers; Yugoslavia with 41% of the teachers without proper qualifications in the subject they are teaching; Sweden with a huge shortage of university-trained teaching staff at this level. In contrast, countries where a parallel system of secondary education persists, with secondary modern schools, for example, the proportion of teachers considered non-qualified is much lower, because primary school teachers can more easily obtain the additional and complementary qualifications.

Higher education has witnessed in many countries what can properly be called an enrolment explosion. If this is taken into account, it must be concluded that the recruitment effort has been gigantic because, in overall terms, many countries have been able to let their teaching staff grow at the same pace as the number of students. But the important factor to note here is that this has only been possible by recruiting relatively more teachers of a lower status as compared to the full professors, thus modifying to an important extent the initial qualification structure of teaching personnel at the higher education level. It is beyond the scope of this chapter to discuss whether traditional training requirements were in fact too "high" and could only be justified in an elitist system, and whether the observed "deterioration" was not unavoidable in view of the mass involvement in the system. While, at the university level, the proportion of full professors with a doctorate has decreased nearly everywhere, it seems that the countries with traditionally very high training requirements for full university professors are precisely those where the supply of teachers has been lagging farthest behind demand and where larger and larger numbers of assistants and auxiliary staff had to be appointed to keep overall student-staff ratios at a reasonable level. In some instances, it was institutional rigidities which prevented existing vacancies from being properly filled rather than because of lack of financial resources.

From this rapid survey it has become clear that educational authorities took up the challenge of the sharp increase in teacher demand in two ways: by immediately taking emergency measures to hold the position and by, at the same time, starting to draw up middle- and long-term policies. The emergency measures consisted of: (i) more intensive utilisation of teachers (within the normal functioning of the existing system); (ii) attempts to enable former teachers (especially married women) to take up teaching again; and (iii) provisionally lowering the level of the various qualifications officially required. The main objective of the longer-term measures was to increase the inflow into the teaching profession of people with the traditionally required qualifications. Particular emphasis was laid on the socio-economic aspects of the teachers' status so as to attract and retain higher education graduates in the face of competition from other branches of activity. The failure to integrate the various measures into a coherent policy, and the fact that it was frequently necessary to keep in force measures which were only intended as provisional, stem in part from the inadequacy if not almost total lack of forecasting machinery in many countries. Statistics both of stocks and flows of teachers are rare and, when they do exist, are of little use because they are not sufficiently detailed. Given the strategic position they occupy, at the crossroads of the quantitative and qualitative domains, the teaching force should have been the subject of reseach and development programmes with respect to training, recruitment and utilisation. In the rare cases when they were done, such studies were badly coordinated, although the need for them became more urgent with the implementation of educational reforms, such as those very briefly reviewed in the first section of this chapter.

All this means that, contrary to what happens in other branches of activity, the lack of qualified manpower and/or its cost implications did not lead to a systematic study of alternative utilisation patterns of real resources used in the education sector as part of an effort to develop new learning and teaching techniques and methods (see also section 3 below). It should be added that, in any case, teachers would have been reluctant to accept such changes because the content of their initial training and the slowness in recognising the need for continuing training left them unprepared for it. In the absence of reliable planning machinery based on research, the education authorities did not grasp the opportunity offered to them to train differently the increasing numbers of young student-teachers they were recruiting precisely to provide mass education. The increased rate of recruitment has rejuvenated the teaching body, and these new teachers are due to spend a long time in the educational systems of the countries in question. Without programmes for systematic continuing training little progress is to be hoped for.

It seems that the pressure of events has prevented educational authorities from taking anything but a purely quantitative point of view. This has resulted in quite an accomplishment in terms of the scale of training and recruitment. But with this approach it has not proved possible to reconsider the use currently made of teachers' qualifications, and what such qualifications should really be. Because it should be clear that what is at stake is the definition of the teacher and the functions he must perform which are largely conditioned by the type of pupils and students he will have to deal with. This problem has remained largely untouched during the period under review.

3. Educational Technology

The term "educational technology" has come to have two quite distinctly different connotations. Many people when they use this expression are referring to the use of hardware, such as audio-visual devices, motion picture projectors, slide projectors, audio-tape units, video-tapes, television and computers. Another group uses "educational technology" to refer to the technology of instruction, i.e., the application of scientific methods and systems engineering concepts to the development of more efficient means of instruction (regardless of whether or not these techniques involve the use of any electrical hardware). The definition of "educational technology" as the technology of instruction has an obvious parallel to the more general use of technology. This definition is rapidly becoming the more common use of the term. Many of the proponents of educational technology contend that, even though present costs may be significantly increased, the consequent advantages (such as a higher rate of student learning, a more uniform mastery of the subject matter required, a reduction in the number of drop-outs, circumvention of the shortage of adequately trained teachers, etc.) have very large economic implications for society. Such arguments have a great deal of appeal and may have very important long-term economic significance. However, this point of view is futile unless society provides the additional funds necessary, and few governments have appeared disposed to do so. Thus far, it appears that the only way that we can economically defend expenditures for educational technologies in most of our educational systems is through a change in the teacher - student ratio or a more even utilisation of the physical plant. It is in these respects that the present discussion is quite obviously related to the survey presented above related to financial and real resources for education.

During the period with which we are concerned, the introduction of educational technology was in the main reduced to the use of material as *supplementary media*. By this we mean material used by the teacher as an aid in making presentations to the class. This includes the traditional blackboard or its modern equivalent the overhead projector, photographic slides, motion pictures, audio-tapes, etc. Since the teacher is still around as usual, the use of this hardware as supplementary media is bound to bring an increase in unit costs. This increase would not be an evil in itself if the effectiveness of this teaching process would be higher, i.e., if pupils would learn more or better, or equally well in less time. But this is very difficult to evaluate and there is, as so often, no general agreement on this point. In addition, certain gains in effectiveness, if they occur, do not always have a significant impact on costs or other resource inputs because of the rigidities inherent in school systems. For example, there is not very much point in mastering a subject quicker if the duration of teaching the subject is one academic year for everyone. It is obvious that many initiatives to introduce new techniques are jeopardised by these overall rigidities. It is extremely important that the question of effectiveness be addressed because classroom use of such media can be very expensive. The annual expenditures for audio-visual equipment and materials in the United States today (around 1970) is about $250 million for equipment and $300 to 400 million for curriculum materials.

More interesting and promising as compared to supplementary media is the *instructional use* of media. By this is meant a situation in which the entire presentation of the material is done through the media. There is no direct involvement of the teacher in the teacher-learning process other than to assign the material, answer questions when the students request assistance, and evaluate their performance. Media that can be used in this way include educational television, programmed texts, motion pictures, computers, and even standard texts. This more "radical" way of looking at educational technology has been, and still is resisted in all countries, not only because of its costs but above all because of the fundamental changes it is bound to bring into the entire educational process. The biggest barrier may well be that there has not been a meaningful professional role defined for the teacher in such circumstances. They are not fulfilling the traditional role for which they were trained: the organisation and presentation of the subject material to a class.

In two very comprehensive monographs (*The Teaching-Learning Paradox* and *The Medium May Be Related to the Message*), Robert Dubin of the University of Oregon (U.S.A.) has summarised the results of forty years of research on the relative effectiveness of different instruction techniques at the college level. These include the lecture, small group discussions, combinations of lecture and small groups discussions, supervised independent study, unsupervised independent study, and television instruction. The conclusion that he draws from these studies is that: "... these data demonstrate clearly and unequivocally that there is no measurable difference among these distinctive methods of college instruction when evaluated by student performance on final examinations." Such a conclusion obviously directly contradicts many people's theories and biases. However, he shows that, time and again, reliable research data have consistently shown no significant difference. Dubin draws the pertinent conclusion from these studies that the choice of instructional technique is not a question that needs to be resolved on the grounds of educational effectiveness. He argues that his review of the research demonstrates that this question is simply an administrative decision that can be made on the basis of purely economic considerations.

Finally, a few words will be said about the use of the *computer* as an integral part of the instructional process, either to teach or in some other way help the student to understand the subject matter being presented. The most publicised area is that of Computer Assisted Instruction (C.A.I.), where a student is working at a computer console and in which the computer is controlling the presentation of the instructional sequence to the student. This mode of presentation is an extremely exciting one for the individualisation of education because of the capability of the computer to carry out a very involved branching sequence based upon an analysis of the student's earlier responses.

But computerised instruction techniques are still very much in the development stage and are quite expensive. It appears that there are three conditions which are necessary before these costs become reasonable: (i) large numbers of students must use the curriculum so that the development cost per student is very small; (ii) the terminals must be effectively loaded throughout the day; and (iii) the terminals must be designed to provide those functions which are most useful without all the "frills" that we might like to have. Evidence from the United States indicates that if one were heavily to load some of the commercially available systems, the resultant cost would be $1.50 per student hour — which is competitive with many of the costs in American universities. Competent American authorities do not exclude the possibility that, within the next ten years, terminals will be available which can reduce this cost to something like 35 to 40 dollar cents per student hour.

In spite of the publicity it has been getting and the almost mystical attraction it exercises on many minds, the educational technology revolution has not yet occurred. As we have seen, the present functioning of the educational sector, a very labour-intensive sector with, indeed, rising unit costs, should constitute a favourable ground for technological innovation. In practice, as we have seen, things are not so simple because educational technology, viewed as an alternative technology of instruction, implies a radical break with current teaching and learning methods and, therefore, also implies profound changes in the role of the teacher. Furthermore, some of the more widely and wildly publicised media cannot stand the test of any cost-effectiveness calculation although, as was suggested, time is working in favour of the more capital-intensive techniques.

4. Concluding Remarks

In this chapter we have attempted an almost impossible "tour de force" — presenting in a few pages an account of the changes which the educational systems of the industrialised countries have experienced since 1950. We have reviewed the changes both in the *scale* of the educational enterprise — students, teachers, expenditure; and in the *structure* and *content* of it — external and internal organisation, equality of educational opportunity, training and recruitment of teachers, technology of instruction. Such an attempt must of necessity be incomplete, but we hope that in the choice of the evidence we have not been biased.

We have seen that between 1950 and the end of the 1960s, and taking the OECD area as a whole, primary education has seen its student body increase by more than 30%, secondary education by almost 100%, and tertiary education by 200%. In the bulk of countries educational expenditures have risen at a rate of more than 10% a year, which is twice as fast as the rate of increase in the national product and one-and-a-half times as fast as the rate of increase in total public expenditure. We have also indicated the huge efforts which countries have made in the domain of teacher training and recruitment, and finally we have outlined the current possibilities and limitations of educational technology. Several conclusions stand out:

(i) The unprecedented growth in enrolments at the secondary and university levels has *not* substantially reduced social class differences in educational opportunity. This does not mean that there are not more children from the lower social classes going on to the higher levels of education. It does mean that when the comparison is based on relativities, not much progress has been made. Every social group is getting more education and group disparities have thus remained the same. This can, therefore, be likened to increases in per capita income and the often-observed stability in income distribution.

(ii) Structural changes have been taking place in many countries leading to less differentiation at the secondary education level (trend towards comprehensive education) and more differentiation at the higher level. However, these changes are concerned with the institutional or external structure of the educational system. Much more timid is the trend towards introducing changes in the pedagogical or internal structure, i.e., changes at the level of the classroom.

(iii) The preceding conclusion is related to the subject of educational technology, understood in the sense of the technology of instruction. The hesitations here are not only to be explained in terms of costs and benefits, although we will be the last to underestimate this aspect. As important, if not more, is the fact that educational technology will only make sense if it revolutionalises what happens in the classroom.

(iv) This leads us to a final conclusion. In the classroom as currently conceived, we find a teacher who has a certain idea of his role and his function, largely based on the training he has received in the very educational system. Although due respect should be given to the quantitative efforts made by countries to let teacher training keep pace with the enrolment expansion, it must be emphasised that no start was made during the period under review with re-formulating the role and function of the teacher in the light of the new developments which will be with us tomorrow.

Having passed in review this fantastic (for once this expression does not seem too strong) development of the scale of education, one cannot escape a feeling of suspense. At the end of the 1960s, the quantitative development of school systems have reached a point where they are ripe for important and far-reaching qualitative changes. Many ideas, developments and innovations are awaiting their chance for large-scale implementation. We have mentioned a few timid forerunners which are being tried out in some countries, but on the whole educational systems have remained basically the same. It is this combination of the steamroller of quantitative growth, which continues its road unfatigued, and the growing recognition that alternative educational systems, methods and techniques are possible and perhaps necessary, which create this suspense in mid-air. In Part Three we will come back in much more detail to the future necessities, possibilities, and limitations.

IV

Continuities and Discontinuities: Conclusion of Part One

We have discussed the "more of the same" approach which was implicit in many of the writings in the fields of the economics of education. Gunnar Myrdal's (1968) critical assessment of the work on "investment in man" is not only valid in the South-East Asian setting: "The investment approach entirely ignores the fact that institutional and attitudinal reforms, which depend on political decisions rather than budgetary considerations, are needed to make investments in education 'pay off,' and the broader consideration that the success of educational programs depends on the policies pursued in all other fields as well as the direction of the educational programs themselves" (page 1550). Myrdal continues the argument by stating that the judgement to devote more resources to improving health and education is probably correct as far as it goes, but that it is vague and does not clarify the really important issues, namely: "where should health and educational programs be directed, how far should they be pushed, what means should they employ, and what other policy measures are needed?" (page 1551).

In the previous chapter we have shown that the single most important phenomenon on the educational scene during the past ten to twenty years has been the increase in the scale of the educational enterprise, which corresponds quite unambiguously with the "more of the same" approach alluded to above. To be sure, structural changes, of the external type, have become more widespread during the 1960s but the goals and objectives of education have remained basically the same. In other words, during the period under consideration the continuities of educational policies, educational outlooks, educational practices, etc., have by far outweighed the discontinuities. It is true that the impressive growth in enrolments can in itself be called a discontinuity, hence the well-known expression "educational explosion." This makes the question why not more pronounced discontinuities have occurred in goals, outlooks and practices an even more pressing and intriguing one.

1. Three Models

It is possible to imagine three, what might be called,"value models of education." We will call them the continuity model, the intermediate model and the discontinuity model. The *continuity model* implies no basic changes in objectives, outlooks or processes. The educational system, according to this model, should be left as it is, except for routine changes now and then. The system does not adjust to changes occurring in society at large, except in terms of numbers and hence of scale. In this model, the school is lagging behind the developments of its environment, at least in those cases where we are not in the presence of a completely static society.

In the *intermediate model*, there is an interdependency between education and society, which is effective in the sense that the educational goal structure is dynamic: depending on developments in society at large, certain educational goals gain or loose in terms of the emphasis they get. This, then, points to a relatively passive attitude of education in the interdependency relationship: education will always lag somewhat behind developments in society, but will eventually catch up. However, within this intermediate model we find another variation in which it is the educational system that in certain respects precedes development in society and, thus, contributes to accelerated societal change. In the first variation, the intermediate model tends towards the continuity model in that, at that extreme on the continuum, education will tend to resist change as long as possible, and only introduce minimal changes when the pressures become really strong. In contrast, the second variation tends towards the discontinuity model in so far as, in its extreme form, the education system is considered strong enough an independent force to change societal structures and habits. Examples of changes in the priority structure of educational policy objectives are: a growing emphasis on equality of educational opportunity in many countries and a trend towards putting more stress on individual development as a major goal. The most interesting and challenging question with respect to the latter objective is whether education can create and respond to new patterns and models of individual development, without which the orientation to social and economic goals will continue to generate social discontent and individual frustration.

In its more independent and forerunner variation, this model can imply basic breaks away from the past with respect to educational structures, curricula and teaching methods.

The *discontinuity model* implies, first of all, a belief that, given the introduction of appropriate changes, the educational system can have a profound, independent effect on societal beliefs and value structures. It may, of course, also mean the adaptation of the educational system to a society, the belief and value-structures of which have changed beyond recognition from those predominant in the region of the world we are concerned with. Whatever the situation may be, the discontinuity model means that educational goals have changed basically, for example, in the direction of placing more emphasis on the students becoming effective thinkers and learners, developing inquiry and problem-solving skills, acquiring social skills, and developing emotional awareness and self-identity. Reduced emphasis will be placed on absorbing specialised information and developing specific vocational skills. Less attention may also be given to grading, credentialling and otherwise labelling persons. At the limit, it may also mean the transformation of educational structures and content to an extent that the individual person is given the information, the methods and the tools to genuinely control his collective environment and individual destiny.

2. The Decade of Lost Opportunity?

If we apply the above very general framework (which will be further developed in Part Three) to past and current developments as described in the previous chapters, what conclusions can be drawn? According to the three models, the various inter-relationships between education and society can be summarised as follows: (i) education adapts quantitatively; minimal qualitative changes; (ii) education not only adapts in terms of scale, but also qualitatively in terms of goals, structures, etc.; however, it does so with a time-lag in relation to societal changes; (iii) same situation as in the preceding case, but instead of reacting with a time-lag, education takes the initiative without preceding the corresponding societal changes too much; (iv) education makes a qualitative jump with a view to changing the belief and value structure of society at large; and (v) education makes a qualitative jump in order to catch up with societal changes.

The work on, and the impact of, the economics of education, in its narrow interpretation, can quite definitely be seen as an attempt to subordinate education to the needs of society and, more precisely, to the needs of the economy. This, combined with the booming individual demand for education, has resulted in the increase in numbers, as reviewed. We have also seen that several structural changes were introduced, in particular at the secondary level. However, it was noted that this trend towards comprehensive education at the secondary level has not yet been accompanied on any significant scale by changes at the level of the classroom. Structural or other changes at the primary and tertiary levels of education have not been as important as those that have been introduced at the secondary level. All this seems to indicate that past trends in education conform to the continuity model and, at best, to the first variation of the intermediate model, relationships (i) and (ii) above.

The structural and other changes reviewed in the preceding chapters were introduced in the first place because of the pressure of numbers and for reasons internal to the educational sector itself, but also in order to stimulate and further the objective of equality of educational opportunity. We have shown that the formidable educational expansion observed has not changed to any considerable extent the situation with respect to group disparities in educational participation. Although progress has been made, the inequalities have persisted. Even in systems with high rates of participation in upper secondary and higher education, such as those of the United States and Japan, marked class disparities persist and, especially in the United States, regional and ethnic differences in participation rates have recently been given considerable publicity. Further, systems that have recently reported dramatic increases in enrolments (France, The Netherlands, Sweden, United Kingdom), and explicit educational policies to reduce disparities, have found these disparities to be very tenacious. Thus, also here the continuity model seems to fit the observed situation.

It could be argued that educational policies had to concentrate fully on the quantitative expansion with which they tried to keep pace and by doing so, stimulated further, according to the mechanism described in Chapter I. There was, therefore, neither time nor resources available to introduce important qualitative changes into educational goal structures at the various levels of decision-making. The machine was on the rails and rolled on and on. A moment's reflection will make it clear that the way things have been and are going, there may be no end to the quantitative expansion of education. In the United States, 6% of the relevant age-group graduated from high school in the beginning of this century. In the early 1970s, more than 80% completed their twelve years of education and if this trend continues, the United States will have reached the goal of universal twelve years' schooling by the time they celebrate the 200th anniversary of the Republic. Now, of course, the next target would be universal schooling covering fourteen years, then sixteen years and so on and so forth, *ad infinitum*!? And while one tries to reach this ever-evasive horizon there is neither time nor resources for rethinking the place and weight of education in society. Until something somewhere explodes.

It has only been in the latter half of the 1960s that it has been possible to observe the distinct symptoms of a movement towards the second variation of the intermediate model and even towards the discontinuity model, relationships (iii) and (iv) above. The move towards more active forms of the intermediate model is reflected in more imaginative and experimental educational policies for equal educational opportunity; the questioning of the relevance of many traditional educational objectives; the possibilities which are now being recognised in educational technology; the stress being put in more and more countries on educational innovation, etc. Potentially, this could lead to important "discontinuities in continuity" within a few years. On the other hand, the phenomenon of what came to be called "university unrest" — although in its various manifestations it reflects various of our models — can be equated in its most extreme form to a full-fledged discontinuity model. It is also an illustration of the lost opportunities when the only and exclusive concern of educational policy is to provide more of the same education to growing numbers.

In one sense, what has been achieved in the past ten to twenty years is exceptional and worthy of praise. So many more young people now have the opportunity to pursue further education as compared with older generations. But in approaching one goal, in this case a quantitative one, many "unexpected guests" have invited themselves. These new and unexpected problems have not been identified with sufficient clarity, and even less acted upon.

Tackling these problems in the 1970s will not be an easy task, since the past decade has not faced them squarely. In how far we are now better equipped to do so will be the major theme of Part Three. But we turn first to the efforts that *have* occurred in the field of educational planning.

Part Two

The Decade of Educational Planning?

V

The Educational Planning View at the Beginning of the Nineteen-Sixties

If there is one activity which has expanded more rapidly since 1960 than education it is educational planning. During the early 1950s, educational planning as a systematic, regularly organised activity hardly existed. The role of the national ministry of education was to administer the system and to ensure that it ran smoothly on a day-to-day basis. This explains why many of the countries with decentralised educational administration felt little need for any federal authority dealing with educational matters, and why, for example, the U.S. Office of Education was little more than a data-gathering agency. At the end of the 1960s, educational planning units have been established in a majority of countries, both within ministries of education as well as in other official bodies. There has been a rapid development of planning methods and forecasting techniques and much progress has been made in terms of the information base.

It is no coincidence that the emergence of planning came at a particular point in the history of education, namely at a time when the essential problem became the one of facing the pressure of numbers and, thus, of the quantitative expansion of the system. Against this background, described in Part One, the reasons why educational planning has expanded so fast become easier to understand. A first important point is that, although educational systems function to a large extent on the basis of individual choices, these choices are frustrated unless the system is efficient in the sense that it provides an effective path for the development of the individual through a series of institutions. In other words, the system in some sense must be planned. At the same time, there has been a growing recognition that the educational system as a whole must respond to both economic and social needs. This too leads to some measure of planning in the common interest. A second central consideration is that the public authorities (whether at central or local level) have major responsibility for administering the system. This also implies a responsibility for the effective use and management of the resources placed at the disposal of the system by the community. Finally, the educational system shows this peculiarity, that its parts are highly inter-related and changes occurring in one part very quickly affect the other parts.

Take all this in combination with the development in enrollments and it will be clear that it has become more and more difficult to have a policy (in the sense of making choices about the purposes, development and administration of the system) without having planning. The preceding considerations also explain that educational planning came to deal mainly with the question "how fast should we expand?" This question inevitably led to heavy emphasis on forecasting and to the incorporation of these forecasts in plans of quantitative expansion. The statistical basis for such forecasting thus became an inescapable point of departure. These are the essential questions and developments around which educational planning in the 1960s has grown. They also explain why educational planning in the past decade has been dominated by technical and methodological discussions, largely related to forecasting of the global needs for expansion and their incorporation into the educational plan.

1. Educational Policy Objectives During the 1950s and 1960s

The striking fact up to about the mid-1960s has been the attempt to quantify — and thus, it was thought, to operationalise — two general educational policy objectives. The first one has been described in the following terms: "to provide adequate education for all individuals and groups to the highest level they demand." The second has been stated as "to provide society and the economy with the trained manpower resources required for optimum functioning." An extensive literature has grown over the last 10 to 15 years related to planning techniques for the quantification of these two broad objectives. These techniques are discussed later in this chapter. At the same time, a certain number of structural changes were introduced (as reviewed in Chapter III) which in the main were meant to attain internal educational objectives, but also with a view to meeting a third and much more ambitious policy objective, namely equal educational opportunity. However, these structural changes were frequently proposed and defended on the grounds of the first two general objectives.

Looking back at the 1950—1970 period, the *implicit goal structure* of the educational polity has been dominated by the first general objective. We have witnessed a stunning race, which is still going on, during which educational policy measures have been continuously outpaced by the individual demand for education. Still in retrospect, it can be asserted that the second broad objective — the one concerned with economic and manpower requirements and which had an apparently predominant position in the *explicit goal structure* during the early 1960s — has in reality mainly served as the "objective" argument in favour of allocating additional resources to the educational sector. In other words, the second goal has served as an important educational lobby in favour of the first goal. This was easy because during the period under consideration the results of the quantification of both goals pointed in the same direction, "more." As to the third general objective — equal educational opportunity — it was rather equated with the first objective mentioned above, i.e., with individual demand for education, because as late as the early 1960s there was still a widespread belief that the expansion in enrolments would automatically bring with it a reduction in group disparities in educational participation. This has resulted in a passive policy towards the equal opportunity goal.

At the beginning of the decade three "planning methods" had been developed in relation to the first two objectives mentioned above. Each of these methods was meant to provide guidelines and criteria for the future development of the educational system, particularly of its quantitative aspects. These methods have already been briefly mentioned in previous chapters (in particular Chapter II) but it seems fitting, before dealing with them in slightly more detail, to quote the description of these approaches as presented in the *World Year Book of Education 1967*. That issue was concerned with the subject of educational planning, and it succeeded very well in catching both the ambiance and the dominant outlook of the beginning of the decade in that respect:

> First comes the social demand approach, of which the (British) *Robbins Report on Higher Education* is a splendid example. Attempts are made to forecast the future demand for places, taking account of demographic and social trends. The assumption is made that the provision of more education will of necessity benefit the economy so that the additional costs will not prove too heavy a burden. Consumer choice is given wide scope, partly because it is difficult to force young people to study subjects in which they are not interested and partly because it is exceedingly hard to forecast five or ten years in advance what kinds of training will be needed in a

> rapidly changing economy. It is evident that this approach commends itself to those who favour a permissive social climate, who are attached to traditional cultural values and who work in societies where public opinion has great influence.
>
> Next comes the manpower-requirements approach. Here the fundamental idea is that total production should grow as fast as possible, even if this involves some limitation of personal choice. Modern production needs educated workers trained in the right skills. Is it possible to estimate ten years in advance how much of each kind of skill a country will be able to employ? If so, how can the manpower be allocated and trained? The difficulty, of course, is that new kinds of industry continually come into existence and new kinds of specialisms are needed. The danger is that the aims pursued may be so narrow as to be self-defeating. Nevertheless this approach recommends itself in part because it leads rather quickly to the employment of quantitative data and in part because it stresses the employment aspects of education which are often overlooked.
>
> The cost—benefit approach, on the other hand, is a direct one: Work out the costs of various types of education and compare them with the returns, both to the individual and to society. Think of "expenditure" on education as a form of investment that is justified by the higher productivity and earnings of educated people. The calculations will then give a guide as to what sectors will best "pay off." These are the sectors to be developed (page 5).

The impetus to educational planning in the beginning of the 1960s came primarily from the economists and from their desire to harness education to economic growth. This meant that the function of educational planning was seen, above all, as that of quantifying some specific socio-economic indicators and the interrelationships between them. To a large extent, educational planning was considered identical with forecasting one or more easily quantifiable "goal" variables, such as the demand of students for education or the need for manpower of the economy.

2. Educational Planning Methods

We have seen that the educational planning view at the beginning of the 1960s was dominated by two basic policy objectives and supported by three methodological "pillars of wisdom." Normally, in the *élan* of a new venture, it could have been expected that the relatively small number of pioneers in this field would have combined their efforts in a harmonious and complementary manner. Nothing has been less true. During several years the emerging educational planning world was shaken by the sado-masochistic relationships of "mutually exclusive" thinkers, each carrying its pillar of wisdom with it as a weapon. We have already anticipated this debate in Chapter II. Here we would like to touch on some of the more technical aspects, starting with the two "economic" approaches.

It would be superfluous to explain once more in detail the methods used in the manpower approach and those adopted in the cost-benefit or rate-of-return approach. For this we can refer to the extensive literature in this area, the bulk of which is mentioned in the *World Year Book of Education 1967*. It is, however, essential to examine the critique addressed to each of these approaches. The main criticisms addressed to the manpower approach centre around the absence of cost-benefit analysis and, consequently, of a way of basing decisions on alternatives, and around the fact that the results of forecasts based on this approach are liable to large margins of error. The rate-of-return approach is being objected to as being a micro-economic and marginal concept applied to macro-economic situations and to average values. It is also argued that it would be mistaken, in many societies, to assume that factor prices are equal to productivity or opportunity costs, and that the use of cross-section material concerning earnings, age and qualifications to predict future earnings ignores the dynamics of sectoral and occupational structure. Moreover, and this is related to some of our observations in Chapter I, there are clearly other factors, next to education and age, influencing income levels. This would seriously limit the significance of the concept of average wage level for persons of a given educational level in a given age-group. Around this average, on which the rate-of-return approach is based, we would find a dispersion, probably of considerable proportions, in wage levels according to social origin, ability, sector of economic activity, etc. A study of this dispersion would seem essential in order to confirm or deny the importance of these factors in relation to those of age and educational level taken jointly.

The manpower approach, on the other hand, is situated in a Leontief universe where a network of technological relationships and coefficients is spread and where prices do not enter. The rationale of this approach was set out by Parnes:

> The rationale for according manpower forecasts a prominent role in assessing educational needs is perfectly straightforward.... The creation of a new steel works, for example, is meaningless unless provision is also made for the scientists, engineers, managers, technicians, skilled workers, clerical staff, etc. necessary to operate it. Since one of the functions of the

educational system in a society is to provide its work force with the abilities required for productive activity, it follows that that system must be reasonably well geared to the production requirement of the economy (page 73).

On the other hand, and this is worth repeating, the rate-of-return approach puts all its eggs in the wage basket and ultimately will say that each person or group of persons will earn the salary it deserves.... The conceptual framework of this approach holds more or less true according to the country under consideration. It would obviously be foolish to adopt such an approach in a country where, for example, the government has bound itself by law to employ any university graduate from whatever faculty or with whatever specialisation, within one year from graduation, at a fixed and relatively high salary. This may be an extreme situation, but it is a well-known fact that the salary structure in many countries does not necessarily reflect the countries' actual hierarchy of skill needs. Some advocates of the rate-of-return approach would then suggest the use of shadow prices — at least in those cases where the estimates of the rates-of-return are used not only as a measure of the *ex post* efficiency of investment in education, but for planning purposes as well. The use of shadow prices is often adopted in economic planning, when one has the impression that certain prices are distorted through imperfections in the market mechanism. But in the present case, how else can one, in the final instance, determine the shadow price for salaries of the various skill and/or educational categories other than by finding out their relative priority in terms of economic development needs! Thus we are back, basically, at the manpower approach. Let us, however, suppose that we have detected a country in which all the conditions are fulfilled for the rate-of-return approach to be perfectly valid. In that case, it remains, nevertheless, true that because one examines present salary differentials, one can only expect short-term signals from which no long-term conclusions can be drawn.

After these remarks on the rate-of-return approach, it should be added immediately that the results of a manpower-approach forecast, based upon technological relationships, hang indeed in thin economic air, not only because of the absence of an optimalisation procedure, but also because in most cases very little evidence is presented in these studies as to the problems of the "transition period," i.e., of how to get from the present occupational and educational structure of the labour force to the required one. As we observed already in Chapter II, the only indication presented in these studies, in the most favourable of circumstances, refers to the expansion of the various levels and branches of education necessary to reach the occupational and educational targets. However, very little or no attention is being given to the functioning of the labour market in general and to the salary and wage structure in particular. In other words, too little attention is given to motivation, attitudes, incentives, wages and social constraints. This partial approach has degenerated frequently in a situation where the manpower forecasts pointed in one direction, while the "social demand" of the individuals took quite another, because the incentives schemes, the salary structure, the social status attached to certain jobs pushed them in that direction. We are faced here with exactly the opposite kind of difficulty to the one noted above with regard to the rate-of-return approach.

The above remarks clearly point to the desirability of combining both approaches by adopting their soundest aspects. This would mean combining the forecasts of occupational and educational structures of the labour force with a thorough study of the actual functioning of the labour market mechanisms with specific attention to wage and salary differentials. Such an analysis would allow us to find out what needs to be changed in terms of incentives and relative wages and salaries so that the "technological" manpower forecasts can get their feet on economic ground. Conversely, such an analysis may very well result in considerable changes in the manpower forecasts originally made.

Another perfect example of mutually exclusive reasoning, in this case between the social demand approach and the manpower approach, is characterised if not caricatured by the following passage of the *Robbins Report on Higher Education* (1963):

> In principle, the problem of estimating the number of places required can be approached in two ways: by considering what supply of different kinds of highly educated persons will be required to meet the needs of the nation, or by considering what the demand for places in higher education is likely to be. We have decided that the second approach presents the sounder basis for estimates.
>
> We have found the first approach impracticable. For, while it is possible, for a number of professions and over a short term, to calculate with a fair degree of precision what the national needs for recruits will be, we have found no reliable basis for reckoning the totality of such needs over a long term.... Here we would only emphasise that, although we have not made national needs the main basis of our estimates, this must not suggest that we have any doubt of the value to the country of a greatly increased

stock of highly educated people and of the absolute necessity of a great increase in the present provision of places in higher education if this country is to hold its own in the modern world (page 48).

The phrasing of this passage suggests that the two approaches are considered to be alternatives and it is not clear how the Robbins Committee would have proceeded if the first had not been found impracticable. Would one approach have been preferred to another, and if so, why? Would the approaches have been reconciled in some way? If both approaches had been pursued separately, how would the Committee have responded to conflicting results? These questions do not get a clear answer in the *Robbins Report on Higher Education.* Indeed, the problem of different approaches to educational planning cannot be reduced to a mere technical issue. It should be discussed in the first place on the conceptual level. But clearly, in the background there is the fact that these approaches represent quite different "philosophies of education"; this is probably the deeper explanation behind the debate. At the conceptual level, one of the first persons who made a clear plea in favour of looking at the complementary relationships of the approaches was Mark Blaug (1967) in a well-known article "Approaches to Educational Planning." It seems fitting to close this section on educational planning techniques at the beginning of the decade with one or two quotes taken from the conclusion of this article:

If the demand for educational inputs depends in any way on its price, and this will necessarily be so if there is any substitutability between educational inputs, changes in supply are just as capable of altering that price as changes in demand, and therefore the quantity demanded of educational inputs is not independent of its supply. It follows that manpower forecasts must always be combined with social demand projections. Similarly, social demand projections by themselves are not a safe basis for educational planning. The tendency to upgrade skill requirements when the labour market becomes favourable is a well-attested phenomenon. It seems to have definite limits, however, as witness the incidence of "intellectual unemployment" in many countries. As we combine forecasts of demand with projections of supply, we start thinking quite naturally of earnings associated with education as indicators of impending shortages and surpluses. And since the costs of training various types of specialised manpower differ considerably, we will be led to consider variations in earnings in relation to variations in the costs of education. This is rate-of-return analysis, whether we call it that or not. By making such calculations on a year-to-year basis we keep a continual check on labour markets for highly qualified manpower and gradually develop insights into the ways in which education interacts with economic growth....

> We have come to the end of our story. The message has been that social demand projections, manpower forecasting and rate-of-return analysis are reconcileable and in fact complementary techniques of educational planning, but not as these approaches are presently conceived in the literature. Above all, they must be combined with specific educational reforms and an active manpower policy designed to minimise the burden of administrative planning decisions (pages 286—287).

3. Differences in "Basic Philosophy" or Temporary Differences in Emphasis?

We have already observed on several occasions that the development of the educational system has been more or less "autonomous," in the sense that educational planning has been concerned mainly with forecasting educational expansion without influencing it. This is what we shall later call "reactive planning." By and large, this development was mainly in line with the goal on which the social demand approach is based, namely satisfying the demand for education of the pupils and their parents. As to the role of the other approaches, it can be safely said that in practice the cost - benefit approach was practically never used by educational planners as an instrument in the decision-making process at the macro-institutional level. Moreover, with the growing recognition that many of the benefits of education are difficult to quantify in economic and monetary terms, an increasingly sceptical attitude has arisen towards rates-of-return results for decision-making. As mentioned earlier, the main purpose of the manpower approach seems to have been to provide the "objective" argument in favour of allocating additional resources to the educational sector.

It is not surprising, therefore, that the debate around the three approaches appeared to many as having relatively little policy relevance, a view which was re-inforced precisely by the "mutually exclusive" attitude on the part of the enthusiastic advocates of each of these approaches. However, the debate has implications which go far beyond the small circles of planning experts: for or against selection for university entrance, for or against (more) private financing of education. These questions, which are far from being solved, are an indication of the fact that the debate engendered in this way was not a mere "academic" dispute. Another illustration of the practical relevance of the debate has been touched upon in Blaug's conclusions above: Whatever the relative merits of these approaches, there will always be a labour market, i.e., a place were the supply of the degree- and diploma-holders from educational institutions will come up against the demand from the economy, both being forced to adapt one way or another.

This begins to give us a clue as to the deeper reasons behind the debate and which are related to the fact that the approaches — in particular the social demand and the manpower approaches, when interpreted in an extreme way, — reflect opposite basic philosophies of education. For example, in the Soviet Union the economic needs play a decisive role, and the educational system, particularly of course its upper-secondary and tertiary branches, has been firmly linked to the economic-technological locomotive. This is illustrated by the following quotations, which are taken from a 1967 UNESCO report on *Educational Planning in the USSR*:

> In the planned economy of the USSR, the indispensable condition for development, *including that of public education*, is to draw up a summary balance-sheet of labour resources. The object is to ensure their most rational use so that sufficient qualified workers and specialists will be available and full employment achieved (page 85).
>
> Such educational development in our country also accords with the task of communist instruction in the USSR; it is based on calculations of the demand for skilled workers and specialists and on the actual possibilities of expanding the physical plant of educational establishments, and it will ensure in the future a steep rise in cultural and technical standards and in the prosperity of the Soviet people (page 176).

In this case, it is clear that access to the higher rungs of the educational ladder is primarily determined by the manpower approach, and that not too much account can be taken of the individual and family demand for education. Although the situation seems rather clear cut, in reality it is a little more complicated than would appear at first sight. What follows applies mainly to specialised secondary and higher education, since basic primary and lower secondary education are planned as everywhere else according to social objectives, as reflected in the stipulations with respect to compulsory education. From the quotations above, it becomes obvious that Soviet planners attach much importance to the rational utilisation and full employment of their qualified personnel. Rational utilisation and full employment should not be interpreted in a global sense, but rather according to levels of skill and qualification. The "basic philosophy" implications are, therefore, that education should expand according to the forecast job opportunities, in order for every school leaver and graduate to find the relevant opening on the labour market in line with the expected and stipulated occupation-education relationships. This can and will, of course, result in more persons applying for, say, university education than will be admitted, in line with the manpower needs five to seven years hence. However, so the Soviet rationale goes, because of rapid rates of economic growth and the parallel upward shifts in the occupational structure of the labour force, the number of persons admitted to higher levels of education will also increase rapidly. Thus, an ambitious goal as equal educational opportunity, at high overall levels of participation, will eventually also be reached in the Soviet Union, but always in a balanced phasing with the developments in the economy and on the labour market.

In the countries with which we are mainly concerned here, the "basic philosophy" which guides educational policy decisions is more ambiguous, although "ambivalent" is probably a better word to characterise the situation. This was already suggested above, when we quoted the British *Robbins Report on Higher Education*. Another illustration of this state of affairs is the formulation of educational policy objectives, as it can be found in the report of the OECD, *Educational Policy and Planning: Netherlands*:

> (1) To develop positive moral and civic values and cultural attitudes among all people and to provide them with the skills necessary for self-fulfillment, so that they may appreciate and contribute to the cultural experience of society. To develop not only understanding of tradition but also the flexibility needed to innovate and accept innovation. To provide for the continuous broadening and deepening of these qualities among people.
>
> (2) To maintain the freedom of religious, social and other groups to pursue and intensify their own development. Such private groups in Dutch society have a constitutional right to carry out activities such as education as an extension of their beliefs. It is through these groups that the Dutch people attempt to express and develop their ultimate life values.
>
> (3) To provide education for all individuals and groups to the highest levels that they demand.
>
> (4) To provide society and the economy with the trained manpower resources for optimum functioning. Within the framework of satisfying the first three major goals, the educational system is required to respond to projected manpower needs.
>
> (5) To develop a large and increasing capacity in people to adjust themselves to the career and work changes demanded by modern technology.
>
> (6) To promote the free development of science, providing support for scientific training and research activities whose results are available for innovation in society in general and in the economic sector in particular (pages 26-27).

Objective 3 corresponds to what we have called the "social demand" for education, while 4, 5 and to a certain extent 6, reflect the economic and manpower needs of society for education. On the other hand, objectives 1 and 2 could be called "cultural objectives." The above objectives are typical for the Western countries, in the sense that we are always in the presence of a list of goals among which can always be found the economic-manpower aspects on the one hand, and the social-individual aspects on the other. It is, however, difficult to know in advance what the relative influences of each of these objectives will be on the specific educational policy of a country. In other words, the priority structure within the educational policy goals is not always clear. In retrospect (we have already touched upon this point and the Robbins quotation confirms this) it can be maintained that in the highly industrialised countries the "social demand" aspects have heavily ouweighed the manpower aspects. But again, this has been facilitated during the past period because both types of forecasts pointed in the same direction. Whether this will continue to be the case in the future is an open question to which we will come back in Part Three. But this much can already be said at this stage: It is not unrealistic to imagine a situation, in countries which maintain a precarious and rather "passive" equilibrium between the various educational policy objectives, that social demand will considerably overshoot the manpower needs. This may well lead to individual frustrations, mal-utilisation of highly qualified personnel and mis-allocation of scarce resources. The planning debate in the beginning of the 1960s was about the priorities in the educational goal structure; about fears of putting too much emphasis on one goal at the expense of another. The attempts to reconcile the "approaches" were based on the conviction that, for different goals to be met simultaneously, compromises must be made and a solution should be found which maximises economic growth, while minimising individual frustrations and mis-allocations of resources.

4. Concluding Remarks

We have tried to bring back some of the atmosphere which characterised the educational planning world in the beginning of the 1960s. In the presentation of the facts we have certainly been biased by the specific vantage point which was ours during the period, and we do not claim to have given a complete picture of the situation — in the next chapter, we will attempt to elaborate on this. Our sole objective here has been to recall the big debate about the approaches to educational planning which, although very often crude, unsophisticated and sometimes even intellectually dishonest, cannot be dismissed as either unimportant or outdated. Hopefully, we have made clear at least that much. What can and must be said is that the debate, which purported to be about educational *planning*, was singularly incomplete, because it did not go beyond the quantification of certain educational *policy goals*. In doing so — and this was suggested in the final chapter of Part One — it may have diverted the attention from other educational goals which, although apparently less easily subject to quantification, are not for that reason less important. Obviously, the first practical steps of educational planners were destined to go beyond the forecasting aspects.

VI

The First Steps

1. The Organisational Development of Educational Planning

In the late 1950s, special government agencies for educational planning could be found in only a few of the countries with which we are concerned. For example, within the Dutch Central Planning Bureau a special branch was charged with the task of educational planning. Parallel to this, a so-called Research Department in what was then the Ministry of Education, Arts and Sciences was concerned with the regular forecasting of the number of pupils in primary education and the corresponding demand for teachers. In France, the Planning Commissariat, established in 1946, obtained in 1951 an expansion of its mandate to cover the field of education, and a special commission was set up within the Commissariat for this purpose. This commission has carried out the preparatory work on the French Second Plan (1953—57), the Third Plan (1958—61), etc., concerning the educational sector. In Sweden, the need for coordination of the activities of the various Royal Commissions, working on problems of educational policy, led to the establishment in 1960 of a Planning Department within the Ministry of Education. However, a considerable part of the work on further plans for different sectors of the educational system was still undertaken by *ad hoc* commissions, usually well-equipped with their own planning staff.

In the beginning of the 1960s, Svennilson, Edding and Elvin (in their Washington Report on *Targets for Education in Europe in 1970*) cited France as "an outstanding example of advanced educational planning." The bulk of the work was still carried out by the Commission de l'Equipement Scolaire, Universitaire et Sportif within the framework of overall French economic planning. The work of this Commission was described in some detail by Raymond Poignant, who was then its rapporteur. He describes the work in progress in 1963 on the preparation of the IVth Plan:[1]

> In France we have the good fortune (as we think) of working within a general plan. The forecasts form part of a whole and are published by the Commissariat Général du Plan .... The work fits into a larger whole which naturally simplifies conclusions. As an example, the Government waits for the educational study in order to take decisions with regard to the allocation of school equipment during the next four years .... The preparation of the Plan, the drafting of the report and its execution are carried out on a national scale by the civil service as a whole. The report is based on enquiries carried out among all local authorities, so that the educational authorities in the various provinces, departments and separate establishments are associated with the preparation of the Plan from the outset. The Report is then summarised in a document put before Parliament; this is the General Plan for Economic and Social Development, containing a chapter on education, accompanied by applications for funds for school buildings, primary schools, secondary schools, vocational schools and universities. Parliament studies the Report, discusses it and, after lengthy discussion, generally adopts the Plan.
>
> Of course, there is always a gap between what the "Commission du Plan" asks and what the Government decides, but the gap is steadily narrowing. Drawing up a Plan is not a matter of defining an ideal, but of adjusting limited possibilities to limitless requirements, and there is clearly a difference between making forecasts, determining requirements and financing them. And unfortunately, only 85 or 90% of the funds requested are normally granted.

Poignant went on to describe the related work of the Manpower Commission but admitted that "even in France there is still no very close link between the plans for educational development and the projections of the active population."

Svennilson and his collegues found the British situation with regard to educational planning very different: "Whereas France can traditionally rely on forms of centralised administration, the tradition in Great Britain is one of devolution to local educational authorities, and indeed to schools themselves." Educational planning at that time, and to a large extent since, was equated with the preparation of reports by *ad hoc* advisory committees. The most important in recent years have been the Crowther Report (1959) on the education of children between the ages of 15 and 18; the Albermarle Report (1960) on the Youth Service; the Newsom Report (1963) on secondary education of average and less-than-aver-

---

[1] In a mimeographed document presented to an OECD working meeting in 1963.

age ability; the Robbins Report (1963) on higher education; and the Plowden Report (1967) on primary schools.

However, despite the devolution of responsibility to local authorities and individual schools and universities, and despite the work of the *ad hoc* advisory committees, the Department of Education and Science has a clear responsibility for general direction and it is increasing its rôle as a forecasting, planning and policy-making body. In particular, it normally provides secretariat and research facilities to the *ad hoc* committees. Indeed, it can be claimed that one function of these committees is to put across to the public, in the guise of informed opinion, policies which might be less acceptable if they emanated directly from a government department. Some of the forecasting and planning functions were formalised in 1966 with the creation of the Planning Branch, whose responsibilities were defined as: (i) the control of planning services; (ii) the coordination of various elements of policy; and (iii) special studies on long-term planning. The Branch has responsibility also for the Department's educational research programme and its aim is "to use the available funds specifically as an instrument of policy and to coordinate research proposals so as to make the maximum contribution to policy formation."

Another country which has made extensive use of *ad hoc* advisory committees is Norway. One of them, making proposals for the period to 1970, reported at about the same time as the Robbins Committee in Great Britain. Other bodies which have been important in Norway, as in some other countries, are the Research Councils. In the case of Norway, the Government Research Councils and, in particular, their Joint Board, were involved in fairly extensive planning activities, mainly related to secondary and higher education. However, as in many other countries, such *ad hoc* planning and forecasting activities proved to be inadequate in a period of rapid educational expansion, and a Planning Department was established within the Ministry of Education in 1964. The immediate task of this group was the "preparation of a programme for the period 1966—1969 of activities in fields covered by the Ministry of Education, as part of the general four years' programme of the Norwegian Government."

Concerning Sweden, Svennilson *et al.* had this to say in 1961: "...a forecasting unit with a large research staff has been established within the Labour Market Board. It investigates long-term trends in the demand for various types of education and training. Special planning problems, such as the extension to nine years of compulsory schooling to include occupational education and training, are delegated to Royal Commissions. A special unit in the Department of Education coordinates all planning activities." An important development in Sweden, as in Norway, is "rolling planning." This is a device by which a new four-year plan of public expenditure is made every year and revised in the light of policy decisions taken and exogenous circumstances in the previous year. The most interesting development in Swedish educational planning during the decade is the attempt to introduce "rolling reform," a concept even more ambitious than that of "rolling planning." The need for rolling reform derives from the fact that "to produce their full effect, educational reforms take a very long time, which may run into decades, and no sooner has one reform been carried through than others must be introduced.... The official Swedish view is that in the present-day world delays can no longer be tolerated and that adjustments of the educational system to changing requirements must be continuous." The machinery for rolling reform consists essentially of integrated programmes of research and planning from the Council of Educational Planning down to the individual educational institutions. Flows of information between the various decision-making levels and the public at large are left as open as possible.

One group of countries, which started the decade with virtually no educational planning machinery but which, for a certain period at least, received a lot of attention as they grappled with the problem of planning education for economic and social development, were those that took part in the so-called Mediterranean Regional Project (MRP) of the OECD. In their Washington Report, Svennilson and his colleagues observed:

> The major endeavours by the six countries concerned — Greece, Italy, Spain, Portugal, Turkey and Yugoslavia — to work out their educational needs for the next fifteen years and to provide Ministers of Education and Finance with detailed programmes is undoubtedly one of the most advanced projects of its kind within the OECD area and beyond. Both the work and the costs are shared by the OECD and the national ministries involved. A good deal of research work has already been carried out and the governments concerned have shown themselves to be encouragingly open-minded towards the idea of long-term planning in education.

This experience has been extensively written up elsewhere. The MRP methodology — heavily biased towards the manpower approach — has been exported to all parts of the world. The country reports produced under the auspices of this programme should be considered as planning documents, and not as educational plans for immediate implementation.

Among the countries that participated in the Mediterranean Regional Project, Portugal established a strong technical planning group in the Ministry of Education in 1966. In Spain also a similar group works in the Ministry of Education, whereas in Greece and Turkey educational planning is, in theory, more closely linked to economic development planning, in the former case by being located in the Ministry of Coordination and in the latter by being situated within the framework of the five-year development plans, elaborated by the State Planning Organisation. An interesting aspect of recent Turkish educational planning is the stress put on qualitative aspects of education. This has been relatively neglected in much of the educational planning of the past decade.

The United States is a very special case, partly on account of its vast size and because the Federal Government has constitutionally no power in the field of education. Thus, the picture in the U.S.A. is very diversified; states such as California and New York have educational planning machinery as "advanced" as any in the world, while in some other states it is virtually non-existent. At the same time, educational planning and economics of education as academic subjects, are undoubtedly more developed in U.S. universities than anywhere else. Educational forecasts are made and models are built by hundreds of institutions and individuals.

At the Federal level, three developments may be noted. First has been the increasing expenditure by the Federal Government on education. This rose from about 7% of total educational expenditure in 1960 to 12.5% in 1967. When this is considered in conjunction with the 10% per annum increase in overall educational expenditure throughout the period, it gives the idea of the increase in the amount of Federal expenditure — it doubled between 1963 and 1968. The second interesting development was the Presidential directive in 1965 instructing all government agencies to make use of the programme budgeting techniques developed in the early 1960s in the Department of Defense. This in effect meant that a planning machinery had to be established in the Office of Education (the American equivalent of a Federal Ministry of Education), not directly to plan the development of U.S. education, but in order to be able to develop criteria for the allocation of Federal expenditures. The third development of interest, though not directly governmental, was the establishment of the Carnegie Commission on Higher Education. This Commission would, for the first time, study the whole of the higher education system of the United States and make recommendations on future development.

A similar movement towards some form of national planning in a decentralised system has occurred in the German Federal Republic, and there are indications of similar developments in the two countries which started the decade with absolutely no formal national or federal interest in education — Switzerland and Canada.

2. The Development in the Substantive Area Covered by Educational Planning

In the previous chapter, we noted that educational planning came to deal mainly with the question of "how fast should we expand?" This, in turn, explains why the educational planning debate was dominated by technical and methodological discussions, largely related to forecasting of the global needs for expansion. However, in the concluding remarks of that chapter, we also observed that "even the first steps of educational planners went beyond the forecasting aspects." It is important, therefore, to give a brief account of the content of a "typical" educational planning document. It must be said immediately that much, if not the bulk, of the time of educational planners is devoted to *ad hoc* studies and to routine work, rather than to the elaboration of "comprehensive" educational plans. Moreover, we reserve the term "educational planning document" for prospective studies of educational development, which are a prerequisite for the elaboration of an educational plan.

A "typical" educational planning document of the first half of the 1960s would — in a more or less complete and sophisticated way — be concerned with at least three big domains: (i) pupils and students within the system; (ii) other educational inputs: teachers, buildings, etc.; and (iii) the relationship of the educational system with the other sectors of society. The domain covered by the first two points has also been called the "internal efficiency" of the educational system, because that part of a planning document would deal with the optimal use of teaching staff, equipment and school buildings, with drop-out, repeating and promotion of pupils from one grade or form to another, with the transition from one educational level to another, in short, with what might be called the "productivity" of the educational system. The third point has sometimes been labelled the "external efficiency" or effectiveness of education, because it relates what happens *in* the education sector to the social and economic objectives of a country.

Thus, in the more complete and comprehensive of the educational planning documents, three parts can be distinguished. A first part deals with the analyses of the present situation, and the recent trends, of what happens and has happened inside the education system, in terms of access to and flows through the system of pupils and students and of real and monetary resource inputs. In a second part, the future scale of the education system is assessed, on the basis either of social demand forecasts or manpower forecasts or both. A third part then maps out the future development pattern of the educational system, taking due account of the conclusions reached in the first part with respect to the internal efficiency. It also includes assessments of implications concerning teachers and buildings necessary to meet the forecast numbers of pupils and students, and normally ends up with the financial resources implied by the educational development perspective.

Little needs to be added as far as the content of the second part is concerned. Some planning documents adopted only a manpower approach, others only a social demand approach, and some showed both forecasts side by side. These aspects were sufficiently covered in the previous chapter, so we need not return to them here. Examples of cost—benefit analysis, the rate-of-return approach, are non-existent in educational planning documents. As for the analysis of the internal dynamics of education, some interesting developments have occurred with respect to the student body situation. In many analyses of the late fifties and early sixties one is struck by the primitive nature of the investigations with regard to the developments of the pupil and student numbers. One is usually presented with the trends in the *stocks* of pupils in the various branches and levels of education over a certain number of years, supplemented by calculations of enrolment ratios for very broad age-groups. Very crude approximations were made of drop-out rates by comparing time series of first-year enrolments in a given school cycle with time series of graduates from that cycle. It will be clear that the comparison of numbers of pupils (stocks) at two or more points in time hides important phenomena, such as the proportion of repeaters, pupils who move to a different branch of education, etc. For these very reasons, stock data are rather poor for making social demand forecasts as well. The only way out of these difficulties is to base the analyses and the forecasts on *flow data*. A succinct statement on the advantages of using flow data can be found in a 1967 OECD publication *Methods and Statistical Needs for Educational Planning.* To take a minimum of advantage of such a scheme, the following information would be required in the case of pupils: (i) detailed and accurate information on inflows into the educational system. This means principally reliable demographic forecasts; (ii) estimates of movements of pupils between grades and between different branches and levels of education in successive years. This is necessary in order to obtain accurate information regarding the progress of a cohort of pupils during their educational career. For this we need to know for each grade the rates of promotion, repeating and drop-out; for the last grade the graduation rate, as well as the transition rates to other levels and branches of education; (iii) information, at least at the key transition points (for example, completion of compulsory education, entry into higher education) on individual characteristics of pupils that are likely to affect their transition probabilities (social background, geographic location, intelligence or some measure of previous educational attainment, sex, age, and in some cases, race and religion). This is not only necessary to understand better the actually observed situation, but also to improve the forecasts of future numbers of pupils. In the words of the above-mentioned publication:

> It is not, however, sufficient merely to make global projections of total enrolments for at least two quite separate reasons. In the first place, no educational system is fully "comprehensive" in the sense that all pupils have exactly the same educational experience while they are at school or university. Total enrolments are distributed amongst different types of school, different specialisations, different geographic regions, etc. To be useful, forecasts of enrolments must take account of these differences, and also of the movements of pupils between the different elements of the educational system at each age. Secondly, children themselves are not homogeneous. They enter the educational system from different environmental conditions and with different inherent abilities. As they pass through the different levels of the system, such differences are often magnified rather than diminished .... Thus, while total enrolments are heavily influenced by demographic factors, the actual inflow of pupils into any particular branch of education is determined by a large number of other factors which exert an influence from both the input and the output sides (page 18).

As we said earlier, it is in this domain of pupil and student flows that several countries, for example The Netherlands and Sweden, made considerable advances during the 1960s both in terms of data collection and analysis for the observed situation, and in terms of the elaboration of student flow models for forecasting purposes. In certain other countries, where less systematic effort has been invested in following cohorts through their educational career, the stock data have been improved and refined to a degree that, with certain assumptions, they can be converted into flow approximations. Interesting models have been developed to this effect.

The situation is different, and this was already suggested in Chapter III, with respect to real and monetary resource inputs, in particular the situation concerning teachers' supply, qualification and utilisation, the quality and utilisation of buildings and equipment, and the costs, expenditure and finance of education. As for teaching staff, teacher flow data, along the lines indicated above for pupils and students, would be desirable, and have, in fact, been proposed and recommended in the 1967 OECD publication. However, progress here is very slow, if it exists at all. This may be explained, partly at least, by two reasons. In the first place, in the case of pupils the educational system can be considered as a fairly well-defined system which pupils enter in a fairly steady flow, and within which they move, following a number of quite well-defined patterns determined by the structure of the system. Flows within the system are of a relatively minor importance in the case of teachers and such movements as do take place do not follow a well-defined structural pattern. In the case of teacher flows, therefore, attention is devoted mainly to the teachers entering and leaving the profession and their reasons for so doing, whereas many of the most interesting pupil transfers are those within the system itself. Secondly, the values of the transition coefficients for teachers entering and leaving the profession are less likely to remain stable or to follow well-defined trends. In the case of pupils, the transition proportions are unlikely to change sharply from one year to the next, because most of the fixed facilities remain intact, and new buildings are, in most cases, only a small proportion of existing capacity; furthermore, pupil flows depend very much on the traditions and inherent propensities of the society. For example if in year t_0, families wish to send 5% of their 18-year-old children to the university, they are unlikely to want, or be able, to send 10% in year t_1. However, the proportion of, for example, university graduates who take up secondary school teaching may be subject to many economic and educational policy influences that can change markedly from one year to the next.

Whatever the reasons, the fact is that many educational planning documents have not gone very much beyond the presentation of total number of teaching staff by level and branch of education, some rough calculations of pupil - teacher ratios, and crude information concerning the qualifications of teachers, sometimes by age. In several highly developed countries the total number of teachers at any given point in time is not even known with any degree of precision! Outflows from and re-entries into the teaching profession are relatively unexplored areas. The exact characteristics and the utilisation pattern of the teaching staff are largely unknown. It follows that pupil - teacher ratios are, at most, very approximate indicators, and may sometimes even be misleading. This is particularly the case at the higher levels of education. And then we do not even mention other-than-teaching staff, which is a rather meaningless aggregate in the statistical tables presented in most planning reports. Analogous remarks could be made about school buildings.

Turning to the cost, expenditure and finance side, the picture is not much better. Again, we are normally presented with total public expenditure per year and by level and branch of education. If we are lucky, we also have information on the private educational sector, although in many cases this is still a closed book. The usual indicators shown in the planning reports are educational expenditure as a proportion of gross national product or of national income, and sometimes also as a proportion of total public expenditure. Unit costs are usually calculated by dividing total expenditure per level of education by the number of pupils enrolled in that level. Not very much is shown as to how these unit costs are built up from below, i.e., what are the components and their weights, for example, teacher component, equipment component, administrative component, laboratory component, etc. The information given concerns the expenditure side; educational planning reports do not give any information about the opportunity costs of students: inputs of students' time are apparently not considered a cost.

The foregoing remarks were all concerned with an appraisal of the "typical" content of a part one of a "typical" planning report. As we mentioned already, the "typical" part two was dealt with in the previous chapter and we can therefore limit ourselves to a few words about "the" third part of "the" planning document. In most cases, this part is restricted to the presentation of annual flows over the forecasting period of pupils and students and their implications with respect to teacher, building and financial requirements. There is no critical evaluation of educational policy goals. At the most, an enumeration of existing goals, as exemplified in the preceding chapter, without priority indications. Nevertheless, one sometimes encounters a discussion about structural changes — as in the Swedish case *à propos* the "comprehensivation" of secondary education. Usually, however, the more qualitative and structural aspects of educational development have been absent in the educational planning documents of the early 1960s, and, it may be added, of the 1960s *tout court*.

But, as we noted earlier, the bulk of the time of most educational planners has not been spent on tracing through the long-term development perspectives and implications of educational policy, but rather on *ad hoc* studies and routine work. Whenever a question is asked in Parliament, or from another influential source, about the regional distribution of teacher-training colleges, about the teacher situation in pre-primary education, etc., there is a chance that the educational planning department is asked to prepare the Minister's reply. This is so because the department is supposed to possess all the relevant data. Somewhat more complex educational policy matters are usually *not* given over for analysis to the educational planners. For these matters a committee is often created, but sometimes the planning office may do the calculations, or to put it in a nicer way, it may act as the secretariat of the committee. In between these two extremes, educational planning departments are sometimes asked to write a report about such matters as the role of research in educational planning and policy, the present state of play with respect to equality of educational opportunity, future teacher needs, etc.

3. Concluding Remarks

An attempt was made here to give an overview of how educational planning units have been set up, and what they have set out to do. Two conclusions stand out. The first is that there has been a marked tendency, during the past decade, for official groups to be established with responsibility for national educational planning. The precise function of these groups varies according to the degree of responsibility for education of the national authorities and the extent to which the country is embarking on an active policy of educational development. The second conclusion is that this mushrooming of educational planning activities has been most instrumental in improving the information and data base on which more rational decision-making in educational matters must rest. We emphasise this point because our critical review of planning activities in this chapter may at times have given the impression that the situation in this respect is still hopeless. The situation is certainly far from ideal, but if one compares an educational planning document of the late 1950s with one ten years later, it will become clear that in the majority of cases the statistical base and its analytical treatment have changed beyond recognition.

However, a third, and to our mind most important, conclusion has been implicit in most what we have said here. The contribution of the educational planning groups to policy-making is not at all clear. It has been suggested that they acted rather as passive service departments, with little initiative of their own. In Great Britain and Norway, for example, the planning groups have supplied the research and other facilities for Royal Commissions rather than the substance; in general, they provide the information on which decision *may* be taken rather than advice on the decisions that *should* be taken. This is perhaps desirable; it permits the planners to work relatively unhampered by the vagaries of public and political opinion and permits them to devote their attention to the complex technical issues rather than endlessly debating questions of value judgement. However, it also has its dangers. Of these, the most serious is that just when they are needed most, the planners often have little to say. For example, for a decade they have forecast huge expansions in higher education and they demonstrated that this expansion was desirable from social and economic viewpoints, but they have not given sufficient thought to the content, structure and cost of higher education. The result is that in many countries important decisions are currently being made with very little advice from the groups that ought to be most qualified to give it — which brings us to the inter-relationship between educational planning and educational decision-making.

VII

The Two Worlds

Planning has been defined as a rationalisation technique for decision-making, or as the process of preparing a set of decisions for action in the future. We suggested at the end of the previous chapter that during the 1960s the contribution of educational planning activities to policy making had been marginal, if at all existent. We have seen that a major part of educational planning work concentrated on assessing the future scale of the enterprise, in terms of enrolments, teachers and finance. At the same time a certain number of structural innovations were decided upon and introduced. It has not always been clear what kind of relationship, if any, existed between the forecasts as practised by the planners on the one hand, and structural, curriculum and educational-technological changes on the other. Moreover, it is fair to say that the future consequences of such "qualitative" changes have not been clear either. Thus, and exaggerating only a little, we are faced with the paradoxical situation that, in the case of the forecasts that were made, it is often difficult to see how they have influenced educational policy decisions; at the same time it is equally difficult to detect what the future consequences are of many of the educational policy decisions, because they have rarely been accompanied by even a minimum of consequential analysis. This can be further summarised by the following proposition: On the one hand we have forecasts, some planning and no policy; on the other hand we have policy based on some planning and no forecasts.

The above considerations have led us to choose as the title of this chapter "the two worlds." One is a small world in which people, who call themselves or have been so labelled by others, educational planners, are busy making analyses, forecasts and other esoteric calculations. The other is a bigger world where educational policy decisions are taken through a process which is often even more esoteric than the activities of the "planners." It is our contention that these two worlds have in the main been living in juxtaposition; maybe "subordination" would have been a better word, and this foreshadows one of our theses which we will develop later. But let us, for the moment, stick to the first expression and advance some reasons which may help to explain this juxtaposition of the two worlds. Two major reasons can be put forward: one is related to the degree of technical sophistication of the educational planning activities; the other concerns the organisational and human aspects — we would almost be inclined to write, the psychological aspects — of what educational planning is all about. These two clusters of problems will be dealt with in turn.

1. Technical Aspects

We can do no better than to start this section with a quotation from the concluding chapter of the stimulating book by Armitage, Smith and Alper (1969), *Decision Models for Educational Planning:*

> We have tried to show that "patterns" detected in past data are a highly fallible guide to the future development of the system; observed trends may persist for some time but they are unlikely to be perpetuated forever. What we must attempt to do is to understand how the system "works" and for this we want more than data which only tells us what happened. We must seek, and anticipate, data which tells us *why* it happened. For this a decision model is indispensable.
>
> We started this book from the viewpoint of making descriptions which led to projections. Some readers may have found this too far distant from our principal concern with planning. This approach was adopted because it seemed to be the natural entry point from "traditional" practices and, indeed, awareness of the need for models sprang from the pressure of the increasing number of projection exercises carried out in the recent past. While there is nothing reprehensible in the desire to make computable models which facilitate more, speedier and better projections, we believe that it is unsatisfactory to hold such a limited ambition. A few years ago when computers did not exist to lighten the computational burden, the making of projections was a heroic task. However, the responsibility for making projections and the responsibility for making decisions were divorced with the result that they were virtually separate activities.... We believe that model building should not be confined to the mere extention and perpetuation of established procedure but that a fresh outlook is both necessary and possible.
>
> We cannot subscribe to the system of planning which has probably existed and which has certainly been advocated by some writers in which projections are made in a decisionless vacuum and decisions are made in some undefined way with a few projections as relevant evidence.... So long

as producing projections and making decisions are regarded as two separate activities, it will be possible for the projectionist to avoid the responsibilities of the model builder and for the decision maker to act in a mysterious and possibly irrational way. Since nobody can forecast the future with certainty, the projectionist is careful to disclaim that he is making a prediction and he offers his calculation as the best estimate of the expected outcome of a set of stated assumptions. If time shows his projection to be far from what does happen, he has the defence that there was nothing wrong with his calculations, only the assumptions were incorrect and this was (at least in part), because of changes in Government policy which he did not anticipate as he forewarned us at the outset. On the other hand, the decision-maker, working on the premise that he must have some idea of what the future might be like, will eagerly seize upon any projection as relevant to his decisions. If these decisions were subsequently criticised, he could legitimately blame the misleading projections. So neither party is responsible for ultimate failure and the procedure offers no prospect of improvement. We believe that it is only by bringing all aspects together in decision models that we begin to resolve the problem of *what to do* in a way which is wholly open to reason and argument (pages 113-115).

Several points can be distinguished in this statement. Firstly, educational planning has been frequently restricted to educational forecasts; secondly, these forecasts were mainly concerned with a few "goal" variables and therefore not enough attention was paid to distinguish instrument variables from other variables; thirdly, a central place must be given to model building. In the words of the authors: "it is dangerous to view research into model building as a mere annex to the main problem of educational planning. We have tried to show how it is possible to build into the model the judgements of decision-makers about the uncertainties of the system and how the model can be used as an analytical tool to make decisions. As we see it, the role of the computable model is to link together the collection of data, the working of the system, the formulation of objectives and the decision-making process. All of these must be unified into an operational procedure." Fourthly and finally, the existence of the first two points in combination with the absence of the third, explain the lack of inter-relationship between planning (or projections) and decision-making.

Let us deal with each of these points in turn. Not much needs to be said about the first, because in preceding chapters we have already touched several times on this point. Although it certainly is not true that educational planners have concentrated exclusively on making manpower and social demand forecasts, it remains that they have devoted, in general, the bulk of their time either to forecasting or to working out the implications of forecasts with respect to teachers, buildings and expenditure. This brings us to the second point. The forecasts and educational planning documents showed us what to expect at some future date in terms of enrolment levels and real and monetary resources implications. They did *not* tell us how to get from here to there except again, and even that not always, in terms of student and resource flows over the forecasting period. Nothing, or very little, was said about *how* to get the students in the desirable branches of education (in the case of manpower forecasts), or *whether* the forecast number of students by level and branch was the to be preferred number and distribution of students as compared to some alternatives (in the case of social demand forecasts). In both cases, nothing is said about what instrument variables, i.e., variables under the control of the decision-maker, are available and what their weight in steering the system is. In the last case, moreover, we are in the presence of a really extraordinary *passive* attitude which consists of extrapolating a past trend without exploring alternative educational developments based on alternative educational policy goal priorities.

Nearly all the forecasts of enrolments of the past decade have been, in the last analysis, projections of trends. In other words, enrolments, enrolment ratios, the "internal efficiency" and other variables considered, have been treated ultimately as functions of time, and functions of time only. The mechanism behind this trend remained obscure. It would be to oversimplify it to suggest that educational planners and policy makers are unaware that a vast complex of factors are interacting to cause enrolments in any particular educational activity to be what they are. Numerous reports in many countries have shown that pupils' achievement, and hence the number of qualified school leavers of various kinds, are influenced by a whole host of variables. Among them are innate ability, family income, parents' social status, occupation and education, employment prospects for school leavers with different qualifications, attitudes towards careers for women, the organisation and pedagogical structures of education, the supply and quality of teachers and other resources, the availability of scholarships and other financial incentives, attitudes of peer groups, and so on. Virtually none of this has as yet been put together in any educational planning model. The reasons are not hard to find. Firstly, it is an extremely complex technical task to piece together information on all these factors (each of which involves complex distributed time-lags) into a single coherent planning and forecasting model; secondly, the available data in countries would make it very difficult indeed to make reliable estimations of the parameters of such a model even if it could be constructed. To sum all this up, educational planning and forecasting have been largely concerned with what entered and what came out of the system, but why people entered or did not enter, and what happened between entering and leaving the educational process has to a large extent remained a black box.

The above non-exhaustive enumeration of factors refers to variables which explain to a more or less important degree the educational career of individuals, i.e., both the decision to continue to higher levels of education and their success or failure within each educational cycle. This does not yet tell us anything about what happens to the school leavers and graduates once they have left the educational system. Manpower forecasts, as practised up to now even in combination with social demand forecasts, do not help much to clarify the situation. In most countries, at least until recently, upward shifts in the skill structure of the labour force propelled by economic and technological progress, have developed parallel with the rapid expansion of education and the consequent increase in output of highly qualified personnel, engendered mainly by individual aspirations for continued education. This has meant that on the whole graduates from the higher levels of education have been able to find jobs at a level more or less in line with their expectations, in turn determined by traditional educational-occupational relationships.

One possible consequence of the quasi-autonomous development of the educational system, implied by the social demand forecasts, may well be a gradual "drop" in the occupational choice of graduates. In other words, more and more graduates may have to enter occupations for which so far lower educational qualifications were the norm. This is not necessarily a bad thing as long as this "over-investment in education" is acceptable on social and general economic policy grounds, and the individual person is ready to accept the career and other consequences; for it is also possible that the spread of more and more education to all layers of society, with the consequent possibility of a downward switch in occupational choices of graduates, may cause a drop in the relative financial advantages that go with a degree or diploma (by reducing salary differences according to level of qualification). This again is not necessarily an undesirable development — some political groups have wished such a trend for decades. The fact is that so far salary differences by levels of qualification have remained remarkably stable in most countries, and that (as we have discussed in Part One) the impact of education on income distribution seems to be ambiguous. However, it remains to be seen how the situation will develop if the future rate of increase in the number of graduates were to be far in excess of the absorptive capacity of the economy, given present occupation - education relationships. Of these kind of considerations — which, it will be noticed, are a variant on Blaug's plea for combining manpower forecasts, social demand forecasts and rate-of-return analysis, as presented in Chapter V — not a trace can be found in the educational planning documents of the 1960s.

Imagine then an educational policy-maker who has just read through a "typical" educational planning document. He now knows how many pupils and students to expect over the coming ten years or so, he also knows, if he has read previous planning documents, that this is most probably an underestimate for reasons explained in Chapter I. Moreover, he gets some rough and global estimates of resources inputs and of the development of the skill structure of the labour force. Finally, he may have obtained some interesting information about pupil and student flows through the educational system. Now, what can he do with this information? He could, first of all, decide to gear the education sector to the manpower requirements of future economic and technological development. On the assumption, which is a huge one, that he has full confidence in the technical expertise with which the forecasts of the skill structure are made, he has clear normative planning figures as to the desirable educational development pattern, in terms of the number of students and their distribution by level and branch. Unfortunately, he has not been able to get the slightest clue as to what buttons to press in order to change the motivations of students and parents so that the level and distribution of students approach the desired target figures. But this is anyway a rather hypothetical example, since in the majority of countries such a solution would not be acceptable for political reasons, at least not in its extreme form. So our policy-maker turns to the social demand forecast. What he discovers there is that everything will be the same as at present, except bigger. There will be more students, more teachers, more school buildings, more financial outlays; and all this will more or less continue its course as in the past. Since everything these days is getting bigger, the policy-maker will be inclined to believe this forecast, the more so as he is told that it reflects the wishes of the People. But if there is a nagging doubt in the back of our policy-maker's mind (which admittedly would rather be the exception, given his frantic life and the daily routine pressures), and if he would like to know what other developments are possible, plausible or desirable, he again would not get an answer. Neither does he know anything about the implications of the increase in scale of the educational enterprise on society and societal structures at large. He is condemned to act as Robespierre who, when asked how he shaped his policy, replied, "There go the people. I am their leader. I must follow them." We now know where this has led him to!

In the light of the above observations, it is not astonishing that for these technical reasons alone a gap exists between the two worlds. Now, the third point we have drawn from the Armitage-Smith-Alper comments is that judiciously constructed educational models, and in particular decision models for educational planning, could bridge the gap between the planning and the decision-making worlds. There is no doubt in our mind that such an initiative could indeed, and in principle, remedy to a large extent the technical reasons behind the existence of the two worlds. But are these technical reasons alone responsible for this state of affairs, or are there other, and maybe more fundamental, factors involved?

2. Organisational and Human Aspects

A good way of introducing this section is to present two quotations from the paper of Gareth Williams (1971) (mentioned before in Chapter I). Describing educational planning in France, he writes:

> However, it also appears to have been the case that there has been in France during the 1960s a substantial gap between the educational planning procedures, and the policy decisions actually taken. This showed itself partly in the wide divergence between forecast enrolments in the various plans and actual outcomes, but also in the many reforms, major and minor, throughout the 1960s whose relationship with the Plan is remote, but which undoubtedly affected the educational environment within which planning should have taken place. The most conspicuous of these divergencies was, of course, in the months following the "events" of May 1968 when, for a time, education was in the forefront of national policy and, therefore, perhaps too important to be left to the planners. In the months following May 1968 major reforms of higher education were set in motion, including substantial changes in university administration to encourage "participation," and the establishment of new university institu-

tions in the Paris area to relieve overcrowding in the University of Paris. There were, however, less striking examples earlier, of which perhaps the most notable were the Fouchet reforms of secondary and tertiary education in 1962. These reforms were undoubtedly partly responsible for the under-estimation of secondary education enrolment projections in the IVth Plan. Similarly, the reform of the university structure and baccalauréat were not taken into account by the Planning Commission, although changes of this nature clearly affect the extent of "social demand" for higher education (page 24—25).

In the case of Great Britain, Williams observes:

> It remains true, however, that during the 1960s educational decisions in the U.K. were the resultant of many forces among which the various planning bodies described do not appear to have been outstandingly influential. Britain may be cited as an example of a country which has tried to plan largely by making the right information available to the right people at the right time. In any case the freedom of action of the central authorities is severely circumscribed by the power of the local authorities in primary and secondary education, and the universities in higher education. It is, however, the case that the various (Committee) Reports have played an important role in moulding informed public opinion by bringing the latest available research to bear on major policy issues — the Robbins Report changed the whole climate of opinion about higher education and the Plowden Report seems to be doing the same for nursery and primary education. Since it is public opinion which is ultimately responsible for formulating objectives and implementing policy, it may be claimed that the Reports have served a useful purpose (page 27).

Although the establishment of educational planning as a process and its institutionalisation can, in most countries, be viewed as a major accomplishment of the past decade, it cannot be denied that the place and the weight of the newly established planning units within the educational polity and administration have remained ambiguous and ill-defined. Within the educational polity the intrusion of the planners smacked of technocracy, particularly since contact with the educational community was difficult, if at all sought. Within the educational administration, i.e., mainly the Ministries of Education, the appearance of the planners created problems of competence between the various "policy" departments (primary education, secondary education, etc.) on the one hand, and the planning unit on the other. These conflicts were usually solved to the advantage of the "policy" departments, because of the generally higher hierarchical status of their directors as compared to the heads of the planning units, and also because they had the singular "advantage" of a long existence and of having accumulated a vast amount of experience of making policy without planning. Since their departments and the educational sector they administered still existed — in spite of the absence of planning — this last argument was quite frequently used in the final analysis.

This delicate position of the new educational planning units was not always facilitated by the fact that each time a policy-planning issue of some importance arose, a special Committee was appointed or a special Advisor was nominated to report on the problem and to come up with policy recommendations. This would not be serious — after all, issue analyses need to be undertaken and very often a committee or an advisor of some reputation are best indicated to do so — if the role and the function of the planning unit in their work were clearly defined. But, once again, this has rarely been the case.

The preceding remarks begin to give us some clue as to why, particularly in the early years, the technical work of the educational planners has been so restricted. As newcomers in a complex administration and an even more complex decision-making process, with long-standing habits, symbols and taboos, the educational planners were often told "to mind their own business." The planners, very often indeed unexperienced and parachuted by a Minister who did not always know himself what to expect of them, set out in search of what "their own business" could possibly be. As could be expected, most of them were quickly led to take on those things which the "policy" departments did not do or which they were "allowed" to do. Thus we arrive at the picture depicted in previous pages. The planners were also asked to do some smaller *ad hoc* studies on specific issues — the more important policy problems, as noted, went to Committees or Government Advisors — and the more ambitious and enthusiastic among them started, after some time, to take initiatives of their own and to choose issues which they considered important. All this kept our small planning world quite busy and, to a certain extent, quite happy. The educational planning units settled down, became even accepted, were put in special buildings at a safe distance from the central decision-making points, in short, they were absorbed in the generalised routine. What has happened?

What happened, reduced to its most simple expression, was simply this: The top decision-makers in the field of education did not understand sufficiently that policy is not possible without planning *and vice versa*. If policy can be defined as looking ahead, coordination and the attainment of deliberate goals, then this is very precisely the definition of planning. In the last analysis, an educational policy implies a clear definition of the educational goals and their translation into yardsticks within feasible limits of growth and qualitative improvements of education. In other words, the goal structures must be identified and operationalised. This means determining criteria and priorities, and then defining the global strategies necessary to reach them, with the resource and other implications spelt out. Without clear goal definition, educational planning is exceedingly difficult. The degree of realism and sophistication of educational planning depends on the degree of clarity of educational policy formulation and vice versa. Thus, the first thing that happened, and this applies to a number of countries, is that there was no active educational policy worthy of the name. These countries followed a passive policy, as described earlier, parallelled by "reactive" planning. They followed the events instead of guiding and steering them. The second thing that has happened is that those countries who tried to elaborate active long-term (but mostly partial) educational policies, farmed out the planning to *ad hoc* groups and/or research institutes, without defining a clear role for their (permanent) educational planning units. This resulted in the latter spending a lot of time on *ad hoc* forecasts and small *ad hoc* issue analyses, which in turn prevented them elaborating a general educational planning model in which the increasing knowledge base, the feedback coming from the work of committees or of other groups on the analysis of specific problem areas and educational policy changes could all be incorporated, so that an improving policy-planning framework for decision-making would be obtained over time. The preceding remarks can be summarised by the following proposition: During the 1960s, educational planning has been hampered by (i) the frequent absence of clear policy formulation, and policy formulation was difficult because of the primitive state of planning; (ii) the organisational ambiguities concerning the place and role of the permanent planning units with respect to the many *ad hoc* bodies doing work with planning and policy implications; and (iii) the equally ambiguous status of the planning units within the internal structure of the Ministry of Education.

3. Concluding Remarks

During the 1960s, educational planning stood in a subordinate relationship *vis-a-vis* both the educational policy makers and the administration. Educational planners have not been treated as equal partners in the decision-making process. The phenomenon of the "two worlds" has both technical causes, but above all, so we believe, it is caused by organisational ambiguities and human interrelationships. As we have tried to show, the distinction between policy and planning is logically absurd. It follows that the policy-maker and the planner should be one and the same person. Although the preceding statement holds true at the conceptual level, it is obvious that in the real world a functional distinction must be made which, in turn, has organisational consequences. This distinction is necessary, because of the important amount of technical and coordination work involved in the planning function. It is this inescapable distinction between functions, coupled with the absence of recognition on the part of the policy-maker of the indivisible nature of the two functions, which is the beginning and the end of the ambiguous status of the educational planning units in most countries. If the conceptual indivisibility of policy and planning is accepted, it follows that the person in charge of the function "planning" should have the same status as the person in charge of the function "policy-making". From this it follows, in turn, that the two or more persons in charge of these functions should discuss and work out ideas and alternative strategies as if one were in the presence of complementary characteristics of the same personality. Institutional and organisational settings have to be conceived which maximise the chances of success of this enormously difficult human interaction problem.

We have also shown that the functional and organisational ambiguities have been partly responsible for the rather narrow scope of the technical work of the educational planning units and other bodies involved in educational planning. Clearly, there have also been other reasons of which the lack of a sophisticated data base, the shortage of qualified personnel and the methodological difficulties, are probably the most important. It may be possible that, had educational planners been able to overcome these technical difficulties quicker, they would have enhanced their prestige and status and would have been taken more seriously. But there is clearly some circularity in the argument here. If educational planners have not been more successful than they were, the main responsibility lies in the fact that educational policy-makers have not realised (or if they have, have not drawn the logical consequences) that an educational policy worth the name necessitates strategic planning and vice versa. It is the "vice versa" which indicates that planners and policy-makers are, or should be, on equal footing, and this again was not realised or not acted upon in educational planning activities during the 1960s.

VIII

Educational Planning and Policy in Retrospect

The purpose of this chapter is to bring together in a slightly more systematic way the various bits and pieces touched upon in this Part Two. In doing so we shall try to go beyond a mere summary, in order to set the stage for the more future oriented and constructive contributions we hope to make in Part Three.

1. Stages of Educational Planning: Technical Aspects

In a little booklet called *What is Educational Planning*, Philip H. Coombs sums up the four key features of the typical kind of educational planning that went on in most places prior to the Second World War and for many generations before:

> (1) It was *short-range* in outlook, extending only to the next budget year (except when facilities had to be built or a major new programme added, in which case the planning horizon moved forward a bit further); (2) it was *fragmentary* in its coverage of the educational system; the parts of the system were planned independently of one another; (3) it was *non-integrated* in the sense that educational institutions were planned autonomously without explicit ties to the evolving needs and trends of the society and the economy at large; and (4) it was a *non-dynamic* kind of planning which assumed an essentially static educational model that would retain its main features intact year in and year out (page 19).

Since 1945, the industrialised nations have passed through three educational phases and now find themselves in a perplexing fourth phase, all of which explain why a new kind of educational planning became necessary. Coombs calls them the Reconstruction Phase, the Manpower Shortage Phase, the Rampant Expansion Phase, and finally, the Innovation Phase. Still according to Coombs, the image of educational planning in the early 1960s changed in the following way:

> First, educational planning should take a *longer-range view*. It should in fact have a short-range (one or two years), a middle-range (four to five years) and a long-range perspective (ten to fifteen years). Obviously its vision will grow less precise the farther ahead it looks...
>
> Second, educational planning should be *comprehensive*. It should embrace the whole educational system in a single vision to ensure the harmonious evolution of its various parts. Moreover, it should try to extend its vision to important types of *non-formal* education and training to ensure their effective integration with formal education and with the priority needs and goals of society.
>
> Third, educational plans should be *integrated* with the plans of broader economic and social development. If education is to contribute most effectively to individual and national development, and to make the best use of scarce resources, it cannot go its own way, ignoring the realities of the world around it.
>
> Fourth, educational planning should be an *integral part of educational management*. To be effective, the planning process must be closely tied to the processes of decision-making and operations. If isolated in a back room it becomes a purely academic exercise whose chief effect is to frustrate those involved.
>
> Fifth, (and this proposition was slower to become evident) educational planning must be concerned with the *qualitative* aspects of educational development, not merely with quantitative expansion. Only thus can it help to make education more relevant, efficient and effective (pages 33-34).

Very wisely, Coombs added, "Like the Ten Commandments, these five propositions soon enjoyed universal endorsement in principle, but the problem was to get them obeyed." If one thing has become clear from the preceding chapters, it is that there exists a wide variety of educational planning practices, both between and within countries. These practices include various combinations of the features mentioned above, referring both to the characteristics of early educational planning and to those that became accepted during the 1960s. It does not come as a surprise, therefore, that today "educational planning" is the label for many activities in the field, and that the question of what "educational planning" actually is or means is not always easy to answer. Given this mild confusion, it does not seem inappropriate to distinguish different stages in the educational planning activities of the 1960s. Such an attempt must necessarily imply a certain abstraction and arbitrariness. Thus, for example, the stages which we are about to present are not based on the experience of any single country nor do they necessarily follow chronological events. What we have done is to look back at the past decade — embracing the whole educational planning experience of the industrialised nations —

and try to put some order in the diverse activities we could observe. This means that a given country could very well claim that it had all planning stages already operating at the beginning of the 1960s, while another country would still be struggling with, say, stage two at the end of the decade. All we can claim is that an attempt is made to order the stages in terms of increasing complexity of the educational planning process.

The first stage could be labelled the "single value forecasting" stage. We have already described this experience in earlier chapters and we do not need to dwell on it here. As its name indicates, the emphasis in this stage is on the quantification of one or two easily quantifiable (which does not imply any value judgement on accuracy) "goal" variables, such as individual and family demand for education and/or the educational needs derived from manpower forecasts. This is the stage where one quantifies *where* the educational system has to go in terms of numbers, but one does not know *how* to get there, or *why* one should get precisely there and not somewhere else.

The second stage could be called the "internal dynamics" stage. Here one starts talking about applying systems analysis techniques to what happens within the educational system. Rather than putting the emphasis on the external pressures that exercise an influence on the schools and universities, the focus of attention is switched to the intricate interdependencies between the different levels and branches of the education sector itself. The technical planning work during this phase resulted mainly in the elaboration of student flow models, such as those by Moser and Redfern, Armitage, Smith and Alper, and Thonstad. They were primarily set up in order to examine the internal efficiency of the system — in the restricted sense of the different transition, repeat and dropout rates — and, by the same token, to obtain a better basis for making social demand forecasts. This led, therefore, to some sort of a new stage in which the first two phases were combined, and much more explicit attention was given to possible bottlenecks within the educational system and which might stand in the way of attaining the quantitative target figures.

In a third stage, which we may call the "optimisation attempt" stage, the model builders became bolder and tried to combine and reconcile the different approaches to educational planning within the context of some kind of an optimisation model. Examples of such attempts are those by Jean Bénard for France, and by Irma Adelman and Samuel Bowles, who have made tentative applications of their models in developing countries. In the case of the Bowles model, the objective function is defined as "the contribution of the educational system to future national income, measured by the increment in discounted lifetime earnings attributable to additional years of education." It combines the flow-model—social-demand approach with the rate-of-return approach. The models of Adelman and Bénard are both attempts to reconcile the rate-of-return and manpower approaches. As Adelman states:

> Philosophically, the model formulated is a cross between the manpower requirements approach to educational planning and the benefit-cost approach. As in the manpower requirements approach, the model described generates its demand upon the educational system from the production side of the economy and uses fixed labour-output coefficients for each class of manpower and for each sector of the economy.... There are also some similarities with the cost-benefit approach; the extent of resources to be devoted to education is determined in the present model by comparing the marginal social benefit of each type of education with its marginal social costs.

Very briefly, Adelman's model consists in optimising investment in education simultaneously with investment in physical capital in the other economic sectors, allowing for a certain number of linear constraints representing the limits imposed by the technological and socio-cultural environment. Bénard's model also takes "the form of a sequential linear programme extending to the whole of a country's economy and treating education as one of this economy's sectors or activities. Its purpose is to determine optimum allocation of mainly physical resources between educational activity and economic activities. This optimisation is arrived at by maximising a social preference function subject to constraints." In this model the activity of the education sector is defined by means of a production function connecting inputs (pupil flows, teachers' work, depreciation of premises, etc.) to the output (graduates), subject to two additional constraints related to minimum growth of the educational system and maximum budget for educational expenditure. Graduates have to satisfy the requirements of the other sectors of activity; as regards their "prices," in this case current market earnings, these are introduced into the model explicitly. If we have taken up some more space for this third stage, it is because, contrary to the two preceding stages, its content had not been dealt with in previous chapters.

We propose to call the fourth phase the "planning as a process" stage. While earlier, as we have seen, planning was often given a rather specific and restricted meaning, such as the quantitative definition of goals, or the implementation of specific reforms, or the yearly management of a system, more recently the tendency has become that of including all such activities under the planning concept. Thus, the planning process came to include:

(i) the setting of objectives;
(ii) the design of alternative strategies to reach these objectives;
(iii) the evaluation of these strategies with a view to ascertaining the extent to which they are in accordance with the objectives and the priorities between the objectives, taking into account various side-effects and constraints, such as resource limitations and implementation possibilities;
(iv) the establishment of short- and long-term plans, as well as decision-making, implementation and evaluation processes.

In this fourth stage, planning was still viewed as a one-directional process, proceeding, for example, from the setting of an objective to the definition of a strategy to reach the objective, and then to the implementation phase. An evaluation phase was sometimes, but not always, attached at the end of the planning period. The process was essentially one-directional, also as to the decision levels involved. One proceeded from general policy decisions at the highest level to the definition of strategies and estimates of resource requirements at lower decision-making levels. This one-directional character of the process made that the image of planning remained a relatively static "one-shot" affair. Educational planning still was a "wait-and-see" activity: The goals were set, the strategy designed, implementation followed its course undisturbed

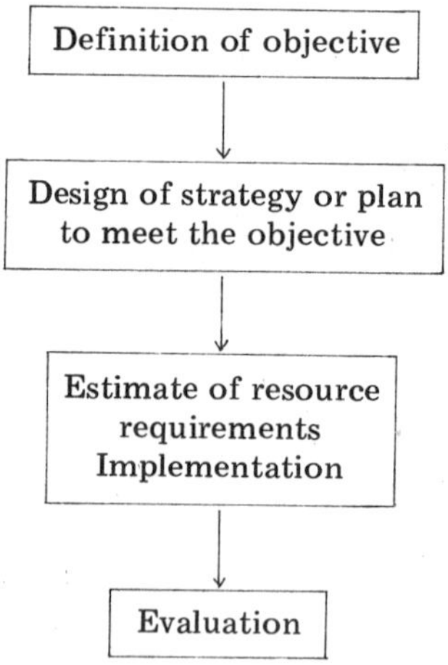

Figure 1

during the time period laid out by the plan. Evaluation came after the process was terminated.

This brings us to the fifth and last stage, and also at the limit between the 1960s and the 1970s. Whilst the fourth stage can now be labelled the one-directional variety of the "planning-as-a-process" phase, the fifth stage is its "continuous approach" variety. The need for a change from this one-directional, discontinuous approach has several causes. There is a growing recognition that many systems and activities, and above all education, have multiple objectives. More precise definitions of these objectives, and of the priorities between them, require information about the extent to which various strategies can contribute to reaching these different objectives, and about the resource requirements, implementation difficulties and side-effects of these strategies. Logically, there is, therefore, a need for an iterative procedure, for instance, in accordance with the scheme outlined in Figure 2. The need for carrying out planning activities on a more continuous basis is imposed by the increasing speed of change in society. Earlier, as still exemplified in the fourth stage above, one could decide on a reform and then, later on, when experience had been gained about its effects, and new problems had become apparent, one could start anew. Today, problems have to be foreseen and dealt with at an early stage, and reforms and plans need continuous revision. The inescapable uncertainty about the future has to be taken into account explicitly in the planning process. To achieve this purpose, there are a number of different procedures, such as rolling forecasts and plans, decision-making models men-

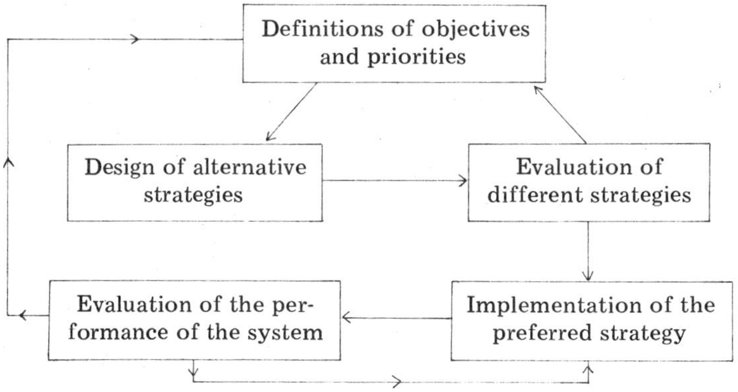

Figure 2

tioned in Chapter VII, sensitivity analysis, etc. By sensitivity analysis we mean investigation of the sensitivity of the solution of a problem to various uncertainties in basic data, environmental conditions, etc. One tries to find a solution which is "acceptable" for all the different possibilities regarding the uncertain factors, even if it is not optimal for each or any of them. In Chapter VI we touched already briefly on the subject of rolling plans and rolling reforms. Instead of fixed-term plans, such as five-year plans renewed every five years, we now have, in the fifth stage, rolling plans. These imply a more frequent revision of the plans based on new information and an addition of a new time-period to the planning horizon. Rolling multi-year plans renewed each year are now in use in various sectors in the United States and in some Scandinavian countries.

Whilst the first three stages were exclusively concerned with the technical and analytical aspects of educational planning, the two variations of the fourth stage implied also organisational adaptations in the light of growing technical complexities. In this connection, it is proper to say a few words about the role of *ad hoc* studies and *ad hoc* bodies in educational planning. An analogy with general economic planning could help to clarify the issue. Jan Tinbergen, in his book on *Development Planning*, devotes a chapter to "the functions of development planning." He distinguishes the following categories: perspective plans, medium-term plans, one-year plans, preparatory research work, pre-investment studies, the formulation of projects, the setting of rules and standards, and *ad hoc* advice to the government. Of this latter function, Tinbergen has this to say:

> Because of the information and experience acquired in fulfilling its other functions, the planning office is particularly well qualified to advise on certain special questions of economic policy. These are in particular those problems in which the interdependence of the various sectors of the national economy are involved or in which the consequences are of importance to the general development of the country.... The planning office may also advise the government on its decision on new projects initiated by outsiders, such as foreign firms, which were not envisaged in the plan; or its decision on new discoveries of natural resources, such as petroleum or natural gas (page 62).

In other words, the planning units are eminently qualified for these kinds of studies *if* they are fulfilling the other functions as well, and precisely *because* of that. In the case of educational planning, we have seen in previous chapters that often many of the other functions are undertaken by *ad hoc* groups (Committees), and that the permanent planning units are frequently involved in *ad hoc* studies! Such a state of affairs could almost be classified as a special stage, were it not that we are faced here with a pure organisational matter. This leads us to the second topic of this chapter.

2. The Communication Issue between Planning and Decision-making

The rapidly-increasing institutionalisation of educational planning activities during the 1960s can also be seen as an aspect of the tendency of all human activity to become more and more conscious. To quote Tinbergen again:

> Whereas in the past the State often acted, in accordance with the principle of *laissez-faire*, only after a natural catastrophe — a war or some other grave crisis or difficulty — the conscious introduction of "thinking ahead" has gradually led to the practice of forming an idea of the situation that will most probably prevail at some future period of time. This thinking ahead is now known as forecasting and the techniques involved in forecasting of this type have continued to improve in recent years. We have progressed from the rather naive method of forecasting by extrapolating the line of a graph to the much more sophisticated method of forecasting based on a knowledge of the operation of social forces. This knowledge, which was initially mainly intuitive, has itself become more explicit with the passage of time (page 43).

One of the more serious doubts about educational planning during the past decade, which we expressed earlier, lies in the difficulty of seeing what policy influence it has had. In Chapter VII we advanced both technical reasons and organisational and human reasons for the dichotomic nature of the relationship between educational planning and the educational decision-making process. Here we shall elaborate on the organisational and human aspects, in terms of the communication issue between educational planners and decision-makers.

Implicit in most definitions of planning is the idea that planning and decision making are not only two separate activities, but that there is only a one-way relationship between them. This is, for example, the case when planning is defined as the process of preparing a set of decisions for action in the future. The political decision-makers are supposed to take some fundamental decisions (for example with respect to the ultimate and derived aims of their policy), which the planners accept as data for the working out of alternative means to reach those ends. This has led to the creation of an "image" of the function of planning based on the assumption that a clear-cut distinction between planners and decision-makers could be made and was desirable.

It would appear useful to take some perspective, and to examine several alternative relationships between planners and decision makers, as these seem possible, plausible and/or desirable. In order to do so, we will use the concepts developed by Habermas on the one hand, and Churchman and Schainblatt on the other. Habermas presents three concepts of communication and cooperation between planners and decision-makers: he calls them the decisionistic, the technocratic and the pragmatistic concepts. In the case of the *decisionistic* approach, planning is a relatively independent activity from decision-making. The planner is considered a technical expert who plays a professional role and who gives objective information to the decision-maker. The latter, who plays a political role, may or may not use this information in taking his final decisions. Given the passive and subordinate position of the planner inherent in this concept, there is more than a remote possibility that planning remains rather "trivial" and has little impact on actual events. The *technocratic* approach, on the other hand, takes as its starting point that the development of scientific and technological knowledge enables the determination of single, optimal solutions. At the other extreme of the decisionistic concept, according to which the planner passively prepares certain strategies which the decision-maker is free to accept or to disregard, the planner actually takes the decision himself. According to the technocratic concept, by definition, there is no room for political, heuristic decision-making by politicians. There is no room for alternatives, or rather the planners have squeezed all sub-optimal alternatives out. In such circumstances, all that the decision-maker can do is to authorise the algorithmic conclusions ("decisions") of the planners. On the other hand, the *pragmatistic* concept neither puts all the stress on the social power of the political decision-maker (decisionistic approach), nor does it sell out to the planners (technocratic approach). On the contrary, it is based on a close communication and cooperation between planners and political decision-makers, which should result in a partial overlapping of their functions.

Churchman and Schainblatt propose four concepts of communication and cooperation to analyse the relationships between planners and political decision-makers. They are the concepts of separate functions, of communication, of persuasion and of mutual understanding. In the *separate functions* world, the planners and decision-makers work in juxtaposition, similar to the situation according to the decisionistic concept. The planner works on the scientific aspects of the problem and feels only responsible for the development of one or more solutions, but not for their successful application. The political decision-maker will accept or reject the solutions offered. There is no interaction necessary between them. It is the political decision-maker who defines the problem and who decides according to his own selection criteria. On the other hand, within the second and third concept of cooperation, the political decision-maker defines the problems as above, but this time the selection criteria are being developed by the planner. In other words, the decision-maker "learns" from the planner which decision will be optimal, or preferable. Within the *communication* concept, the decision-maker plays the active role in this learning process, and tries to understand the activity of the planner. Within the *persuasion* concept, the planner tries to find ways in which to overcome the emotional resistance of the decision-maker towards innovations which are necessary as a result of the planner's activity. This means that the planner tries, by formulating his solutions, to take into account the psychological disposition of the political decision-maker. The fourth concept of cooperation, the concept of *mutual understanding*, requires that the definition of problems and the "rational decisions" be the result of close collaboration between planners and decision-makers. Their activities cannot be regarded in isolation from each other. This concept corresponds to the pragmatistic approach of Habermas.

If we have insisted somewhat on the above concepts, it is not because they excel in subtle analysis (particularly in the summarised form in which they are presented here), but rather in order to clarify certain issues which we discussed in the second half of Chapter VII. In our opinion, these concepts do clarify the com-

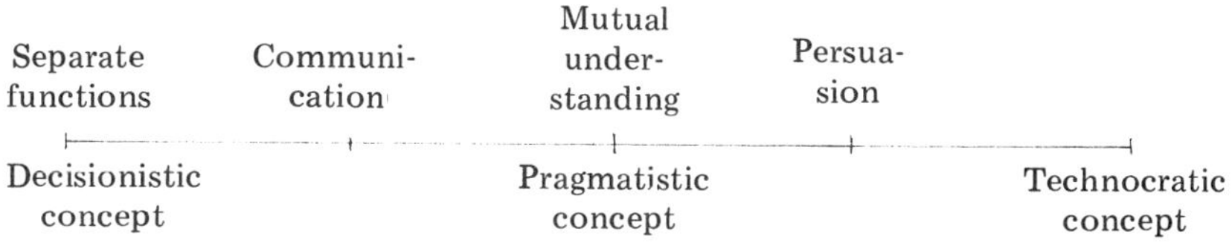

Figure 3

munication and organisation issues, precisely because of a certain naivete in which extreme situations are presented. Taking the various approaches together, we can express them as depicted in the continuum in figure 3. The debate is, of course, about where in the real world the different educational planning experiences are situated along this continuum. It is clear that we will rarely encounter actual planning experiences that can be classified at the extremes of the continuum: either as fully fledged technocratic or as one hundred per cent decisionistic experiences. It is probably true that the majority of countries would find themselves somewhere between the pragmatistic and the decisionistic concepts, i.e., on the left half of the continuum. Even more precisely, the bulk of them will be situated between the communication concept and the decisionistic (separate functions) approach, and closer to the latter than to the former. However, it is interesting to note the conscious or unconscious attempts to bring educational planning over to the right half of the continuum. This is, for example, the case each time educational planners try to put forward the point that the scope for political decisions is largely fictitious. This tendency is frequently inherent in the often-used correlation analysis between, say, national product and educational expenditures, or between per capita income and enrolment ratios. The correlation approach implies often the technocratic thesis of a "Sachzwang" which ignores the learning capacity of social systems and rejects planning as a conscious change of the social system. The educational system is treated as a static system; decisive characteristics such as adaptability and possibilities of manipulation are ignored. This type of "historicism" assumes a pre-determined behaviour of the system, and its conscious or unconscious use implies a technocratic claim towards the political decision-maker.

Still in the context of the "right half of the continuum," an interesting phenomenon can sometimes be observed, mostly in developing countries and particularly in the Latin American setting. We refer to attempts by educational planners to generate their own sources of social power, for instance, by enhancing the complexity of the plan. This way of strengthening his role as a planner *vis-a-vis* the political decision-maker in a technocratic way or by persuasion is probably used as a countervailing power in the face of the decisionistic position. Guy Benveniste has observed such a situation: "In a study of educational planning in a Latin American country I found that the educational planners had been able to acquire considerable influence within the Ministry of Education simply from the fact that they had in due time developed a unique network for information gathering, far superior to the one available to the leadership of this ministry."

Finally, let us turn back to the "left half of the continuum" and indicate another reason for the lack of clear policy influence of educational planning. An important problem arises, indeed, in the field of forecasting, and in particular with respect to the "social demand" forecasts. The difficulty in question arises because of the existing dichotomic relationships between educational planners and decision-makers. This difficulty, which is not limited to educational planning, has been denounced many times. We will give two examples. Ragnar Frisch asks the question: "How can it be possible to make a projection without knowing the decisions that will *basically influence* the course of affairs? It is as if the policy-maker would say to the economic expert: 'Now, you expert try to guess what I am going to do, and make your estimates accordingly. On the basis of the *factual information* thus received, I will then decide what to do.'" According to Gottfried Bombach,

> ...a clear separation between autonomous and instrument variables is essential. Instrument variables are entirely within the scope of the authority which requires projections as a basis for some sort of optimum policy. Let us assume that the government has asked for a projection. It is obvious that such a projection can be carried out only if the intentions of the government as regards the use of instrument variables are already known, or alternatively, if the government wants to know the results of the projections in order to make its decisions. This again means the use of instrument variables on the results of the projections. It demonstrates the well-known "vicious circle" of projection (page 203-204).

Analogies in the field of educational planning are obvious. Instead of asking, "how many students do we want in 1980?", political decision-makers often ask instead, "how many students do we have in 1980?" thereby implicitly assuming that the reasons for university attendance are predetermined one way or another, and ignoring the comprehensive socio-economic context in which educational planning has to take place. This dilemma is particularly acute in "social demand" forecasts for education. In the case of these forecasts, it can legitimately be asked why this future educational expansion pattern and not one or two others? Clearly, this question cannot be answered when one does not know where to go in educational policy terms, i.e., without an active educational policy. In contrast, manpower forecasts provide decision-makers with educational planning figures, i.e., with targets. But here the difficulty is that one does not know exactly how to steer the educational system towards these targets, because not enough is known as to the number of instrument variables at the disposal of political decision-makers and their importance in influencing educational expansion patterns. The same holds true, of course, for other planning figures based on different or complementary criteria other than manpower considerations. And thus we have come back full circle to the inter-relationship between the technical difficulties of educational policy and planning, and the communication issue. In terms of the knowledge about the causal factors behind the educational growth phenomenon, substantive advances have been made (as will be outlined in Part Three). But for this progress in the technical domain to have any effect it must reach the political decision-makers through a sustained dialogue with the educational planners and research community. This, in turn, implies drastic changes in the communication process between planners and political decision-makers. Therein lies the real challenge for educational policy-planning in the 1970s.

Part Three

Plenty of Room at the Top?

IX

The Present View of Educational Expansion: Growing Insights and Perplexities

If we want to influence what happens with and in the educational system, we must know something about the causal mechanism behind its growth and dynamics. We have seen that most educational forecasting models in the 1960s were based on a few definition equations — using only the most obvious and global variables — and that, if any behavioural equation was included, the explanatory variable in most cases was "time." This kind of trend extrapolation portrays the development of a given variable as a function of time without making an attempt to analyse the relationships implicitly assumed. The primitive nature of the forecasting models is not necessarily a reflection of the knowledge one has about causal relationships. In trying to explain the observed situation, explanatory variables which are themselves extremely difficult, if not impossible, to forecast, must frequently be brought into the analysis. A distinction should, therefore be made between the attempt to explain the observed situation, and the usefulness of the relationships established for forecasting purposes. With these remarks in mind, we will first review the growing insights obtained in the educational growth problems and, by the same token, the limitations and possibilities for the school to be instrumental in reaching given educational and social policy goals.

1. Some Macro-Sociological Evidence

It may be a convenient starting point to look first at the macro-sociological studies, which set out to explain regional differences in educational participation. A number of these types of studies have been conducted in various countries in the past. They were designed to serve different purposes and this had, of course, an influence on the choice of the dependent variable finally retained. Thus, for example, British and Dutch studies had as their principal purpose the explanation and prediction of the *inflow* of students into certain levels of the educational system. A Norwegian study concentrated on differences in regional *transition rates* from one school level to another. A German study was more concerned with the educational opportunities of *disadvantaged groups* and used a limited set of explanatory variables. In France and Yugoslavia studies are available which analyse the regional disparities in school *enrolment ratios*. The number of regions with each country being considered varies widely. In Yugoslavia, only 8 regions were distinguished, and in France, 21. In other studies, a considerably greater number were treated: The Netherlands, 89, Great Britain, 145, and Germany, 566. In Norway, data for over 800 areas were used.

The independent or explanatory variables used in these studies to account for regional variation in educational participation vary from country to country, but they generally pertain to three broad categories: demographic (such as rate of population growth, density of population, degree of urbanisation); socio-cultural (racial and religious composition of the people, educational level of the population, and availability of school facilities); and economic (standard of living, income, industrialisation and occupational structure of the regional labour force). Students' abilities are sometimes considered in these studies, but no account is taken of students' aspirations, nor are governmental school policies and practices regarded as explanatory variables.

Let us review the general conclusions which can be drwan from such macro-sociological studies. Among those studies adopting the *educational level* of the population or the parents in a region as one of the explanatory variables, it is the factor that correlated most highly with educational participation. The *occupational structure* of the regional labour force comes in either as the best or as the second best explanatory variable, depending on whether or not the educational level of the population is included in the analysis. This rather strong relationship between socio-economic factors and school participation may not so much be an economic relationship, as one which accounts for differences in life styles and mobility aspirations. At least, this is suggested by the weaker association of *income* with educational participation as compared to that of either educational level or occupational structure. Although a moderately high correlation coefficient with per capita income is obtained in The Netherlands, much lower coefficients measuring the same relationships are found in Norway, Yugoslavia and France. A small negative coefficient is obtained for Norway when income *growth* over a five-year period is used as the independent variable. Some measure of *population or urbanisation* was included for several countries. In The Netherlands, the percentage living in towns with more than 5,000 inhabitants was correlated 0.75 with educational participation rates. Moderate to low correlation coefficients were obtained in France and in Yugoslavia. The number of inhabitants per square kilometre in regions of Norway correlated 0.47 with school participation. The influence of *religion* has been investigated in The Netherlands and in Germany. In The Netherlands, neither the percentage of Dutch Reformed nor of Catholics in the total population showed any noticeable correlation with school participation. In Germany, the percentage of Catholics was likewise unrelated to enrolment ratios. The *average distance from home to school* in The Netherlands correlated 0.74 with participation. In a multiple regression analysis, however, it added very little to what was already explained by the occupational and educational background of the population in the region. In Norway, France and Yugoslavia, the number of schools in the region was introduced as an explanatory variable. This factor seemed to be uncorrelated with school enrolment ratios. The number of schools and the distance from home to school may be less critical than the size of schools for school participation. The British study used some variables to describe the "quality" of schools; these variables, some relating the school and class-size, correlated moderately with participation rates. Finally, the correlation coefficient between school expenditure per capita and school-going in Yugoslavia was small, and the association disappeared when school expenditures per pupil were substituted in the analysis.

Only two of these studies used some measure of the *ability* of the students as an explanatory variable with rather opposite results. For The Netherlands, the percentage of army recruits in high intelligence classes correlated 0.71 for boys and 0.76 for girls with school participation. For Great Britain, on the other hand, the mean verbal test score at age 11 correlated 0.18 with participation of both sexes, and this correlation coefficient was not statistically significantly different from zero. Since the ability measure for The Netherlands was for adults rather than children, it may have caught a different dimension of ability. In fact, the occupation index and the ability variable had a correlation coefficient of 0.80, indicating that the two variables may be measuring the same socio-economic phenomenon. On the other hand, the ability measure used in the British case is based on testing at an age prior to the period of participation and is directly related to the sample of children for whom school progress has been charted. It would appear, therefore, to be a more valid measure of ability and the insignificant correlation coefficient suggests little, if any, association of the variables. However, the research is too limited to reach any definite conclusions.

Since many of the explanatory variables used are highly inter-correlated, their inter-relationships in their effect on the dependent variable were analysed in the studies of The Netherlands and Norway. In The Netherlands, the occupational index was highly correlated with income per capita, percentage having an income greater than 6,000 guilders, degree of urbanisation, distance to school, and percentage in high intelligence classes. The highest multiple correlation coefficient for any set of these variables combined exceeded that for the simple correlation coefficient for the occupational index alone, by only 0.03. In the case of Norway, the education of parents was highly correlated with income per capita and population density. The highest multiple correlation coefficient was but slightly higher than the simple coefficient for parents' education (0.64 vs. 0.62). It is, therefore, obvious that underlying the regional variations in school participation is a general socio-economic factor or set of socio-economic factors which differentiate one region from another, and which facilitate educational participation for some groups and impede it for others.

This rather obvious finding, that variations among regions in socio-economic composition of the population probably account for most of the variations among regions in school attendance, does not negate the fact that there are unique factors within each region which explain some of the distinctive school participation patterns of the area. These may include the historical-cultural traditions of the region, its school policies, and other natural and social environmental effects. Thus, and without denying the fact that the occupational and educational structures of the population are important determinants for regional enrolment rates, changes observed within social group participation across regions indicate that such factors as job perspectives in the region (related of course to migratory trends), distance to school, etc. are important secondary variables.

2. A Theoretical Excursion

If the explanation of regional disparities in education lies mainly with socio-economic factors, and more precisely with differences in regional occupational and educational structures of the population, what, then, accounts for socio-economic disparities in educational participation? At the theoretical level, an explanatory analysis of social disparities in educational participation can follow at least three routes. It can be: (i) a broad analysis of the relationship between sweeping social changes and disparities in educational participation, emphasising such factors as educational expansion and economic and social change; (ii) an "ecological", or middle-range, analysis which associates the average or distribution of characteristics of social categories with the pattern of educational disparities; and (iii) a more focussed analysis which stresses individuals as units of analysis and which identifies causal mechanisms or processes of a socio-psychological nature.

The theoretical route which seeks explanation through analysis of broad social trends offers a first basis for understanding the existence and trends of social disparities in education. As we have seen in Part One, the available data indicate that the educational expansion in the industrialised countries since the close of World War II has not had a significant effect on regional and socio-economic disparities in school participation. At least, all social categories seemed to have shared in the expansion but the separation of participation rates between the categories has largely been maintained. The basic disparity among groups has not become altered by educational growth, although all groups have benefited from educational growth. The major exception to this generalisation is that in societies, or at school levels, where the saturation point in school participation is being reached, democratisation of participation occurs. For example, in most countries participation rates at the lower secondary level are high enough, so that differences among social categories are small — although in many European countries children are enrolled, already at that level, in educational branches which are very different in terms of their goals, content, methods and thus, in terms of their implications for further schooling. In the United States, Canada and Japan, the complete cycle of secondary education (high schools) is coming close to attaining a near-maximum level and social disparities in participation at that level have diminished. This points up the fact that educational expansion has a sequential effect on educational levels and educational disparities, beginning at the lower levels and progressing to the higher levels. It would not be expected, according to this line of thinking based on observed developments, that educational inequalities at, say, the higher educational level could be removed until inequalities at the secondary level had been eliminated. But even then other disparities, of a more qualitative nature, arising from social selection among secondary school graduates would probably be found.

Clues to the existence and maintenance of educational disparities can also be found in the nature of systems of social stratification. All nations are perceived to have institutionalised inequalities which become perpetuated by the differing ideologies of the various strata and the greater political power of the advantaged strata. At the same time, education comes to be viewed by the more privileged classes as both a potential and an actual avenue of mobility, and opportunities for education are made freer for these classes than for the less privileged classes. In addition, the culture of the upper and middle social strata defines education as a desirable goal for personal intellectual enrichment as well as for economic motives. However, these advantages and these goals came to be viewed, more and more explicitly and massively, as desirable by the lower strata as well. Thus, the growing and persistent demand for a greater share of socio-economic satisfactions from the lower social classes has led to a re-examination of social inequalities and of the factors which produce them. The strain on the part of the advantaged and more powerful groups between maintaining the desired advantage for themselves for the added rewards it brings on the one hand, and granting better statuses to the lower strata, out of a sense of democratic values and moral concern on the other, presents a very real dilemma. Until recently, the strict maintenance of social disparities in educational participation suggested that the desire for continued advantage was by far the dominant factor among the privileged strata. The gradual erosion of disparities in school participation in recent years, in certain countries and at certain levels of education, could be brought about in one of several ways: by a shift in the balance of values concerning the maintenance of status distinctions and democratisation which now places more weight on the latter; or by a belief among the privileged groups that the importance of education in economic achievement may have been over-stated and that more education for the lower strata will not diminish income differences; or by the realisation that educational participation is only one dimension of the educational process and that other educational inequalities can be substituted for disparities in educational participation (for example, in terms of kinds and quality of education received) in a way that would not endanger the present stratification system.

Educational disparities are also, to a certain but obvious extent, a consequence of educational policies in different countries, regions and local areas. Many studies have shown that educational policy-makers are drawn from the ranks of the advantaged strata and they are prone to maintaining the existing social order and enacting school policies which will accomplish this. Educational policy can continue to impede democratisation or it can hasten it, either by removing barriers to educational participation for some groups or by speeding up the attainment of the saturation point in participation and providing a chance for the less-advantaged strata to "catch-up." The latter approach, of course, involves enormous investments in education in a relatively short period of time and a favourable outlook on universal education.

3. The Educational Process and Educational Opportunities

When we reviewed the macro-sociological evidence with respect to regional differences in educational participation, the focus of attention was on inflows, transition rates or enrolment rates at a given point in time. The same holds true for the studies that attempt to measure social disparities in educational participation. A first question that arises is, where during the educational career of the individuals, do these social group disparities become important? A second question concerns the factors responsible for social group differences in school achievement. A third question, to be reviewed in the next section, has to do with the problem of the relationship between education on the one hand, and occupational career and earnings on the other. The kind of studies on which this discussion is based is a mixture of what we called above "ecological" analysis and "more focused socio-psychological" analysis.

The longitudinal studies at our disposal indicate that, already at the primary level, significant and systematic differences in achievement by social class occur. For example, in the Douglas study English children were tested at the age of eight when they have normally been at school for about two years. Quite substantial social class differences already appeared at this early age. After a follow-up study of these children, Douglas concluded that these differences generally remained constant when tested for pure intellectual capacity, but tended to widen when tested for school subjects. The main characteristics of the development of the pupils' test scores are decided by the age of eight, if not earlier. These gaps in school achievement which exist right from the start (and we will have more to say about their causes in a moment) are, of course, an important factor in explaining that transfer and drop-out rates are socially biased. In France, for instance, one sample shows that five years after the completion of compulsory schooling, 556 out of 1,000 children of farm labourers will have left the educational system, as against only 27 out of 1,000 children of higher administrative, managerial and executive workers. However, a more detailed study of the different transfer rates shows that variations in school achievement are not the only cause of these disparities, as could be expected. At equal achievement levels, pupils do not apply for transfer to academic secondary schools to the same extent in all social groups. Even at the highest achievement level, these transfer rates vary between the social classes. Thus, we must note two points. First, the proportion of under-achievers will be systematically higher, the lower the social class. Second, drop-out and transition rates will be respectively higher and lower among top achievers from lower social classes as compared to those from higher social classes. In the latter case, even pupils with below average achievement may continue to the higher levels of education. Clearly, differences in motivation and family stimuli play an important explanatory role in these different behavioural patterns.

All this means that the differences observed at the university level are the outcome of cumulative social differences at lower levels of the educational system. Some of the data at hand suggest that at the higher levels of education, the selection process becomes socially less biased. But this fact must, of course, be considered in conjuction with the earlier selection process. We can, therefore, conclude that achievement in primary school, transfer rates to academic secondary schools, and drop-out rates in secondary schools, go a long way to explain social group disparities in educational participation at the post-compulsory level.

Having established this, the next logical step is to determine what factors influence school achievement. In what follows, we will attempt to assess the relative importance of genetic factors, family and social environment characteristics, and of the school and teacher variables in influencing achievement as measured by test scores. In other words, the problem we want to throw light on concerns the relative influence of (i) what has happened to the individual *before* school, and (ii) what happens to him *in* school. This can be further summarised by stating that the problem is to determine the respective weights of school and out-of-school factors on school achievment. We shall start by looking at the genetic versus the other factors. The debate about the influence of genetic versus environmental factors on I.Q. and on school achievement was revived again by Jensen's long article, "How Much Can We Boost I.Q. and Scholastic Achievement?". Most researchers in this field have been preoccupied with the influence of genetic and environmental factors on intelligence quotients, rather than on school achievement. Although intelligence tests have been traditionally associated with achievement in school, there is far from being a perfect correlation between I.Q. and achievement test scores.

This is not the place to go into a long and technical discussion about this controversy. Our intention here is to sum up the conclusions, as we see them, based upon the available evidence. These conclusions are as follows: the genetic factors are, of course, important in explaining differences in school achievement, probably more so than any other single factor or complex of factors. But they are not all-important. For our purposes, the important question is not what proportion of variance is explained by genetic as against environmental factors, but what the potential for increasing intellectual capacity by educational and social policies is. In order to give a rough answer to that question, we make the following assumptions which are based on the existing literature and giving the benefit of doubt to the "genetists:"

(i) Genetic factors account for 80% of variations in I.Q.;

(ii) I.Q. has a simple correlation coefficient with school achievement tests of 0.7 to 0.8, thus accounting for 50 to 65% of the observed variations in achievement scores;

(iii) The genetic factors influence achievement only via I.Q.

Thus, the genetic factors would be responsible for 40 to 50% of the variations in achievement scores, leaving 50 to 60% for all other factors, i.e., mainly the family and social environment characteristics and the school and teacher variables. Our next step will, therefore, be (bearing in mind the place and weight of the genetic factors) to examine the relative importance of the other factors on school achievement.

In Chapter I we quoted the conclusion of the Coleman Report with respect to the relation of school versus family background factors. European studies focusing on the same problem area confirm that social background factors are probably much more important for school achievement compared to what happens in the school. The likelihood of changing the achievement pattern through social policy measures would, therefore, seem to be greater than by educational reforms. However, there are a number of facts which may have led to an underestimate of the role of school and teacher variables in the studies on which the above conclusion is based. First, the statistical and analytical methods used in these studies have been criticised. There is a certain arbitrariness in the manner the total variation is accounted for and is apportioned between the different groups of variables to the detriment of the school and teacher variables. Second, the school variables used in most of the studies come closest to what, in the case of the social background variables, has sometimes been labelled "material circumstances," as opposed to other, more psychological factors. In this respect, it looks as if some improvement has been made in the recording of the home environment, which seems to have greatly improved the explanatory power of these variables. On the other hand, it is possible that the school and teacher variables adopted are still too crude to register the amount or the lack of stimuli a child, and for that matter its parents, encounter in the school. This problem of incentives and motivation is crucial. To illustrate this point from the family and social environment angle, we can refer, among others, to evidence from the Plowden Report (1967). In that report, two kinds of social background variables were distinguished: "home circumstances" and "parental attitudes." It turned out that, what really makes the difference between the impact of social background and of the school, is the massive influence of the psychological home variable "parental attitudes". The studies of the influence of the school must also become more "qualitative" to be on the same footing as the home enquiries. Third and last, there is also the possibility that the school variables vary so little within a country that a regression analysis will not give any result, the few deviant cases being submerged by the mass of conventional and uniform school situations.

Moreover, these studies can, of course, only measure the effect of the different variables within the limits of their actual variation at the moment of the enquiry. They cannot say what would happen if we moved outside the present system. A distinction must, therefore be made between the effects of school variables within the existing educational system, which seem to be small, and the unknown effects of moves outside it. Thus, in spite of the outcome of the regression analysis, the Plowden Report was very optimistic about what the school could do. This was based on the finding mentioned a while ago, namely that what counted most in the home situations were not material circumstances, which the school admittedly cannot do much about, but the attitudes of the parents. When the children grew older, the attitude variable seemed to increase in importance relative to the material home circumstances. As the attitude variables were to a large extent independent of material circumstances, this could be a new field of endeavour for the school, and for active intervention in general. Many other studies which have analysed the influence of the family and social environment characteristics on school achievement and transfer rates have also often come to the conclusion that the economic situation is not as decisive a factor as the parents' cultural standard and conception of school and society. It may well be that income is a "threshold" variable i.e., only below a certain level will its influence be significant.

In many of the interview type surveys one is struck by the lack of information, uncertainty and even bewilderment, of the lower classes concerning the school and the possibilities it offers. The values and attitudes embodied in the school and in the teaching staff will often be in contradiction with those of the lower classes. Therefore changes in curricula content and more clearly defined vocational goals for tertiary education might increase the motivation of the lower classes to pursue their education beyond the compulsory stage. Some authors (for example, Bourdieu and Passeron, 1964), have found that pupils from working-class backgrounds who stay on at school are closer to those of the middle classes in attitudes and consumption pattern than those who leave early. In how far the school could influence such attitudes is not examined in the studies under consideration, which are restricted to surveying a formal and rather conventional school system.

Another type of study points to more specific areas in which the school can act to improve pupil achievement. One concerns the evidence brought forward to the effect that inadequacy of linguistic range and control is a very important factor in explaining the low average achievement of working class children. Linguistic inadequacy seems to be a "cumulative deficit." Although this cannot simply be looked upon as a problem of language, a mechanical skill to be taught, since it is a reflection of a whole culture, the school can facilitate, so this particular argument goes, the development of certain abilities by equipping the pupils with an appropriate language Clearly, to achieve anything in this direction, the cooperation of parents will eventually be needed. There is also the challenge made by, for example, Jensen (1969). Things could be learnt in different ways. The present school system applies teaching methods that make use of one faculty, "conceptual learning," which is perhaps unevenly distributed among social classes. However teaching could be arranged to appeal to other faculties that are more evenly distributed, e.g., so-called "associative learning." Another alternative is Benjamin Bloom's concept of "learning for mastery."

These examples as to the possibilities of new forms of educational systems are still speculative. For the time being, we are stuck with the conclusion that the influence of family and social environment factors, taken as a whole, on school achievement, is much more important than that of the cluster of school and teacher variables. To round off this part of the picture, we must now turn to an examination of the school variables individually, in order to see which are the more important ones in terms of their contribution to pupils' achievement.

The available information on existing school systems does not permit any generalisations about the relative importance of individual school factors on pupil achievement. If we distingiush three groups of school factors: "physical setting" (pupil - teacher ratio, size of school and of class, student body composition, etc.); "teachers" (age, sex, quality of staff, experience, etc.); and "organisation and policy" (time for instruction, homework, differentiation, streaming, parent - school cooperation, etc.), we note that one study (the National Survey of the Plowden Report) finds the teacher variables to be the most important feature of the school, but that other studies — for example, the Manchester Survey (Wiseman, 1964) and the International Mathematics Study (Husen, 1967) — consider the organisation and policy group of variables as the most influential. The evidence with respect to class size is only very slightly in favour of small classes. Either size of class is unimportant for school achievement when other variables are allowed for, or larger classes are more effective, at least up to a certain size and for the younger age groups with which the studies under review are mainly concerned. Comprehensive education has a positive effect on the school-leaving age and examinations passed, but no significant effects on achievement. While the quality of the teaching staff is important for pupil achievement, it results less from formal training than from experience and interests. The famous pupil - teacher ratio, according to all the evidence we have surveyed, does not seem to have any influence on achievement. Finally, we recall that the conclusions of the Coleman Report mentioned in Chapter I indicated that teachers' characteristics were more important than other school variables, and that the social composition of the student body was more highly related to achievement than any school factor.

What can be concluded from the above studies is that, within the small independent effect of school and teacher variables on achievement after one has allowed for genetic factors and family and social environment characteristics, an educational policy aimed at improving the school achievement of pupils should perhaps concentrate, not so much on the improvement of material circumstances (including class size and pupil - teacher ratio), as on teacher training, mentality and outlook as well as on school-organisational matters.

What conclusions can we draw from this brief survey about the factors that influence school achievement? Looking at the quantitative results of all the studies reviewed, and cutting a few Gordian knots, we can say that genetic factors account for 45% of the observed variations in school achievement; family and social environment characteristics for 40%; and school and teacher variables for 15%. Within the (important) residual left after the genetic factors have been controlled for, the family and social environment characteristics account for 70% and the school and teachers variables for 30%. On the basis of this evidence, therefore, any instrument variables which can strongly influence school achievement are more likely to lie within the realm of social than traditional educational policy. This might surprise but not necessarily discourage. For one thing, it does not mean that educational policy is ineffective, and secondly, it should be possible to intervene in the factors that lie behind the social background characteristics. Of course, if the intention was to democratise society through democratising educational opportunities, indirect action being preferred in such a delicate matter, it is somewhat disappointing to find that one of the best ways of democratising the school is to democratise society!

But any conclusion from the above studies must include a

reflection on the theoretical knowledge of educational processes on which they are based. It becomes clear, in the light of the studies reviewed, that the theory of educational processes must be improved in two important ways. First, the structure of the educational process must be better specified; current educational theory offers only very crude insights into the functional form of relationships among educational inputs and outputs. While it is possible to identify several correlates of school achievement, it is not possible to indicate whether these effects are linear, additive or independent. The argument that ability and quality of educational experience somehow interact is sufficiently appealing not to be summarily dismissed. Second, as important as the need to develop an adequate theory of education, is the requirement that the theory be operational. Much of existing educational theory is essentially circular (e.g., defining teacher effectiveness by student achievement). Student ability and motivation are two important variables that are also circularly defined. More operational formulations of educational theory by educationists, as well as more objective and direct measurement of variables, are necessary before useful applications of the "production function concept," on which the above studies are based, can be made to education. Next to the large-scale empirical research reviewed here, the alternative approach to enlighten educational policy is to improve the usefulness of micro-level educational action research. This alternative has several attractions. The more disaggregative the analysis, the more policy information may be obtained from the research. Educational changes which are *a priori* valuable may be experimentally instituted and the consequences evaluated. There are also limitations in these kinds of pilot experiments: absence of cost - effecttiveness analysis, lack of integration of micro-level educational research into a general model of education, etc.

4. Educational Opportunities, Educational Growth and "Life Chances"

So far we have discussed the relative effects of the educational process and of the out-of-school variables on the educational achievement and "survival" of the pupils and students. We have seen that the out-of-school factors seem to carry a much heavier weight in the explanation of how the individual fares in the educational system than the school and teacher variables. In spite of these results, we also know that all social groups have benefited from the past period of educational growth, and that many more youngsters from the lower social classes now have and take the opportunity to push their studies higher and higher up the educational ladder. Logically, therefore, our next problem is to ask ourselves what this increasing amount of education means in terms of the "life chances" of the individual and, more precisely, in terms of his occupational career and personal income. Do people leaving school with equal educational but differing social backgrounds get the same kind of jobs and can they be found in the same income brackets? On the whole, the information available on this subject considers "educational level" as determined by the number of school years or by the certificates and/or degrees obtained. The level of school achievement attained at given stages of the educational system is, thus, generally disregarded. It would, of course, have been preferable to consider both "educational level" and achievement. As it is now, when the occupational chances and the earnings of people from different social backgrounds having reached the same "educational level" are compared, we do not know to what extent, if any, the occupational and earnings differences can be explained by differences in school achievement. Thus, the role policy measures aimed at improving pupil achievement can play in equalising occupational opportunities cannot be estimated. However, we do know from some studies that even at equal achievement levels, social disparities in occupations may persist. For example, the English interview study conducted by Douglas (1968) shows that the occupational aspirations vary between the social classes, even for pupils at equal ability levels.

In a first instance, the evidence available concerning the occupational choice of school leavers and graduates leads us to advance the following hypothesis. As long as a given level or type of education can impose restricted admission practices — whether admission is restricted because few people are eligible, or because out of the many eligible only a minority is allowed entry, is indifferent to the reasoning — there will be close to a one-to-one relationship between that particular educational level and occupational opportunities. In more mundane terms, when we have to do with a "good" educational level or branch (because it is "restricted"), the bulk of the entrants will be from "good" social backgrounds, and when they leave they will enter "good" jobs. Obviously, already during those "restricted" days, a minority among the entrants will come from the lower social classes, and they benefit also from the one-to-one relationship between social class - school - job. However, as soon as admission to this educational level or branch, for one reason or another, becomes more general and less restricted, the relationship between that educational level and occupational opportunities becomes looser, and the importance of social background greater. In other words, it looks as if in this latter case, education becomes gradually less important as an explanatory factor in the occupational "choice" of the individual, but the one-to-one relationship between social background and occupation remains: The student from the higher social class will still tend to get the "better" jobs, but this time the graduate with a lower social class background will be squeezed more and more into the "other" jobs.

One piece of empirical evidence comes from the English longitudinal study of Himmelweit and Swift (1969), based on a sample of 600 pupils who in 1952 were 13 to 14 years old. In 1963—64, when they were 25 years of age, their occupational situation was investigated. An interesting difference was observed between those who had attended grammar school and those who had gone to secondary modern school. The distribution by occupational groups of the pupils who had finished grammar school was very similar across social background, working class children being only slightly less successful. However, the kinds of jobs that fall to children coming from secondary modern schools turned out to be much more dependent on social origin. Himmelweit and Swift thought of the grammar school as a "strong" system having well-defined goals and methods. Such a system will orientate its pupils in certain directions irrespective of the attitudes of parents. The secondary modern school is not such a "strong" system and the outcome will be conditioned to a larger extent by family background. Although this interpretation is not necessarily wrong, it does nothing more than present one possible effect of a restricted as contrasted with a more generalised school system. However this may be, the results are in line with our hypothesis.

The above effect of school on occupation has apparently little to do with ability. A certain number of pupils had been assigned to grammar schools, although their general level of ability was a great deal below the average. On the other hand, some pupils had been allocated to secondary modern schools, although on tests they showed ability which would have permitted them to go to grammar schools. In spite of this, both these groups followed rather closely the occupational patterns of their respective type of school.

A Swiss longitudinal study (Girod and Tofigh, 1965), followed 2,500 children born in 1942 - 43 through school and the beginnings of occupational life. The majority of pupils left school before the upper-secondary education stage. According to a five-point occupational scale, it appeared that, at these low levels of education, the differences in social origin do not have any marked influence on the first steps of the occupational career. Most children become workers, qualified or not. The percentage becoming qualified clerical workers increases with the level of instruction at about the same rate for each social class.

As to the evidence concerning university graduates, we have mentioned in an earlier chapter the admittedly very crude international comparison on occupational and educational structures of the labour force which suggested that the more university graduates are "available" the more they can be found in all the (non-manual) occupational categories. According to our hypothesis, graduates from the lower social classes should be over-represented in the "lower" occupational categories.

Let us now look at some information with respect to the relationship between education and earnings. Insofar as there is a positive correlation between occupational level and earnings, our hypothesis should be valid for this second relationship as well. One of the more interesting pieces of evidence available is reported by Torsten Husén (1969), on the basis of a follow-up study made in Sweden. A sample of 1,500 pupils in the third grade of elementary school has been followed since 1938. In 1964, when they were 35 years old, practically the entire group was contacted again and from about two-thirds information could be obtained with regard to their earnings. As can be seen from Table IX-1, mean income increases, within each status group, with the length of education. However, at each level of education, there are more or less important income differences among the social classes, with the exception of those who have elementary schooling only. For example, with 11 to 14 years of education, the son of a professional worker earns on average 35,000 crowns a year, while the corresponding average for the son of an unskilled worker is 18,000. For the children of unskilled workers, extended schooling from junior to senior secondary school does not appear to be very rewarding: a substantial increase in salary comes only after having attended university. In general, those from status group 1 earn more than those from status group 4 on the next higher educational level. Husén concludes that earnings are determined to a greater extent by social origin than by length of formal schooling and ability.

TABLE IX-1
Mean Taxed Income (in 1000 Swedish Crowns) by Level of Formal Education and Social Class

Years of education	<8 years Elementary Schooling only	8-10 years Junior sec. schooling	11-14 years Senior sec. schooling	>14 years University
Social class				
(1) Professional, Managerial	15.0	23.1	35.5	45.4
(2) Sub-profes-sional, middle-level	14.9	18.0	24.4	34.5
(3) Skilled workers	16.3	18.6	21.8	28.0
(4) Unskilled workers	15.6	17.6	17.9	29.7

Source: T. Husén (1969), *Talent, Opportunity and Career*, Stockholm.

These data on earnings corroborate Girod's conclusions with regard to occupational choice. At the very lowest levels of education, the labour market situation, whether judged by earnings or occupations, is very similar for people with different social backgrounds. Of course, it must be remembered that only a small minority of the children from the upper classes leave school at this early stage. This evidence requires a reformulation of our original hypothesis, which should be amended as follows: when a level of education is universally attended, many pupils will tend to continue to maintain their "educational differential." Those who leave at this "early" stage will have the same occupational opportunities irrespective of social class, it being clear that there will be very few pupils among them from the middle and higher classes.... More important is the suggestion from the Swedish evidence, that even at moderately restricted levels of higher education, social class plays immediately an important role in the determination of earnings. This seems to contradict, therefore, the English grammar school evidence. This point is important enough to merit some further, and somewhat speculative, discussion.

It has often been suggested that the educational system is really only a social device for "screening and labelling" individuals according to their social background. If this were to be the case, any attempt to increase the independent effect of the school to offset social class differences might have no effect: either the "best" schools would continue to be identified according to the high social origin of their students (independent of the school characteristics), or some other social device would take over the "screening and labelling" function of schools. This screening and labelling function is sometimes referred to as the "sheepskin effect," the idea being that the mere possession of a degree will be taken by employers as proof of productivity. This issue was examined in the United States by Hansen, Weisbrod and Scanlon, in an article called "Does Schooling Really Count?".

Still in the United States, a paper by R. Weiss (1969) would seem to lend support to this screening and labelling hypothesis. In a carefully designed study based on U.S. 1960 census data, Weiss found that, for non-whites, there was no significant relationship between additional years of education and earned income. It might be argued that, in the case of non-whites, a stronger screening and labelling device displaces the use of the educational system for such a function. The social class of non-whites being identified in the employers' minds by their race, identification by educational degree is ignored. There are, of course, simpler explanations for Weiss' results. To consider only measurement problems, there is the likelihood that conventional measures of educational resources for non-whites, whether in terms of years, test scores or expenditures, are in reality poor substitutes for measures of the quality and quantity of the resources that do reach and educate non-white children in those skills that they are interested in learning, in order to make a living in a society marked by severe racial discrimination. This source of errors in measurement is compounded by more customary types of reporting errors, which are also probably more serious for non-whites. Both types of errors could cause a "no effect" verdict for education. Another explanation is that, although education does increase the productivity of non-whites, employer and/or market discrimination against non-whites increases as the education of non-whites increases. However, in seeking alternative explanations of the empirical findings, we should not ignore the possibility that Weiss' findings lend support to the "screening and labelling" hypothesis about education.

At this point we should draw attention to the fact that this "screening and labelling" argument could provide a consistent set of explanations for the findings on the school characteristics — school achievement relationships versus the rate-of-return results, a paradox which we discussed in Chapter I. If schools do not really function in the sense of creating greater economic productivity beyond that determined by the social background of the individual, but if more years of school, or more schooling per year, tend to be correlated with higher social background, then schools would act as a "screening and labelling" device to indicate higher socio-economic background, which employer seek. Thus, even if schools as such do not necessarily increase productivity, people with more years of school or attendance at "better" schools would receive higher incomes, and this would give the results reflected in the positive findings in terms of rates of return. To the question why the children from high socio-economic status go to school at all, or at least go to school longer, one answer would be: for consumption benefits. Of course, authors of studies on the rate-of-return have attempted to take this kind of factor into account by making allowances for "ability." However, it is widely agreed that these ability adjustments are inadequate as controls for innate ability. Further, "ability" may be less responsible for the favoured position of the children from higher social groups than the acquisition of "social graces" or "connections."

From the rather heterogeneous data presented here, we can draw one or two tentative conclusions. The educational requirements of many occupational categories are often so loosely defined that persons with widely differing qualifications can enter the same occupation. The upper classes seem to know best how to take advantage of this situation. It might be that the occupations in question are only open to them, and that they have, to a certain extent, created this situation. Even during an economic expansion, when the number of top positions increases and cannot be filled to any substantial extent by highly educated people from the upper status groups, they seem to be filled more readily by persons from the upper classes with lower qualifications than by persons from the middle or lower classes with more extensive education. The few exceptions where people from different social groups have equal occupational or earnings possibilities, or where education is clearly linked to social mobility, are in situations where (i) the school system is highly selective (and there is no guarantee that this would not change if the system became less restricted); and (ii) the very lowest levels of education are considered — or, more generally, those levels where universal attendance prevails — which for the majority of children of higher status groups are not the final educational stage.

However, these facts should not be interpreted to mean that extended education for people of modest social origin would not improve their occupational and earnings opportunities. The data indicate that they would, although the reaction of the labour market to a greatly increased output of highly qualified personnel may reduce the benefits. What education seems incapable of doing is to erase the influence of social background on occupational and earnings opportunities. Thus, equal participation rates in education will be consistent with unequal occupational chances.

5. Concluding Remarks

When we speak about educational growth and expansion, we eventually speak about growing educational opportunities for more and more people with very different characteristics — be they genetic or environmental. When we speak about educational growth and opportunities, we must eventually ask for the purpose, and thus we must speak about the role of education in a person's out-of-school life. These two points have been the guidelines for steering us through this chapter. It is also because of these two points that stress was put on (i) what the school can do in the face of the external factors that determine the characteristics of the child before he enters the education system, and that continue to exercise their influence during his school career; and (ii) the influence of education on what happens to the individual once he has left the educational system. In both cases, the available evidence suggests that the independent effect of the school is much smaller than that of the external, societal factors. This finding leads us to the following reflections on educational growth, educational opportunity and "life chances."

In the industrialised countries, everyone completes *n* years of education. Of course, *n* varies from country to country. In some countries it may be 6 years, in others 8 or 10, and in the United States *n* will soon be 12. In all countries there is a widespread and deeply held belief that education is a powerful force in shaping the subsequent "life chances" of any individual. It is believed, in other words, that education is a powerful and useful means for the attainment of upward social mobility. This is, of course, the economic and social rationale behind the pressure for equalising educational opportunities across social classes. Now, if we take these two observations together — the fact that universal schooling is achieved at the *n*th level, coupled with the belief in the socio-economic benefits of education — we have one of the most powerful explanations of the driving force behind educational expansion. At the same time, we come to the perplexing insight that this expansion could go on *ad infinitum*, without ever reaching the socio-economic objectives which lie behind the goals of educational expansion and equal educational opportunity. Let us illustrate these assertions.

What happens when a country is well under way to reaching universal education at the *n*th level? Two inter-related phenomena can be observed: the first is that the socio-economic advantages associated with the attainment of that educational level will disappear as one approaches the target of universal education at that level, and the second is that, precisely because of this, the pressure to continue to the next higher level will gradually increase in order to benefit again from the socio-economic advantages that will now be associated with the next higher level. We could say that at the *n*th level the principle of zero-correlation has set in: if everybody completed a given level of schooling, then the correlation between completing that level and any subsequent social differences that may arise (income, occupational opportunity) would be reduced to zero. Under such conditions it can only be at some point beyond the *n*th level that there can again exist any correlation between the level of education attained and any subsequent indicator of social standing or social mobility. And so the pressure for more and more years of education will spiral upwards. Moreover, as we have suggested in the present chapter, it seems to be the case that democratisation only sets in once the saturation point has been reached for the higher social classes. In other words, at whetever level the point of zero-correlation is reached, the last group to attain that level will, in general, be from the lower class. This proposition can be reversed by saying that by time the "group of last entry" completes the *n*th level, the principle of zero-correlation will set in. The promise and the hope held out will not be satisfied. What was believed to be a sufficient condition for improved opportunities and "life chances" will turn out to be only a necessary condition. Failure to complete the *n*th level for the "group of last entry" will prove to be increasingly more disastrous for the individual, but success, by the same token, will be less consequential than it has been for the other groups. The prospect is for a fresh cycle of frustration.

It will become necessary for members of the group of last entry to go on to yet higher levels of education. And so the pressure for easier access to higher levels of schooling will be on, and those pressures will conflict directly with the selective character of these higher levels. The typical response in institutions under such pressures of conflicting roles is to find a means of escape. What we would expect, in short, is that the society would develop techniques for releasing the "head of steam" to avoid an explosion. This will generally be done by a diversification and re-structuring of the higher levels of education, thus creating qualitative differences. And so, at the end of the rope, we come back to the observations made during our "theoretical excursion" concerning differences in kind and in quality of education which, for the upper classes, is another means to escape the principle of zero-correlation.

X

The Present View of Educational Expansion: Goals and Strategies

In the previous chapter we were concerned with the mechanism behind educational growth and with what the various social groups "get out of" education; in this chapter the emphasis will be on current thinking about educational policy goals and on alternative educational strategies designed to reach these goals. In dealing with the subject of goals and strategies we will, of course, constantly keep in mind the possibilities and limitations of present educational systems as reviewed in the preceding pages.

Let us recall that two viewpoints about the overall objectives of educational growth have dominated the scene in the 1960s: (i) the view that education should be provided for all to the highest level they demand, and for which they are qualified; and (ii) the view that a rapid expansion of the educational system was justified to provide the necessary manpower for expanding economies.

The latter is still an important objective in the developing countries, but in the highly industrialised part of the world, the social justification of growth is becoming more important as income and educational levels attain new heights. Indeed, the greater attention being given to the social objectives of education in national policy-making could be seen as part of a general re-emphasis on social objectives in the allocation of resources in the industrialised countries. It should be noted in this connection that education has to compete with other social objectives, such as health, housing, transportation and improvements in the national and urban environment. In these circumstances, it is important that the objectives of education, and their changing priority structure, be identified, clarified and defined in order to provide a clear guide to efficient resource allocation and utilisation. First, we will discuss changes in educational policy goals in the 1970s; second, alternative educational strategies to reach these goals, and finally, in a third section, we shall take a longer-term view and say a few words about alternative educational and societal futures as a means to explore longer-term changes in educational goals, in line with social change.

1. Changing Educational Goals in the 1970s

In the concluding remarks of the previous chapter, we suggested that the main driving force behind educational growth has been the principle of zero-correlation coupled with the belief in the economic and social efficacy of education. This has resulted in increasing pressures for giving higher priority to the goal of equal educational opportunity. We have assisted, in the latter part of the 1960s and in certain countries, at a swing towards a more active policy directed towards the *equal educational opportunity* goal. It has become quite clear, as exemplified in Chapters I and IX, that by giving people from very widely different family and social environment characteristics access to the same schools and the same curricula (i.e., the same educational opportunity), the results in terms of *educational achievement* vary substantially and systematically according to social groups. The conclusion is, therefore, more and more drawn that, to overcome background disadvantages, the goal of educational policy will have to broaden the equal educational opportunity concept to include also equal school achievement. However, many objectives pursued by educational policy are not end-objectives, but serve as inputs to attain wider social objectives. This clearly applies to equal educational opportunity as well, and so we are back at our conclusions reached in the previous chapter. One of the strongest common assumptions in most Western societies is that education is the key to upward mobility. This common belief in the efficacy of education as a means for individual social advancement has been combined with a growing social consensus that education should be used broadly as an instrument for social change, i.e. a large-scale opening of educational opportunities through governmental intervention should be a principal, or even "the" principal instrument for the transformation and progressive modernisation of societies. In earlier chapters we have made an attempt to juxtapose pieces of evidence from several areas of the economics, the sociology and the psychology of education. Our survey certainly was not comprehensive and, perhaps, in the selection of points considered important, it was mis-representative. However, it is shown in these chapters that the juxtaposition of empirical evidence does raise a number of substantial, unresolved issues. The big question put foward by these chapters is, "What if the efficacy of education as an instrument for change is not as clear as the common belief would suggest?" If educational systems have basically assumed a reproductive function (Bourdieu and Passeron, 1970), preserving or even reinforcing the structure of society, the pressure for change is being diverted into "futile" educational activity, which will, in fact, not generate change. These doubts will either have to be dispelled or, if the doubts are substantiated, our understanding of the educational process will have to be deepened to the point where we can transform education into a truly effective instrument of social and economic progress. In how far the swing towards *active* equal educational opportunity strategies will or can increase the efficacy of education, is one of the main subjects of this chapter.

Socialisation and *individualisation* are also seen as important educational policy objectives for the 1970s. Education is *par excellence* an institution which is on the bridge between the individual and society. The rapid economic growth, technological advance and social change of the last decades have transformed the relationship between the individual and society, and to a more or less significant degree torn down the national, class, professional, ideological and religious supports which provided the social framework for the individual. If the educational system is to succeed in relating the child and the young person to his society, then the curriculum, teaching methods and the relationship of the school to the outside world must be changed to cope with the new realities. The ability of individuals to find a constructive role in society will be more dependent than in the past on the self-consciousness and understanding which education can provide, on better knowledge and understanding of the choices faced by society, and in a certain sense on a "critical" view of society (which may be defined as a sense of freedom from "blind" social forces). In other words, the socialising role of education is dependent on individualisation — social cohesion and the autonomy of the individual are inseparable. Such a new approach to socialisation would have fundamental implications for the curriculum and methods of teaching.

Individual development may be seen as the central integrating goal for education in modern, democratic societies. All other goals find their specific meaning in relation to it. Equity, for example, must respect the reality that the creative development of individuals takes place in the workplace as well as the school, and access to education to achieve adult as well as youth aspirations will thus become increasingly important. Secondly, the opposition between economic efficiency and the development of the individual is too simple-minded in a society where individuals without qualifications are social casualties. The debates of the 1960s opposed quantity and quality on the one hand, equity and efficiency on the other. These conflicts are, in fact, a consequence of the idea that economic growth is an end in itself. Within this framework an "efficient" educational system is seen as one which advances personal or national income. If in the 1970s economic growth is looked upon more as a means to a wider range of economic and social objectives, the efficiency of the educational system will refer to a wider range of objectives. The restatement of the problem will be: how can education use resources so that it is effective in achieving whatever goals society sets for it? Socialisation, as we have seen above, cannot be achieved in modern conditions of rapid change without self-conscious and socially creative individuals. Moreover, an educational system which fails as a learning process for the individual will fail whatever the priority it gives to the other objectives.

The most challenging question, therefore, is whether education can create and respond to new patterns and models of individual development, without which the orientation to social and economic goals will continue to generate social discontent and individual frustration. Educational structures, curricula, and teaching methods, must respond to these new models of creative individual development. The links between education, work and leisure that they imply is likely to be a central issue in the policy-making of the 1970s.

The above discussion of goals makes it clear that any statement of educational goals is bound to deal with values about which there may be a lack of social consensus, or values which are only meaningful when translated into action in the schools by those involved in the schools. Thus, the necessity of making goals more explicit cannot be translated simply into targets for national policy — they have to be reflected in processes which reach into the school and local community. This poses a difficult problem. Indeed, if the process of making goals explicit is more likely to reveal different sets of values to which different groups in society would give priority, the idea of a social choice between one constellation of values as opposed to another is problematic. It is also questionable whether the notion of a hierarchy of goals is operationally useful, since different social groups will obviously order their priorities differently.

It is for these reasons that the question of "whose goals" is as important as "what goals," and that the process of public discussion through which goals are identified is as important as the technocratic process through which they may be "operationalised." In sum it is a question of how the democratic process can function in relation to such choices. In order to get to grips with this problem, it is necessary to make a distinction between those goals which call for general political decisions about the allocation of recources, and those which are rather a reflection of values which cannot necessarily be reflected in such political decisions. For example, equity and economic efficiency can only be realised through general political decisions about the allocation of resources in relation to objectives. As such, the process for determining such goals is bound to be the normal political process. But at the same time, it must be recognised that neither can be successfully attained unless translated into the specifics of school practice, and there is in consequence a major problem of involving teachers, parents and students in the definition of goals and their translation into action. The goals of socialisation and individual development, on the other hand, are fundamentally concerned with the curriculum and teaching methods. The implicit values behind them are those of the society at large, but the political process as such cannot do more than provide "guidelines." In this area, therefore, the formulation of explicit goals depends on the creative participation of teachers, parents, children and students in the framework of their local communities, schools and universities.

In sum, the question of "whose goals" can only be answered by a process which includes two main features: (i) the normal political process with explicit machinery for translating the allocation of resources into action and change in the schools; and (ii) the "grass roots" process whereby general social values about educational content and method are materialised by a process of participation in which teacher—parents and children are involved.

We shall come back to these issues both in section 3 for a wider and longer-term perspective, and in the next chapter as far as the policy-planning aspects are concerned. But first we turn to an overview of the educational strategies and changes which are being introduced, or which are envisaged, in view of attaining the above goals.

2. Alternative Educational Strategies and Educational Technology

Here we want to do two things. We shall first present four educational strategies which have been designed mainly, but not always exclusively, for attaining the equal educational opportunity goal. Second, we come back to the subject of educational technology — in the sense of the technology of instruction, as described in Chapter III — in order to see which possibilities have already developed and which could be of potential use for the goals of socialisation and individual development.

Alternative educational strategies for equal educational opportunity

It is possible to distinguish three theoretical approaches to an explanatory analysis of social disparities in educational participation: they may be labelled the cultural theory, the educational theory, and the structural theory. The first puts relatively more emphasis on the characteristics of the population before entering the educational system, such as the family - pedagogical environment, i.e. the attitude towards education, the language spoken in the home and by the peer group, the education of the parents, etc. The second puts more emphasis on the school and teacher variables and could be called the optimistic theory, because it assumes that the influence of the school could be increased in relation to that of the non-school external factors on which the other two theories concentrate. Lastly, the structural theory lays emphasis on economic and social constraints, and broadens the concept of the effects of education to include, for instance, the effects of education on jobs and on income.

Each of these three approaches is clearly a partial one, and a general theory would have to embrace them all. But there is little doubt that recent strategies aimed at equalising educational opportunities have been inspired mainly by the educational theory. The most important of these strategies are reviewed below.

(a) Pre-school training. Pre-school training has been in use, in one form or another, for some time. More recently, special programmes have been designed coordinating as much as possible this pre-school training with primary school in order to bring children into an appropriate educational environment before the start of compulsory education. One of the better-known examples is "Head Start" adopted in the United States. This project

is designed to enrich the lives of children during the years when they grow and learn most quickly — the years when they are learning how to learn. Children of the poor generally reach school age lagging far behind their middle class contemporaries in their ability to perform and absorb in the classroom. The schools as they now exist fail to close this gap. Because the relative handicap of those children who start out behind remains almost constant, their actual lag in educational achievement grows greater through the school years. Head Start has rightly focused our attempts to ease this gap on the pre-school period of life.

All such programmes are based on the assumption that the intelligence level, which is an important factor in determining school achievement, is not fixed genetically, but is responsive to environmental influences during the first formative years. In this connection, the effects of the Head Start programme are being evaluated thoroughly. Reports suggest that the programme has not proved as effective as had earlier been thought, and that, so far, its long-term effects have been slight. One of the early findings was that Head Start children appear to "fall back" after entering the regular school system. The reason for this is not yet clear, but it may be that non-Head Start children just "catch up." Research has shown that every child shows an initial spurt in aptitude when it first enters school, and it may be that in Head Start children this spurt manifests itself in the pre-school programme, while in non-Head Start children it appears in the regular classroom. However this may be, the fact remains that the findings are not conclusive, and that the whole problem of pre-school training is much more complicated and fraught with frustrations than was thought previously. (Little and Smith, 1971).

(b) Compensatory education at the primary level. With compensatory education, the emphasis shifts to the early years of schooling proper. Here, the main effort is directed towards modifying traditional curricula and teaching methods as well as introducing a range of educational supporting services so as to enable socially disadvantaged children to make contact with the outside community. In this connection, the importance of language development as a precondition for later school performance in all subjects is being increasingly stressed.

In the United States, Title I of the 1965 Elementary and Secondary Education Act has provided very large funds to improve education in areas with large concentrations of children from low income groups, and the Follow Through Programme has been specially devised for such children who have also participated in a full year of Head Start or similar pre-school programmes. The Froomkin and Dugan report (1969) published by the U.S. Office of Education evaluates Title I as follows:

> The implication that school resources are not being rearranged in a very effective manner to achieve the expected cognitive gains of students can be deduced from the analysis of disparate reports submitted by localities in connection with Title I. These reports imply that very little change in reading achievements has occurred as a result of the implementation of Title I projects. Granted that these reports are fragmentary and only report achievement of a small proportion of projects, our impression is that the projects which reported had a higher than average investment in resources. Hence, the other projects probably showed even bleaker achievements gains. The reports for 1967 and 1968 indicated that less than one-fifth of the Title I participants achieved a significant gain in reading, roughly two-thirds showed no change, and the rest showed some loss. It is also interesting to note that the majority of gains were attained in the higher grades. This is contrary to popular impression. Thus, it would appear that Title I programmes which motivated older children were more successful than the remedial programmes at a lower age.

Some of the more experimental compensatory programmes attempt to change the organisation of the school and of the classrooms. A case in point is the More Effective Schools Programme (MES) in New York City. This has reduced the number of pupils per teacher by more than half so as to increase correspondingly the attention given to the individual pupil. But there has been no evidence to show that such a measure would change the relative positions of the privileged and non-privileged pupils. After two years, the pupils in MES schools exhibited the classical pattern of increasing academic retardation. This is, of course, in line with the now well-documented fact that a drastic reduction in the pupil—teacher ratio is a necessary but not sufficient condition of effective compensation. As pointed out in the final evaluation of MES by D.K. Cohen (1969):

> Despite the...organisational changes, little has happened in the way of innovation or re-structuring in the basic teaching process. Observers noted that a majority of lessons they saw could have been taught to larger classes with no loss in effectivenes.... All levels of staff noted that the basic weakness of the programme, or their major disappointment with it, centred about the functioning of teachers, which they attributed to inexperience and lack of preparation.

The general criticism of the American Compensatory educational programmes is that they have concentrated heavily upon the deficiencies of children and neglected to give serious attention to the deficiencies of schools. As noted by Cohen, "So much has been made of the deprivations children are supposed to have inflicted upon the schools that hardly any serious thought has been given to the institutional deficiencies of schools which regularly are inflicted upon children". Most programmes provide additional services which are supposed to make up for the cumulative effects of poverty and discrimination, but they leave the rest of the educational system unchanged. In that sense, one could say that they are piling wooden ploughs on wooden ploughs.

It may be added that the American programmes emphasise equality of educational opportunity between races and tend to lose sight of the gross inequalities of educational opportunity between one social class and another. European programmes will, of course, have to concentrate more on the latter aspect. [1]

(c) Comprehensive education at the secondary level. Comprehensive education at the secondary level has been introduced in some countries and is being considered in others. It represents a more or less radical break with the traditional selective system which prevails in most countries. Its consequences cannot be easily compared internationally, because the meaning of comprehensive education varies from one country to another.

In terms of organisational differentiation, one can distinguish between *track differentiation*, in which the pupils are assigned to different lines of study in the same type of school; *class differentiation*, in which the pupils have, on the whole, the same curriculum, but are divided into parallel classes on a certain grade level according to some criterion of general ability, such as achievement, test scores, grade point average, or intelligence test scores; and differentiation by *ability grouping or "setting,"* in which the pupils within a given grade are grouped and re-grouped in parallel classes in certain subjects according to their progress in these subjects. This means that they are re-grouped for each subject. An example of the first type of differentiation is the organisation of grade 9 in Swedish comprehensive schools and the various lines of the continuation schools. An example of the second type of differentiation is provided by streaming in British comprehensive schools.

There may also be *pedagogical differentiation*, i.e., differentiation exclusively within the framework of the class. Thus, a class may be divided into two halves according to pupils' ability in a

---

[1] On this whole aspect, see again Little and Smith (1971).

given subject, with the teacher instructing one half at a time. Or it may be possible, particularly if self-instructional material is available, to give individual tasks on which each pupil can, in principle, work at his own speed and at his own level of ability. Pedagogical differentiation (which should rather be called individualisation) can, of course, be applied to any school structure.

The change from a dualistic or parallel system, in which pupils are divided at an early age according to "talent" and "wishes," to a comprehensive system, in which this selection is postponed to a later stage, has been brought about by a combination of economic and socio-political factors. Economic, because the rigid selective system is suited to an economy with a relatively small professional élite, whereas economic and technological changes of the past twenty years have produced considerable shifts in the skill structure of the labour force, resulting in an increasing demand for highly skilled personnel. Socio-political, because, rightly or wrongly, education is being increasingly seen as the democratic substitute for inherited wealth and social position.

In contrast with pre-school training and compensatory education, which are in the main additional activities leaving the educational system unchanged, the comprehensive school could be part of a general educational policy aimed at tackling the problem of the socially underprivileged and based on the assumption that social mobility may be brought about through the development of the individual. However, and the American example is there to show it, what is most important in this context is the kind of comprehensive school in terms of organisational and pedagogical differentiation, and quality of instruction. As noted earlier, equality of school inputs does not result in equality of outputs. The idea of an improved comprehensive education was expressed by Fantini and Weinstein (1968) in the following terms:

> True process change involves changing the institution of education at its core — the entire system of education from teacher techniques, curriculum content and teacher training to administrative organisation and personnel; from the physical plant to the very attitudes and philosophy which underlie the entire educational system. In short, an up to date process can only come about by constructing *a new model*, a model based on the belief that institutions must adjust to *people*, rather than the other way round. In essence, this requires a change in the behavioural roles among educational personnel within the system. Educational personnel must be willing and able to recognise that there are *no human failures*, only programme and institutional failures (pages 228-229).

Comprehensive education is not a panacea; its success in promoting equality of educational opportunity will depend largely on the right mix of organisational and pedagogical differentiation with a view to exploiting to the maximum potential talent and minimising as much as possible the drawbacks due to differences in culture and environment.

(d) Recurrent education. The idea of delaying part or parts of education until a more mature age is gaining increasing attention in several countries. Tradition holds that as much education as possible should be squeezed into the early years of life. The prevailing notion is that a total of, say, 16 years of education should be given between the ages of, say 6 and 21. In contrast with, but by no means in opposition to, this notion is the idea that education could be spread over a much longer period, that, for instance, a total of 16 years could be given between the ages of 6 and 30, or 6 and 40.

The reasons for such a spread are manifold. There is the question of motivation and attitudes towards education. Many talented people are diverted from education at a young age by lack of motivation and even prejudice in their home and their environment but become motivated at a later stage in their lives, after having had the opportunity of comparing themselves with others in a work environment. Many young people would simply prefer to leave school at, say, 16 if they knew that a guaranteed and increased possibility exists to resume their education at a later stage in life. Then there is the question of the flexibility of the educational system. Spreading the educational period over a longer time span would make the educational system much more responsive to changes in the labour market and, at the same time, give the individual more flexible opportunities for his development.

At the Sixth Conference of European Ministers of Education held at Versailles in May 1969, Olof Palme, the then Swedish Minister of Education, gave an important address, from which we have extracted the following passages:

> We may already assume that we shall not be able to afford an educational system with large elements of recurrent education if youth education is allowed to continue developing at an unchanged rate. The first question we must ask then is the following: Where can the restriction be set in the first place? A restriction of school education, including upper secondary education, would presumably hit pupils from lower social groups. For reasons of equality we, therefore, cannot refrain from a youth education for all of 11—12 years as normal length. Moreover, upper secondary education in one form or another will certainly be needed to satisfy the labour market's increasing demand of trained manpower.

The only remaining material possibility is therefore to reduce the growth of post-secondary education in order to enable adult education to expand. This thought may appear absurd to many. The solution I have in mind, however, is not to take from the one and give to the other. Let us regard instead, the entire education coming after school education as a unit, organisationally, and from the point of view of resources. Of course I do not intend to deal with all questions and problems connected with such a radical structural change. I believe, however, that here is the central issue of educational policy in the times to come. And since this issue is indeed very closely connected with the development of secondary education I find it appropriate to touch upon some of its more interesting aspects. I think that the best way for me to illustrate the question at issue is to assume — as a hypothesis, representing an extreme, this I am fully aware of — that all post secondary education is organised on a recurring basis, that all people, after completing upper secondary education, go out into a job, that after some time at work they take another period of education, then return to a job again, pass through another period of education and so on.

A system of this kind would have considerable consequences on upper secondary education because in such a system upper secondary education would be the basis for both entry into the labour market and for continued education. It would, among other things, be necessary to give a vocational bias for all lines of upper secondary education, even to those which today essentially lead to higher education. On the other hand, there would still be a need for a large element of general theoretical subjects as a basis for recurrent education.

After having touched on the difficulties, limitations and possibilities of this idea of recurrent education, Mr. Palme mentioned some of the effects on individuals and society which the alternation between education and occupational work may have:

For the individual, recurrent education ought to have several advantages. We all have a need for variety, whatever our occupation is. The student with educational neurosis and the person in working life with symptoms of stress would both perhaps get to grips with their problems if they were given the opportunity of a change of activity for a time. Leisure time would be used by many in a more valuable way than now and the individual would have a better opportunity to get to know his aptitudes. Absolute individual failures would be less common, as everybody would have a repeated second chance.

Recurrent education should help us on the way towards *equality* in society. The interplay between different human activities would result in their being regarded in various respects as on an equal footing. The understanding between different social groups would increase as people had more similar experiences. The relations between the generations would improve.

Contrary to the three previous strategies reviewed here, the recurrent education model has not yet been tried out. It should not be equated to existing schemes of adult education. Indeed, the return of adolescents and adults to education is at present very difficult in practice and only few have the necessary surplus of energy and perseverance to accomplish studies, alongside their occupational work, some or many years after they have left school. The existing schemes do not change the basic education model at all and cannot be expected, therefore, to satisfy the needs of those young people who do not conform to the prevailing institutional framework or pattern of education.

The introduction of recurrent education would constitute a radical departure from this framework and would clearly have widespread effects on all other sectors of education. Organisational and pedagogical differentiation along some of the lines traced above would have to be introduced at the secondary level to give it more flexibility, and thus enable people to resume their education at any time. In fact, recurrent education is a strategy that comes closest to a total reform of the educational system.

Coming to the end of this presentation of educational strategies, we are led to reflect on them in the light of what we said in Chapter IX, and particularly in the concluding remarks. The first two strategies reviewed have set out to increase the educational achievement of the lower classes. It has become clear that they have not always been successful in this endeavour. The third strategy — comprehensive education at the secondary level — aims rather more to increase the intake of young people, although the more ambitious comprehensive school versions also attempt to look at the output side. But whatever their aim — diminishing inequalities in school achievement or diminishing inequalities in educational participation — and whatever their results, it will be clear that these strategies do not solve the dilemma of the "principle of zero-correlation." It could even be claimed that the more successful these strategies are, the quicker will the "fresh cycles of frustration" succeed one another and the more the majority will be pushed to spend ever longer years in the educational system. In other words, educational strategies that are relatively successful in meeting the equity goal in terms of scholastic performance, will very soon exacerbate the problem of the economic and social efficacy of the sequential increase in years of schooling. This is particularly true for the lower social classes, because of the "law of last entry" which will continue to function and be valid in the framework of these new strategies. Indeed, any type of compensatory, i.e., more effective, education originally intended for the less advantaged social classes will also be adopted by the other classes, who will benefit at least as much from it. This, in a nutshell, is an illustration of the qualitative cycles of frustration which await us behind the quantitative ones.

This pursuit behind the same economic and social efficacy of education for everyone should come to an end at some point. The Sisyphean nature of this process is to no small extent the result of the sequential build-up of the education system. Historically, the educational structure has grown by adding new cycles and new levels, which are supposed to be taken one after the other without interruption. The equal educational opportunity goal coupled with the principle of zero-correlation creates intensification and growth throughout the system. Intensification, as exemplified by the preschool and compensatory strategies; growth, through the introduction of comprehensive education at higher and higher levels which, in turn, will push up the level at which the principle of zero-correlation sets in. This results in additional efforts of intensification at the lower levels which increase the pressure at the higher levels, and so on and so forth, in a ring-dance of madness. The only strategy which seems to be able to bring this rat race to an end, is the one of recurrent education as described above. This strategy, without neglecting the equity goal, does away with the sequential nature of the educational system, after a basic period of schooling at the primary and secondary levels. We will come back to this idea of recurrent education at the post-compulsory level — which appears, in the light of what was said above, as well as in Chapter IX, as the only realistic educational strategy — in the final chapter.

It might be argued that we have put too much stress on the economic and social efficacy of education and that, in doing so, we have forgotten that after all the main goal of education is to educate. It is obviously impossible to disagree with the idea that the schools are there to educate the people. However, it would be a relatively new idea to see this as an end objective and not as an intermediate objective in view of the "life chances" of the individual. We shall also come back to this point in the final chapter. In the meantime, we turn to a closer examination of alternative possibilities of how the school can educate the people.

Educational technology

In Chapter III we touched already on the subject of the technology of instruction. In the concluding remarks of that chapter we suggested that new means of communication require a radical review of the teaching—learning process, i.e., a radical review of what happens in the classroom. We have seen that most countries have relied on structural changes in the educational system to achieve a more truly educated society. Only now are they beginning to realise that quantitative growth, structural reforms and a longer school life will not produce the desired results if the traditional teaching—learning process remains unchanged.

In most countries the system of learning is teacher-based: The system depends on the teacher and on what he is doing. From the learner's point of view, learning is mainly passive and quietness must prevail in the classroom so that the teacher may be heard. The lockstep of the class, whatever its degree of homogeneity in ability and achievement, dominates the teaching—learning situation, and determines the content and pace of the lesson. Furthermore, dependence on the teacher implies a fixed timetable with lessons of equal length. Consequently, a teacher-based system imposes on an adolescent in his most active years a docility few adults could sustain, a docility enforced by an apparatus of entreaties, threats and commands that constitute an inadequate form of motivation. Moreover, the fixed timetable discourages individual exploration and personal experience of learning. It should be said that among the thoughtful teachers there is general dissatisfaction with the present system; equal dissatisfaction with the results is felt by those who expected much in the shape of higher standards from an increasing quantity of, and expenditure on, education.

It is of course true that intensive efforts have been made in recent years to remedy the defects of class teaching: books for schools have become far more attractive in layout, illustration and colour; film-strips, tapes and other aids make occasional red-letter periods possible; above all, curriculum development teams have produced admirable materials for teachers, and have provided a more genuinely active role for children than was allowed by classroom teaching and conventional laboratory exercises. Yet, these improvements leave the essentials of class teaching unaltered. The source of instruction and interpretation and almost constant guidance remains the teacher, whether live or transmitted, single or multiple. The subject - teacher - class - period structure of the traditional timetable still contains the instructional process, which in general remains passive, communal, externally and closely organised, quite unlike the pattern in many nursery schools or even more and more primary schools. The problem is indeed most serious in secondary schools.

By an environment-based system is meant a shift in emphasis from the teacher teaching to the learner learning in an environment where technological aids as well as the teacher are available as resources. It is not helpful at this stage to consider the merits of any particular technique or device, especially since educational technology has been equated in many people's minds with media gadgets, seen in relation to the existing system of learning (where the market lies), or as a threatening mechanical substitute for the teacher within the existing system. It is more profitable to illustrate what is meant by taking one example: the use of broadcasting as part of an environment-based system. A broadcast normally used in a classroom is simply part of the teacher-based system. In certain circumstances (in Sicily, for example) broadcasting has been used extensively as the prime means of instruction but the mode, the system of learning, has not changed: there has simply been a shift from the teacher on the dais to the teacher on the screen. Suppose, however, broadcasts are made available in recorded form: then, with suitable printed accompaniments they may provide excellent "packages" for a radical change in the system, from teacher-based to environment-based learning. Thus, the essential difference between such an attempt and conventional teaching lies in the relationship of the learner to the source of instruction. In practice, of course, a learner in school does not have to submit to constant instruction nor, on the contrary, is he likely to be left absolutely free to learn independently from books and objects and people around him. Teacher-based and environment-based are two extreme poles: good sense will lead us to settle in some habitable region between them. But which of the two ways we take, the direction we lean in, will have extensive implications. At present, our books, classroom arrangements, furniture and equipment, curriculum, streaming and setting, disciplinary requirements, timetabling, all reflect and facilitate class teaching; if we shift to an alternative system of learning we shall find all these elements subtly, and not so subtly, changed.

In general, "packages" are essentially prepared materials which may involve, for any particular subject, any or all of a variety of media broadcasts, film loops, strips or slides, tapes, textbooks or booklets. The difference between packages and more sophisticated learning systems is that the former provide only the "core" for a learning system together with suggestions for further exploration on related topics. They leave the teacher free to incorporate class lessons in his subject, thus enabling him to use his skill in teaching in the way that the good teacher has always done, to provide the stressing of cardinal points, the extra examples, the illustrations on the board, the parallels with everyday experience, the quizzing of students round the room. This also means that a package course, although providing a learning environment richer, more flexible and more varied than a teacher can produce working alone, is only a part of this environment. Care must be taken that "packages" are not used to excess. Pupils can, of course, work through a package on their own but not all will be prepared to do so: It is in any case important to realise that the complete loss of communal and social elements in learning is undesirable. There is nothing more depressing than to see pupils and students tied to their individual boots, like pigeons in front of their holes.

The implications of an environment-based system of learning on the classroom organisation are, or could be, considerable. So long as children learn chiefly from the lips of a teacher the argument for making the classes in which they are taught as homogeneous as possible is strong. While the snags of streaming are now well advertised, it does not follow at all that unstreaming in itself is enough or even better. If put into an unstreamed class and then taught in the usual way the less able child may well feel more bewildered, exposed and depressed than ever, while the more able are hindered by "over-learning." Any worthwhile attempt at varying pace in a single class or group depends on suitable materials for more independent work being provided. A central problem in education is motivation. Presumably we shall continue to require that learners pursue certain studies, the pleasure and purpose of which elude them. But the degree of compulsion is, in part, a function of our teaching method. We gather learners into groups of about thirty and take all thirty along the route we lay down, point by compulsory point. By allowing more choice (between subjects or within a subject, in the use of time, in materials, in activities) independent learning can encourage a more responsible and a more active attitude to learning and a more personal involvement.

Educational technology, as understood here, is concerned with the design, organisation and evaluation of learning systems. Learning systems involve the production of course materials which will make the student relatively less dependent on the constraints of time, space and staff. Environment-based course materials can contribute directly to:

(i) Stimulating the trend towards individualising instruction: for example, printed learning packages for individual use in conjunction with audio-visual aids and/or other material assignments tailored to meet different learning styles. The material allows the student to progress according to his own motivation and knowledge, stimulating enquiry behavior and creativity (though it must be added immediately that existing material often still fails to meet the latter conditions).

(ii) Coping with mass student enrolments and contributing to the equality of educational opportunity: for example, learning systems which imply the use of mass media (such as television, radio or computer) in conjunction with printed material can serve innumerable students at the same time over great distances, and they can be constantly repeated. Computer-managed information systems may also in the future expeditiously undertake administrative and counselling tasks for a large number of students.

(iii) Democratising the learning situation: there are three aspects to this. In the first place, the procedures for developing course materials necessitate defining the educational objectives to be achieved by the learner. In current practice, not only are objectives vaguely conceived, but they are also approached without the active involvement of students: discussion between all partners in the process about the importance and worthwhileness of objectives would give older students a better understanding of what and why they are to learn and also a greater insight into the goals of education. Secondly, self-contained learning packages, aimed at active student participation in the learning process, also give students responsibility for the timing of their learning, a responsibility which they so far have not enjoyed. Lastly, these learning systems assign new functions to the teacher while freeing him from old ones: they are likely to reduce, to a great extent, the old autocratic relationships in the classroom.

All revolutions, by their sudden and excessive promotion of change, carry within them the seeds of their own destruction; new techniques and new methods in education are in danger of the same fate unless their limitations are overtly stated and understood. Educational technology interpreted in the widest sense cannot be grafted on to existing systems, but will lead to fundamental changes whose purpose is the provision of a better education. The difficulty is that, although, for example, we know what is meant by a better motor car, it is not easy to define a better education. The performance of a car can be measured, but the objectives of new learning systems (like those of more traditional ones) that are easiest to measure are not necessarily the most important. Many aspects of education — attitudes, ability to solve problems, adaptability to new situations, ability to cooperate with others — follow not so much from the content of the system as from the way in which learning has taken place, that is to say the process. Particular attention, therefore, must be given to ways of assessing what is happening in the course of a pupil's learning, over and above the acquisition of skills and knowledge. This may call for a more ecological approach towards assessment and evaluation (i.e., one that is concerned with the interaction between the learner and the learning environment) of which the standard of achievement is only a part. It is of course not suggested that a concern with less easily measurable goals should lead to the dismissal of those specific objectives which a learning system has set for itself. Knowledge and skills are important and the fault is within the learning system if it fails to impart them as well as, or better than, traditional systems.

Finally, we want to come back to the question of individualised learning. As we already suggested above, this is neither practicable nor desirable if the term is taken to describe a system where individual learners are working entirely on their own, proceeding from one piece of work to another as soon as the former is successfully completed — a system which imposes a rigid straitjacket on the learner in the interests of quality control, and ignores the positive effects of interaction between groups of learners and between learner and teacher. This is a misleading but widespread interpretation of the concept of individualised learning. It is perhaps less confusing to refer to independent learning, that is, learning taking place in a flexible framework containing some carefully controlled elements and providing a variety of learning opportunities for different individuals. One pre-requisite for independent learning is a learning resource centre from which material can be selected by the learner or the teacher for the individual's most appropriate route towards stated objectives. There can also be no question that some subjects and some aspects of all subjects are best dealt with by group discussion or cooperative enquiry on a particular topic; undoubtedly the teacher will remain the most important resource of the learning centre and the best guide through a learning system for the individual learner. Independent learning has the advantage that it places upon the learner greater responsibility for his own learning, increases his area of choice and by its variety releases him from the boredom and monotony of one class lesson after another following a similar pattern.

One aspect of independent learning systems that has discouraged teachers is their reliance on the written word, for the substantial proportion of learners for whom this is not their preferred means of communication, the opportunities offered by other media have not yet been fully exploited. Another source of discouragement is the difficulty of introducing independent learning into old or unsuitable buildings and into schools whose equipment is unreliable, out of date or badly maintained. Under these circumstances a greater emphasis on independent learning is difficult to achieve. The limitations of learning systems appear greater than they need be if they are perceived as infallible and unchangeable ways of ensuring learner success. There is a place for a "closed" system in certain fields where objectives can be clearly defined and measured and where the route to them is straightforward and linear. But the number of such fields is limited. A systematic approach does not, however, preclude an "open" system in which creativity and the solution of open-ended problems form a major part. Such systems may consist of only a "core" of pre-designed materials and methods introduced by the teacher, the school or the learner himself.

We hope that it has become clearer in the foregoing pages that a certain amount of progress has already been made towards creating a system of environment-based learning, and that the shift from teacher-based learning to environment-based learning as such is desirable. But in spite of the values inherent in each of them, they are obviously instruments, both of them, with which a variety of goals can be reached. The design of learning systems requires, therefore, the statement of general goals, the definition of specific objectives and a method of ascertaining that the goals and objectives are being achieved. The first is a matter for decision at the political or community level; the second can most effectively be undertaken by the teams who are actually designing the system in consultation with teachers. To ensure that objectives are being met, feedback and evaluation are essential elements in the design. As no learning system can ever be final, there must be frequent revision and continuous adaptation of any completed system. As we observed above, few learning systems will be complete in themselves: most will take the form of a "core" to which open-ended elements can be added by the teacher. His role will change from that of a purveyor of information and an instructor to that of manager, motivator and guide. Methods and media are inseparable and a clear understanding of what the latter can achieve is an important element in the design of a learning system.

Because of the importance of the long-term trends in society for the priorities to be attached to the educational goal structure, we shall say a few words about alternative societal and educational futures next.

3. Alternative Societal and Educational Futures and Implications for the Schools

In recent years a spate of books and reports has seen the light with such titles as *The Year 2000*, *Mankind 2000*, *Europe 2000*, etc. Under the general umbrella of "futurology" a wide and wild variety of visions have been painted of the long-term future state of society and its component parts which, in the main, are as interesting as their respective authors' imagination. In saying this, we do not necessarily wish to pass a pejorative judgement on these endeavours, but we do want to stress that careful scrutiny is required in order to distinguish the useful from the less useful work in this area. In Part Two we had several times an opportunity to underline all the importance we attach to widening the scope of the prospective view for policy-planning purposes. Most long-term educational forecasts up to now concentrate mainly on demographic and economic variables and they assume that the future will not substantially differ from the present except within the limits prescribed by some of the endogenous variables selected for the analysis, and which we discussed in Part Two. They have *not* forced educational planners and policy-makers to systematically speculate about alternative societal futures, alternative educational goals for the future, alternative ways of reaching these goals, nor about complex qualitative aspects of education.

Exploring alternative educational futures does not mean making longer-term forecasts of the type described in Part Two. It does not mean extrapolating the demographic and economic variables to the year 2000 instead of to the year 1980, for example. Neither does it imply doing away with them altogether. It does imply something more, which makes the *alternative educational futures approach* qualitatively and substantially different from the traditional forecasts. Exploring alternative educational futures includes as a minimum the following aspects:

(i) Tracing through the future consequences of current and foreseeable decisions. This amounts to an attempt to determine alternative educational futures resulting from past and current policy decisions. It may be labelled a "forward running" or "exploratory" approach.

(ii) Multi-dimensional goal assessment and alternative strategy considerations. This step implies obtaining a minimum amount of information concerning societal futures, and, also in the light of this information, the design of global educational strategies, indicating how one can move from the present situation towards the direction as indicated by the goal structures. It may be labelled a "backward running" or "normative" approach.

(iii) Two pitfalls must be avoided: on the one hand, statements of policy alternatives based on a simple extrapolation of single variables which over-simplify the direction or complexity of social change; on the other hand, the so-called "creative" definition of normative "futures" which ignores the limitations of resource allocation and of the existing socio-economic structures and values. The main feature of the alternative educational futures approach, besides its very long-term perspective, is its attempt to concentrate on issues, values, and goals and to trace their quantitative and qualitative consequencces back to the educational process.

From the above remarks we can decude three purposes for "futurologic" studies in education. The first is the identification of future consequences of present planning and policy decisions. Important questions in this context are whether these decisions are in line with the goals, and which future alternatives have been excised by today's actions or non-actions. For example, when the Swedish authorities decided, a few decades ago, to go in radically for centralised schools in urban areas and shutting down the majority of the small rural schools, they were motivated by the prospect of certain administrative benefits, and perhaps economic ones as well; since large-scale educational operation would be more advantageous than continuing with the little red school house, the latter ought to be closed down. However, the transportation of young people to large urban schools, which followed from the closures, combined with the abandonment of farms to generate a vast depopulation of the countryside. A subsequent study (Marklund, 1969), showed that small schools offering middle-department courses (i.e., grades 4-6) do not perform worse than the large schools, indicating that the pure educational advantages of doing away with all the many small rural schools at the lower and middle levels have been of dubious value. On top of that, the social and economic impact on sparsely populated areas has been highly negative. Politicians are easily tempted to look for short-term solutions to current problems. This is perhaps understandable considering that they are reminded of their mortality at fairly short intervals, i.e., at the regularly recurring elections. Hence they readily go astray when confronted with situations where they have to choose between that which imperils themselves in the short run and that which imperils the voters, i.e., the society, in the long run.

The second purpose is to go beyond the traditional extrapolation of numerical trends and to include "qualitative" considerations as well. The third purpose of exploring alternative educational futures is to examine possible changes in social and political values. Here questions will have to be faced related to the kind of society that is deemed both plausible and desirable, and to the role of education in helping to bring about such a society. The appearance of tomorrow's society does not follow in any clear-cut and mechanical way from the scientific and technological potentials we have today, and probably not from the ones at our command tomorrow, either. The crux is if and how we intend to use these potentials. That is determined by the social preferences, i.e., by the prevailing values. Medical science can give us formulas on leading a way of life that will keep us in good shape physically and mentally. But nonetheless we put ourselves in situations, both on and off the job, that induce stress and break us down physically and mentally. We allow the waste products of technology to spoil our environment to the stage where it poses health hazards not only for coming generations, but also for ourselves. Will the values that fix priorities and preferences look essentially different two or three decades from now? Will science and technology be more greatly harnessed towards creating a better and healthier environment? And what about notions as to what constitutes the "good life," the life worth living? The protestant ethic, under which everyone was supposed to stick it out to the end, and which suffused the life ideal of a large part of the present generations in the Western World (and in the socialist countries, too, for that matter) may be superseded by another ethic. As long as the "sweat-it-out" ethic dominates, the awarding of marks on the basis of individual performances in competition will continue to dominate in our schools. The curricula can then talk as piously as they wish about group work, cooperation, consideration and social maturity.

Thus, the major rationale of the work on alternative societal and educational futures is that considerable value may be found in analysis which highlights long-term educational issues and the projected consequences of alternative responses to them. One of the basic questions faced by the analysis of societal futures, as suggested above, is whether the operative values which have served to bring us to the present point of development will continue to serve well in dealing with the problems created by that development. Obviously, the goals assigned to the overall educational undertaking, and hence all of educational planning and policy, are centrally affected by the ultimate outcome of the "value-choice" crossroad. Through the investigation of alternative futures, a host of factors which have, until now, been exogenous to the planning process, will be considered as endogenous. Alternative goal structures can be made explicit as well as the choices implied by opting for one rather than another.

A very important problem, as summarised in particular in Chapter IV in connection with the three models we presented there, will remain the relationship between societal and educational objectives and, therefore, between societal change and educational change. Can one expect to change the future educational system in such a way that it becomes a more effective instrument in societal change (the "optimistic view"), or does such an attempt represent an utterly unrealistic view of the potential impact of education, in whatever future form? If so, should the operative values of society change first so that educational goals, structures and content can finally become very different from what they are today (the "realistic view")? The discussion and the evidence presented in previous chapters clearly incline towards the "realistic view."

The basic issue for education is the choice of goals; all else follows. What is it we are trying to do? But for this statement to make sense we have to be using the word "choice" in the sense of a commitment of psychic, human and economic resources in a particular direction. In that sense the choice is not necessarily what the society or its leaders may declare it to be. The choice is, rather, inferred from where the society puts its resources. We could move one step further and argue that the implicit choice of goals can be inferred from the outcomes. Few will want to go all the way with that statement, but it contains an important germ of truth. Evidence mounts that in multifold and unconscious ways humans communicate more than they consciously mean to communicate, and influence events in ways they do not consciously intend. Classical examples are the "Freudian slip" and the self-fulfilling prophecy. Thus, if we find that the operations of the school system tend, in fact, to perpetuate class differences, we are forced to consider the question of whether this is not an inferred, if largely unconscious, intent.

This is mainly to reiterate the point that the goals of the educational system are much more a function of the choices the society has made, or is making, than they are a consequence of the declarations of educational leaders. When George Counts in 1932 issued the inspiring challenge, "Dare the schools build a new social order?" an appropriate answer might have been, they cannot. Looking at this issue in another way, we might say that choices of educational goals are made in the society on at least three levels. First, the society itself makes a pervasive choice regarding the overall direction of its movement. This choice tends to set the constraints on what, in the long run, will be fostered, tolerated or opposed. A movement within the school system which is not aligned with the general drift of the larger society, for instance, is unlikely to persist. Secondly, the society makes a decision as to what tasks will be assigned to educational institutions and what tasks to others. These two types of choices are made largely outside the educational institutions. Thirdly, then, choices are made within the resulting context as to what the more specific objectives shall be, with what priorities they shall be carried out (that is, what resources shall be allocated), and in what manner they shall be accomplished. These choices are determined partly within and partly outside of the educational institutions.

Thus, if the society moves towards what could be called a "second-phase industrial" society (in which the operative values have not changed), we can anticipate increased emphasis on the role of education as playing a major part in accomplishing social goals and alleviating social problems (equal opportunity, racial discrimination, environmental deterioration, etc.). There will be strong reliance on "behaviour shaping" approaches, involving the detailed specification of desired behaviours to be imparted by contingency management techniques. This work will be based on a sound behavioural science infrastructure. The roles of evaluation and credentialling, i.e., assessing suitability for the various vocational and professional tasks which the society requires for its functioning, will probably remain important. Continuing education, in the form of vocational retraining, will also have an important place.

On the other hand, to whatever extent we move in the direction of a "person-centred" (humanised-technological) society, this will be reflected in the schools. Goals will shift towards placing more emphasis on students becoming effective thinkers and learners, developing inquiry and problem-solving skills, acquiring social skills, and developing emotional awareness and self-identity. Attention will be diverted from achieving behavioural objectives to setting conditions for spontaneous learning — especially to fostering feelings of safety and trust, and freedom to explore and inquire, and to providing a responsive environment and directed challenges. Reduced emphasis will be placed on absorbing specialised information and developing specific vocational skills. Less attention may also be given to grading, credentialling, and otherwise labelling persons.

It is the above wider societal framework which provides one possible framework for a discussion on socialisation and individualisation as important educational policy goals for the 1970s. Individualisation as a priority goal is advanced more and more frequently. However, depending on what the operative values are of society, and on whether one can increase the independent effect of the school, it will be a major end-objective or a "derived" objective. Probably nobody would deny the importance and the desirability of individualisation as an educational policy goal. One of the major tasks of schools until now has been to act as a selective device, taking little account of individual desires and aspirations. This has also been reflected in the curriculum and in teaching methods. Individualisation could bring about a major change with respect to this state of affairs. However, the question remains in what societal context this educational goal is being pursued. If we are moving towards a "second phase industrial" society, the socialisation goal will in the final analysis dominate the individualisation goal, because once out of the educational system the individual will have no real possibility of influencing social structures. In other words, individualisation in this case can only be realised, if at all, in narrow educational terms. If, on the contrary, we are moving towards a "person-centred" society, individualisation becomes really a primary objective of policy, because the individual person will have an increased chance to realise his full potential and will be able, through his own choices, to influence existing social structures.

4. Concluding Remarks

It will be recalled that in Chapter IV we discussed three "value models of education": the continuity, intermediate and discontinuity models. And, based on them, we derived five inter-relationships between education and society: (i) education adapts quantitatively with minimal qualitative changes; (ii) education not only adapts in terms of scale, but also qualitatively in terms of goals, structures, etc.; it does so with a time-lag in relation to societal changes; (iii) same situation as in the preceding case, but instead of reacting with a time-lag, education takes the initiative without preceding the corresponding societal changes too much; (iv) education makes a qualitative jump with a view to changing the belief and value structure of society at large; and (v) education makes a qualitative jump in order to catch up with societal changes.

In this chapter we have reviewed a certain number of educational strategies whose main purpose is to reduce existing inequalities in educational opportunity between social classes; we have also looked somewhat closer at the possibilities of changes in the classroom which, besides meeting objectives such as equal educational opportunity, are particularly instrumental in meeting educational goals like individualisation and socialisation. These three educational policy goals have indeed been singled out in the beginning of this chapter as those that will most probably get high priority in the decade before us. In the third section an attempt was made to put this whole discussion in the perspective of societal changes and of changes in belief and value structures. This obviously brings us back to the interdependency between education and society, as schematically presented in Chapter IV.

The naive idea that changes in the educational sector alone could be important and significant enough to alter significantly the society in which it operates must be given up. This rules out inter-relationship (iv) mentioned above. The difficulties encountered with the alternative educational strategies reviewed in section 2 indicate that even inter-relationship (iii) may be an impossible proposition. It is too often forgotten that the Swedish initiative to generalise comprehensive education at the secondary level, an initiative that was taken during the 1960s, came after thirty years of general political reforms. It is, therefore, an illustration of inter-relationship (ii). The American example of the high school is there to show that a generalisation of secondary education to the entire age-group in one form of comprehensive school may do nothing more than introduce qualitative differences along the same social class and ethnic lines as exists in the American society at large. This phenomenon has been documented by several authors and has been called by one of them the "neighbourhood effect". This is not meant to belittle the American effort. What we do want to convey is the idea to judge the effort in its proper perspective and not to jump to naive conclusions as to the independent effect of the school on societal structures and values.

What must be our general conclusion from what has been said in this and the previous chapters? To our mind, the one inescapable conclusion that stands out is the absolute necessity to rethink the place and weight of education in society. In the light of the above observations and the conclusions reached in Chapter IX, should not educational goals put relatively less emphasis on the economic and social efficacy of the educational enterprise, and relatively more on the potential value of education proper for the individual person as a reasoning (and not necessarily reasonable) human being capable of assessing intelligently his environment? To be sure, this is an intriguing and perplexing proposition, even if it is not phrased in mutually exclusive terms. As we said earlier, one of the strongest common assumptions in our societies is that education is the key to upward mobility; this belief combines with a growing consensus that education should be used broadly as an instrument for social change. Now, it is quite clear that individual cases of social mobility through additional years of education abound. Table IX-1, and other empirical evidence, shows (as long as one reads the table "horizontally") that within each social class it "pays" to have additional years of schooling. All this does indeed suggest that the belief of education being an important element in upward mobility is correct. However, two observations must be made in this connection. First, there is no contradiction between the above evidence and the principle of zero-correlation. Second, there is no contradiction either between the above evidence and absence of significant social change, as is shown when one reads, for example, Table IX-1 "vertically." We have said enough in these two chapters to substantiate this latter point and we do not come back to it. But the first point may need some further clarification.

There is no contradiction between the evidence of education being important in upward mobility and the principle of zero-correlation because in most countries universal education (the *n*th level) is still situated at a relatively low level. Consequently, there is still plenty of possibility to maintain education differentials beyond the currently achieved *n*th levels. This is a sufficient explanation for the observed role of education in social mobility. But what do we do if the target of 30 years of education for all has been reached? This is, of course, an exaggerated example for illustration purposes only. But is does make the point that sooner or later the role of education in upward mobility must break down. This does not mean that education cannot continue to fulfil its present selective role for many years to come. History will repeat itself at ever higher levels of education and in ever more excellent "centres of excellence." But the number of socially frustrated individuals will have a tendency to increase rapidly, and long before we have reached thirty years of education for all, the present educational system will have exploded. It is our contention that we are rapidly reaching the point where relatively less resources should be allocated in favour of the quantitative expansion of education in terms of number of years of schooling, and where relatively more resources should go to educating the individual to cope with and to judge his environment.

XI

Educational Planning and Policy Tomorrow

In Part Two we described, in broad terms, the development of educational planning during the 1960s. We reviewed the analytical techniques most conspicuous during the past decade; we also said a few words about the organisational aspects and, finally, we put some emphasis on the phenomenon of the "two worlds" — the lack of interpenetration of the planning world and the decision-making world. Moreover, it has become clear from the preceding chapters that countries are now faced with the unprecedented problem of combining a growing pressure for rapid educational expansion with the reshaping of the entire educational system. One of the major problems of the coming decade will be how this enormously complex process can be planned, managed and controlled, and what administrative changes this will imply.

In the previous chapter we have shown that the process of educational change must respond to complex goals which are those of society at large as well as those of education as such. We also indicated that, because of the different decision-making levels at which the various goals can best be handled, this process must include at least two features. These are the political decision-making process through which the allocation of resources are made which makes changes in the schools possible, and the decision-making process at "grass roots" level which must turn changes in the classroom into a reality, through active involvement of teachers, parents and pupils. The structure of this chapter follows from this. We shall deal successively with: (i) strategic policy-planning; and (ii) the management and administration of innovations and educational change in general.

1. Strategic Policy-Planning

At the highest level of decision-making there will be a growing need for long-term, global and integrated policies. Long-term, because the fast rate of change compels at least some framework of long-term objectives if today's major policy decisions are to be reasonably related to one another; global, because of the inevitable inter-connections between the several parts of the educational system; and integrated, because policy goals in our societies are served by a variety of instruments, of which education is often only one. It is our contention that at the highest level of political decision-making, the role of educational planning should be the elaboration of alternative educational strategies in the light of policy goals, like those mentioned in the previous chapter, for example. Such a position, which we will elaborate in a moment, has two important implications. In the first place, educational policy must be coherent and consistent which can only be provided by a strong policy-planning framework. Secondly, it implies decentralisation of decision taking so that flexibility is maintained, within the global framework, at the local, institutional, classroom and individual level for creative social change and individual development.

The fundamental problem of policy-planning is thus a potential conflict between a necessary highly technical basis if the system is to be effectively planned in relation to future needs, and if "wastage" and conflict within the system are to be minimised, and the creative process of educational change and development in which individual social groups and communities can play an active part in the development and control of education. The implication of the first requirement is that educational policy must in the future be backed by a strong planning function and that policy and planning must be drawn more closely together than they are today. However, this planning function should not be seen as a mechanism for the precise development and control of the educational system, but as a means whereby broad strategies can be examined in a global way and the real alternatives presented for political discussion. The second requirement implies that policy-planning calls for debate and discussion of the major alternatives by the various social groups involved in the educational process and by the public at large. Planning instruments should, therefore, be related to consultative machinery representing all the social groups engaged in education, and to the several ways in which political authorities expose policy alternatives to public discussion. It will be clear that this is a generalisation of the communication issue as discussed in Chapter VIII: We are now concerned not only with the relationship between decision-makers and planners at one level of decision-making, but also with the vertical relationships, i.e., those that exist, or should exist, between the actors at the different levels of decision-making, from the Cabinet to the classroom level.

It was suggested in Part Two that, if planning is to serve decision taking more effectively, the most important need is to make progress in planning as an organised process within the context of total educational policy and administration. The relative accent in the 1960s on planning techniques should therefore shift to an emphasis on the effective organisation of planning. A planning process of the kind we have in mind will take root more easily in those administrations which are so organised that there is a clear relationship between objectives and the deployment and management of resources to achieve such objectives. In this connection, it is interesting to note that several European countries are envisaging organisational changes along output-budgeting or similar lines. This is, for example, the case in The Netherlands and Great Britain and it is anticipated that such changes will create the environment in which planning can function effectively. But whatever the organisational and administrative setting, the planning group should be oriented towards the decision-making process at the highest level of responsibility, and be essentially concerned with the preparation of policy alternatives for examination at the political and policy level. This is another reason, next to those mentioned in Part Two, why the location of a planning function at the highest level in the organisational structure is of fundamental importance.

Educational forecasts in the 1960s did *not* lead educational planners and policy-makers to think systematically about alternative future problems of society, alternative educational goals for the future, alternative ways of reaching these goals, nor about complex qualitative aspects of education. This is one reason for the difficulties in formulating clearly educational policy, although it is evident (as we explained earlier) that other reasons of a political, organisational and technical character are just as, if not more, important. If educational policy is to put more emphasis on the definition and analysis of long-term goals as a basis for strategic decisions, it will be necessary to establish procedures and create structures for discussing and searching for consensus. Organisational characteristics of the decision-making process should change so as to secure (i) a high degree of participation of persons and groups who are directly concerned with educational policy-planning administration; and (ii) a high degree of "transparency" in decisions, which has less to do with who participates in the process than with the procedure that is followed in reaching decisions. This kind of change goes far beyond the output budgeting or PPB frameworks mentioned above.

Whereas educational planning during the 1960s has been mainly "quantitative", reactive and partial in its approach, it should become, during the coming decade, programmatic (as opposed to reactive) and comprehensive. In this context, the comprehensive nature of educational planning has to be seen in two respects. First, it must not only take into account the "quantitative" domain, but also deal with psychological, pedagogical and cultural domains (i.e., "qualitative planning"), which presupposes more knowledge of the functioning of the whole educational process. Second, education is just one element in policies concerning the future development of the economy and society; thus, educational planning must explicitly take into account the intricate relationships between the educational sector and other sectors of society.

Planning approaches of the 1960s assumed a highly simplified picture of both the decision-making and goal-seeking process. We have shown in Part Two that this was to no small extent a result of the communication and cooperation difficulties between policy, planning and administration. The implicit assumption was that the consequences of planning would flow, as if the system behaved as an automatic control process, between planning interventions without conflicts and without feedbacks. A more realistic planning approach would be based on "rolling" planning, feedback mechanisms for continuous evaluation, and in consequence linking the different phases and levels of the decision-making process. Clearly, such an approach would also require additional analytical methods. A structural model of the educational system would need to be related to the decision-making structure and to cope with the relationship between the two. Thus, a more complex set of relationships would require different techniques such as, for example, the use of heuristic programming, (machine) simulation techniques, adaptive control theory, cost - effectiveness analysis, sensitivity analysis, etc. Moreover, new integrative methods would need to be applied to the analysis of decision-making processes, such as simulation games, Delphi techniques, cross-impact techniques. This is not the place to present a detailed discussion of these analytical and management techniques. There exists an extensive and growing literature with respect to the possibilities and limitations of these tools, including those that came into the limelight more recently like the use of Delphi techniques and the cross-impact matrix.

Instead, let us say a few words about the elaboration of alternative educational strategies as a basis for strategic decisions. This is, in our view, the main function of the planning group at the highest level of decision-making. Strategic decisions about education should be increasingly related to long-term goals like those reviewed in the previous chapter. Such goals will very often be formulated or related to a wider governmental context. There is, therefore, a first need for a systematic effort in terms of goal identification. This could be the function of look-out institutes who would, through the exploration of alternative educational futures, identify desirable changes in the priorities of the educational policy goal structure. But active educational policy formulation requires not only that goal structures be identified, but also that they be operationalised and, whenever necessary, revised. Strategic policy-planning can be summarised in these three actions: goal identification, operationalisation and revision.

We have said enough about the goal identification dimension in previous chapters. The "operationalisation" dimension implies the elaboration of global educational strategies to reach the identified goals, and assessing their implications in cost - effectiveness terms. This latter aspect, which we may call in more mundane terms assessing the advantages and disadvantages, requires that the educational strategies be worked out in a comprehensive framework as defined above. It is here that the plea of Armitage, Smith and Alper in favour of educational models (discussed in Chapter VII) becomes important. Indeed, global educational models, particularly when they are computerised, can give us in a relatively short time a first idea as to the implications of a given strategy on the various levels and branches of education. This also illustrates the point that strategic policy-planning puts less emphasis on the elaboration of the comprehensive plan than on the elaboration of specific strategies within such a comprehensive framework. In other words, we have the comprehensive planning framework permanently in the (computer) cards, not as an end-objective but as a means to trace the implications of educational strategies for the larger system. Examples of certain strategies have been given in the previous chapter: pre-school education, compensatory education, comprehensive education and recurrent education. They will serve as an illustration to clarify the above abstract discussion.

The four educational strategies which we presented in Chapter X are meant to "operationalise" the equal educational opportunity goal. They were based on considerations which, although already extensively presented throughout this book, merit to be summarised in the present context. The broad goal which states that educational policy is to "provide adequate education for all individuals and groups to the highest levels they demand," has resulted in a huge expansion of the secondary and tertiary levels of education and, therefore, in an important widening of educational opportunities. However, the evidence also shows that, while all social groups have benefited from the general increase in overall educational opportunity, *group disparities* in educational participation have not changed substantially during the past twenty years. Thus, the policy that consists of "following" individual demand for education can be thought of as a "passive" approach toward the realisation of equal educational chances, based on a conception of equal opportunity by society as that of making available a socially "unbiased" set of educational facilities. However, it has become very clear that by giving people — from very different social backgrounds and therefore with widely different characteristics — access to the same schools and the same curricula (i.e., the same educational *opportunity*), the results in terms of educational *achievement* vary substantially and systematically according to social groups. In other words, it has become obvious that equality of inputs (in terms of school and teacher variables) does not result in equality of outputs (in terms of educational achievement). This is so because of the initial gap in achievement between social groups and because of the subsequent differences in learning rates caused by (i) the above-mentioned differences in characteristics of the population before entering school; and (ii) the small independent effect which school and teacher variables have, in the present school systems, to counterbalance these social background differences. To overcome background disadvantages the goal of educational policy will have to broaden the equal opportunity concept to include also equal achievement (in terms of average achievement by social class and not, of course, in terms of individual achievement), and this can only be attained by introducing a much more active or interventionist approach toward the provision of equal educational opportunity. Hence, the introduction of special pre-school programmes and compensatory programmes at the primary level, for example. This summary has shown two things. First, it is an interesting example of goal definition and the difficulties of doing so. Second, it is indicative of the fact that on the whole the declared policy objective of equal educational opportunity has often been formulated as a statement, but rarely elaborated explicitly (what exactly does one mean when talking about equal opportunity) nor translated into operational terms (how much can one achieve and over what period of time). And this in spite of the strategies reviewed in the previous chapter which, as we have seen, have not always had the expected results. Nor have they been accompanied by any detailed cost-effectiveness calculations, so that their "generalisibility potential" — under the assumption that the micro or pilot projects show significant results — cannot possibly be assessed.

But, as explained in Chapter IX, in any effort to translate policy goals into operational terms further questions must be asked. Many objectives pursued by educational policy are not considered end-objectives, but are supposed to serve as inputs to attain wider societal objectives. This clearly applies to equal educational opportunity as well. Does equal educational opportunity result in equal occupational opportunity or in equal personal income opportunity? If not, what other wider societal objectives are being served by realising the equal educational opportunity goal? Or, conversely, what wider societal implications does the total or partial realisation of equal educational opportunity have? This poses the problem of the economic and social efficacy of education about which we presented our point of view in Chapter IX.

Thus, it will be clear that any attempt to translate the equal educational opportunity goal into operational terms necessitates, besides tackling the definitional problem, an answer to the following twin question: (i) how far can one go, within defined economic, social, cultural and financial constraints, in achieving equality of educational opportunity; and (ii) if one would like to go further, what would this mean in terms of changes required in the economic and social structure of society? The answer to such questions implies an analysis of the inter-relationships between three sets of variables: (i) characteristics of the population before they enter school, i.e., family and social environment variables; (ii) school and teacher variables; and (iii) variables describing what happens to the individuals once they have left the educational system. In short, it implies an examination of the inter-relationships between what happens to the individual before, during and after school. The analogy with the approach we adopted in Chapter IX will be clear.

Coming back to the four educational strategies set out in Chapter X, it will be recalled that in terms of the three theoretical approaches we distinguished (the cultural, educational and structural theories), it was our contention that these strategies are heavily biased towards the educational theory, though in varying degrees. The comprehensive school is, of course, the purest illustration of this theory. Pre-school programmes and compensatory education at the primary level are predominantly concerned with school and teacher variables, though the more dynamic among them touch upon the cultural theory as well, insofar as they pay attention to language and to the family—pedagogical environment. On the other hand, recurrent education touches upon the structural theory insofar as it aims at giving the individual better possibilities in his career as well as enriching his leisure.

We have chosen this example in order to show (i) the problems of goal definition; (ii) the prevailing lack of sophistication in terms of analysing implications and consequences of alternative educational strategies; (iii) the almost total absence of cost - effectiveness analyses; and (iv) the lack of clarity concerning the inter-relationship between the equal educational opportunity goal and the other educational and social objectives. This last point, which is implied in the others, leads straight back to our earlier discussion related to the identification, definition and "operationalisation" of a whole range of goals. The difficulties suggested in our "unidimensional" example will be compounded when we are confronted with alternative goal structures, but the necessity of overcoming these problems is obvious if we want to arrive at clear *educational policy formulation*.

We have argued in this section that at the highest level of decision-making, educational planning should be concerned with working out global educational strategies to meet defined targets, within specified goal structures, and taking the constraints of the environment into account. However, we emphasised that this kind of strategic policy-planning should leave enough room and incentives for initiatives to be taken at the lower levels of decision-making, and particularly at the level of the school and the institution. This is our next problem.

2. Management and Administration of Educational Change

Educational change and innovations cover many activities directed to meeting goals at different levels of decision-making. Thus, an educational strategy like comprehensive education can be called a *structural innovation*. In such a case it is clear that decisions and the power to carry out this innovation should reside at the national level, taking the formal democratic institutions such as Parliament and various national interest groups into the decision-making process. On the other hand, innovations in the fields of curriculum development and educational technology are taking place very differently in different countries, but all have the potential to change the schools drastically. It is also obvious that many important changes in these fields start in the classroom. These different levels of goals, of process and of innovations imply a complex, decentralised and politically-sensitive process for which there is no single or simple answer. Changes in goals, content, means, structure, attitudes and behaviour are not only slow processes, but sometimes painful and always difficult ones. This is not only a result of psychological and sociological problems, but also of the difficulty of arranging effective participation in the decision-making structures. To a considerable extent, the problem of change is a problem of democratisation. Who is participating, not only in the change process, but in the decision-making process? At which levels are decisions taken and by whom? What are the decisions that can be taken at a decentralised level? What part do teachers, students and parents play in this process? The problem of new mechanisms for educational administration is not mainly a question of efficient methods, but a question of values, vested interests, and participation. How is it possible to build mechanisms for innovation that fully take into account the question of democratic decision-making on the one hand and necessary efficiency on the other?

It follows from these remarks that the legislative process will be too broad and blunt an instrument to keep pace with the realities in the schools of the 1970s. In other words, the ability of the schools to take part in a creative process of development will depend on legal and administrative principles which explicitly recognise their role as an agent of educational change. More specifically, this will involve giving an explicit mandate and status to experiments in the schools, creating career patterns and incentives for teachers so that innovation is stimulated, establishing educational information networks which are selective and speedy in their action, and creating services which can play a role similar to the field advisory services in the agricultural field. Within such a framework, development programmes will be much more effective, compared to the situation which prevails today, namely pilot experiments which constitute "change oases."

All this should be conceived against the general background that planned innovation from the centre and creative social change which engages the initiative of those in the educational process have somehow to be wedded. It follows that development work itself should be widespread through the system, decentralised in control, and based in the school and university system itself. Since the accent in development needs will shift over time, programmes with a circumscribed objective rather than institutions with standing functions would be more appropriate. Of course, development programmes would need to be backed up by specialised institutions providing services to all development programmes, e.g., in the fields of educational technology and evaluation techniques. In addition, development work has to be related to a diffusion process, a consideration which would have a major influence on the location and organisational arrangements for specific development programmes. Moreover, diffusion "agents" of some kind are clearly needed in an area, such as education, where the initiative for innovations is, or should be, highly decentralised. This consideration has implications for the role of school inspectorates or any similar corps of educational field advisers.

Thus, for such a development and innovation process to function effectively, several requirements must be fulfilled. First, the central educational authorities must take a clear responsibility for drawing up a development programme or strategy, taking as a starting point the results of the strategic policy-planning work as described in the previous section. Second, a central, coordinating innovation mechanism must be established, possibly with executive responsibilities. Third, the development programmes must be located in, or close to, the education system itself. Fourth, specialist institutions must be set up to provide services to development programmes. Fifth, a diffusion network must be created, based on a service of field advisers.

There are various alternative approaches available to establish such a complex "qualitative" planning process in a systematic way. One solution might lie in the establishment of an executive or coordinating agency for educational innovation, operating outside but linked to central administration, particularly if it is given executive powers. However, it would be clear that both the decisions regarding specific innovations and innovation work itself should be done at different levels in the educational system itself. The responsibility of the innovation agency is to find the right level of decision-making for particular innovations. The problem is to find the level of decision which is nearest to the actual problem, and which at the same time gives the best chance of success. Thus, the establishment of an innovation agency is not a matter of centralisation, but rather one method of flexible decision-making. As described above, it is essential for the innovation agency to build local development centres. These centres should have great freedom to set up locally based innovation programmes, but should also be able to work as the "change agency" for major innovations developed at a more central level.

3. Concluding Remarks

In a nutshell, our argument here is that educational planning in the 1970s will have to put more emphasis on participation, transparency and flexibility. This will imply making a sharper distinction between what is possible to undertake at the highest level of decision-making and what should be left to the lower levels. At the highest level, educational planning should be concerned with working out global educational strategies to meet defined targets, within specified goal structures, taking into account other social as well as economic goals. These global strategies should leave enough room and incentives for initiatives at the lower levels of decision-making, and particularly at the level of the school and the institution. Such a flexible and multi-level scheme will, of course, create some difficult problems of coordination.

Thus, we conclude that the strategic policy-planning mechanism should be a major partner in the definition of research and development needs, but that the undertaking of research and development should be through separate mechanisms; and that strategic policy-planning groups must be able to take a more positive role in research and development work needed for their own purposes (new analytical tools, account framework, output indicators, etc.).

XII

What a Country Spends on Education Depends on Its Values

In this final chapter we shall come back to, and elaborate on, the salient features we have treated thus far in Part Three, standing on the shoulders of the discussions we presented in Parts One and Two. Thus, we shall return to the economics of education; we shall draw some conclusions with respect to educational policy goals; the subject of educational expenditures and finance will be re-discussed, and finally we shall elaborate on one of the educational strategies already presented in Chapter X, namely recurrent education.

1. The Economics of Education Revisited

It is interesting to start this discussion with two quotations from a recent book by Mark Blaug (1970), *An Introduction to the Economics of Education*. Mark Blaug has been one of the more eloquent advocates of the cost - benefit or rate-of-return approach. In his chapter 2 on "Education as private and social investment," he has to face of course the question how much of the additional earnings observed between groups distinguished according to education and age is caused alone by different levels of educational attainment. His answer to the critics who put emphasis on the high correlation between education on the one hand and income and wealth of parents, ability and motivation, sex, race, etc. on the other is:

> Of course, social class origins, native intelligence and community environment are so intimately intertwined with educational attainment that the task of disentangling them can easily be made to look hopeless. But to throw up our hands at the task is to make a mockery of the goal of equality of educational opportunity. If the superior earnings of better-educated people are simply a matter of privileged birth, then apparently schools merely select people for innate ability, putting them through finer

> and finer selection sieves bur adding nothing whatever along the way. Why then advocate more schooling for the underprivileged? It is simply inconsistent to assert, on the one hand, that nature and nurture are so mixed up that their separate effects cannot be unravelled and, on the other hand, to advocate egalitarian redistribution of schooling based on assertions which are only true if most of the determining factors have been unravelled (page 45).

A little later, Mark Blaug rounds off his answer to the critics with this argument:

> To reject the notion that the higher lifetime earnings of the better educated is simply the consequence of class origins and family connexions is not, however, to prove that the better educated are better rewarded because they are more productive. It is still conceivable that the labour market somehow finds it more convenient to use a proxy variable like educational qualification in place of a battery of psychological tests designed to discover the native ability of job applicants. It is interesting to ask oneself, however, what costs would be imposed on employers if the educational system issued no certificates of competence whatever (page 46).

These are not very convincing arguments because they simply throw the ball back in the other camp. It is easy to use the counter argument, "Yes, suppose that the goal of equal educational opportunity is a mockery." The reasoning in the second quotation is even more besides the point. As we have argued earlier, if education acts as a screening and labelling device, employers do not need to adopt "batteries"; they are getting people from a certain social class. The more convincing argument would have been why they ask for educational certificates at all, instead of merely asking for social background.

We have summarised our view on this matter in the concluding remarks of Chapter X. There we observed that schooling does make a difference in terms of earnings *within* each social group — we called this the "horizontal" interpretation of such evidence as presented, for example, in Table IX-1. However, we also noted that the same level of educational attainment appeared to have quite different "earning power" according to social class — this we called the "vertical" interpretation of the evidence. In relative terms, therefore, education indeed "adds nothing whatever along the way" (interpreted in the sense of personal incomes and not, of course, in the sense of what education proper has given to the individual in terms of increased realisation of his intellectual potential). In absolute terms, education adds something both in terms of earnings and in terms of what we shall call "reasoning power." This is by now a familiar phenomenon which we have encountered several times: The fact that all groups are getting more (education, earnings, etc.), but that group disparities remain substantially the same. Thus, there are two distinct and very different questions: When we look at the absolute earning differentials we are concerned with the private rate of return to educational investment. When we look at relative earnings we are concerned with the independent effect of education on economic and social inequalities in general. Finally, there is a third question — implied in the second Blaug quotation — which has to do with the relation of the social rate of return to economic growth. Do positive social rates of return necessarily mean a positive contribution to economic growth? We shall say a few words about each of these questions, in particular the first and the third. The second question has been the underlying leitmotiv of much of what we have said in this book, and will continue to be so in this final chapter.

If people with the same level of education have lower earnings on average when they come from lower socio-economic backgrounds as compared to those from higher social classes, and if the out-of-pocket costs to the individual do not vary substantially across social classes, then we are faced with an equity problem of the type illustrated in our discussion around Table 1-4 in Chapter I. It is interesting to note that such a situation is not necessarily reflected in lower private rate of returns for the lower social classes. That depends of course on earning differentials *within* each social class according to level of educational attainment. The equity argument is the following. If, as we have shown, there is a social bias in educational opportunity in favour of the higher social classes, then public expenditure on education would represent a transfer from relatively poorer sections of society to richer, or potentially richer, people. In such circumstances, the conclusion can be drawn to increase the share of the cost of education involved for the students from higher social classes and/or for those that will later earn more than a minimum annual salary (repayment of loans). We shall come back to this rather complex problem when we discuss the question of educational finance.

Let us turn to the third question. The fact that both social and private rates of return are usually positive does not yet mean that education makes a positive contribution to economic growth. It is true that economic growth is normally measured by the rates of increase of national income; national income is by definition the sum of all earned and unearned income in the economy; there is no doubt that more years of education tends to raise the earnings of those who have benefited from it. It could, therefore, be concluded that investment in education accelerates economic growth. But things are not as simple as that. The fact that people with additional education have on average higher earnings does *not* prove that they command salaries *because* they are capable of producing more goods and services. In the words of Mark Blaug:

> If business men simply pay graduates more because of the snob appeal of a university degree despite the fact that graduates are no more productive than secondary school leavers — "conspicuous consumption" of graduates as we labelled it earlier — the effect is either to reduce profits, or, if profits are maintained, to reduce the earnings of non-graduates. In consequence, the higher earnings of graduates simply redistribute national income without augmenting it. It is exactly as if industry suddenly decided to pay blondes more than brunettes: dyeing one's hair would now produce positive returns in the form of greater lifetime earnings, but this would last only as long as there were brunettes to "exploit." National income would not increase as a result of it. As a matter of fact, it would soon fall, everything else being the same, because hair dyeing involves the using up of resources. But of course as much is true of the provision of education. If the association between education and earnings is simply due to the "conspicuous consumption" of educated manpower, the extension of education would decelerate economic growth as it is now measured, not accelerate it (page 61).

Blaug's argument would have been still more interesting had he opposed graduates from different social backgrounds instead of opposing university graduates and secondary school leavers. But we do not want to go into that now. Let us go back instead to first principles after the preceding relevant, but sometimes confusing, discussion about rate-of-return results and paradoxes.

When a country's production process and, in general, its economic and social life, become more complex, its needs for and the range of highly qualified personnel will increase and broaden. It will be recalled that this truism is the starting point and the rationale of the manpower approach. As from a certain level of complexity many skills need to rest on a broad and advanced level of general knowledge and a minimum basis of specialisation. Hence, the "pull effect" exercised by economic and technological growth and development on the expansion of the formal educational system. But it so happens that these "pull factors" are not the only ones that determine the quantitative growth of the educational system. There are a host of other factors, of which the job expectation is, of course, one, which determine the individual and family (also somewhat misleadingly called, including by us, the "social") demand for education. From the point of view of the labour market, this individual demand results in a "push effect" of graduates and school leavers who want to enter jobs. We have noted that in the past educational expansion was governed largely by individual demand for places, the "push factors." We have also already had a chance to note that this *may* result more and more in a supply of graduates exceeding the economy's requirements, on the assumption that current norms as regards choice of occupation and with respect to earnings are maintained. Should this be the case, it is probable that there will be an upward adjustment of "requirements," a variable proportion of graduates going into jobs which thus far took persons with lower educational qualifications. Now two things can happen. Either the "conspicuous consumption" hypothesis works and graduates continue to command roughly the same earnings, or we assist at a lowering of the economic position of graduates in relation to other categories of employed persons. Clearly, in the light of all we have said in the preceding chapters, *we* know pretty well what the most likely course of events is likely to be. First, the lower social classes will form the bulk of those that "choose" the jobs which up to then had lower educational requirements. Second, this "threat of democratisation" will lead graduates at a given level to aim at further differentiations, either upwards (by taking a second university degree, for example) or laterally, by going to centres of excellence and/or becoming "rare" specialists. The spectre of the principle of zero-correlation casts its shadows a long way before it has fully arrived, and its influence is felt long before the *n*th level has increased another couple of years.

What does all this mean for the economics of education? It will most probably mean that in most countries economists will stop being the advocates in favour of accelerated educational expansion and expenditures. They will show decreasing rates of return for the higher levels of education and increasing rates for the lower levels. They will be asked to look much more closely than hitherto at the financial aspects of education as well as at the productivity and efficiency of the school. The economics of education will become much more micro-oriented, because the macro-analyses will have come too late and, anyway, will continue to be largely ignored because the educational policy goals will not give them a priority status.

2. Educational Policy Goals Revisited

Let us dream awhile and listen to Willis Harman (1972) as he describes the "person-centred" society. The goals of the society include making economic growth meet human needs, achieving knowledge and aesthetic advance, and controlling social problems so that individuals may progress toward their own goals of self-fulfilment. The industrial system is subservient to, and responsible to, these larger purposes of the society. The overreaching goal is the cultivation and enrichment of all human beings, in all their diversity, complexity and profundity.

In the forecasts which describe this society, each individual will be provided enough resources, and in such a way, as to enable him to live in dignity. Underlying the economic system will be the proposition that each free man has the right to a full life, which includes useful, rewarding work and self development. Economic security will not be achieved only by welfare payments or guaranteed incomes. In part, at least, it will be accomplished by an extension of the principle of free goods and services from those already provided (elementary education, library services, fire and police protection, innoculations, lunch milk for children, etc.) to include others (such as re-education for a new occupation, food and nutrition staples, urban transportation, etc.). In the "knowing society" education will be as central to the economy as mass production has been in the past. Thus, education is a valid occupation, entitling the educatee to subsistence as well as the opportunity to learn. A diversity of educational paths will be available, and men will not be judged on the basis of a single uniform academic standard. (Competitive grading, therefore, will assume much less significance.) Similarly, the society will provide a diversity of ways in which a person can win the esteem of others. In other words, economic failure or academic failure will not be equated with failure as an individual.

Lewis Mumford (1965) has analysed the basic attitude shifts that would have to accompany conversion to the "person-centred"society. There are, he says, "serious reasons for reconsidering the whole picture of both human and technical development on which the present organisation of Western society is based.... The deliberate expression and fulfilment of human potentialities requires a quite different approach from that bent solely on the control of natural forces....Instead of liberation *from* work being the chief contribution of mechanisation and automation, liberation *for* work, for educative, mind-forming work, self-rewarding even on the lowest physiological level, may become the most salutary contribution of a life-centered technology."

The society will be a planned society, but planned in such a way as to deepen, not diminish, the freedom of the individual. Opportunity will be provided for real participation in planning by those for whom the planning is done. Management structures will be such that power flows both ways.

The technological level will be high, as in the "second-phase industrial" forecast, but the priorities for technological development will be influenced by human and global needs. The problems of the ghetto and of the underdeveloped societies will not have been completely eliminated, but their solution will have had high priority. As a consequence of these efforts to respond to human needs, and also as a consequence of the way people perceive the goals of society, international tensions will have lowered and internal alienation will have decreased markedly. The military establishments of the industrialised nations will have moved a long way toward cooperation on an international policing role....

Education will centre on developing self-learning habits and skills, problem-solving and decision-making abilities, individuality, sound valuing capabilities, capability of continuous self-renewal, and self-understanding. Education will be much more equated with life, and with the distinction between formal and informal education having become blurred it will be much more a lifetime activity. The significant distinctions will not be work vs. education or work vs. leisure, but work—education—leisure vs. "killing time."

Hutchins (1968) describes "the learning society" as "one that, in addition to offering part-time adult education to every man and woman at every stage of grown-up life, had succeeded in transforming its values in such a way that learning, fulfilment, becoming human, had become its aims and *all its institutions were directed to this end.* This is what the Athenians did....They made their society one designed to bring all its members to the fullest development of their highest powers....In Athens, education was not a segregated activity, conducted for certain hours, in certain places, at a certain time of life. It was the aim of the society....The Athenian was educated by the culture, by Paideia." The Athenian education was made possible by slavery, which was the necessary provider of leisure. But machines can do for every modern man what slavery did for the fortunate few in Athens. The vision of a learning society can be realised. Whether it does or not depends upon the transformation of values.

Michael (1968) argues that drastic changes in education are necessary if we are to be prepared for the future:

> We must educate for empathy, compassion, trust, non-exploitiveness, non-manipulativeness, for self-growth and self-esteem, for tolerance of ambiguity, for acknowledgement of error, for patience, for suffering. In the first place, those social-aid roles, the roles that are meaningful because they relate a person to a person, require such capabilities...The other reason for deliberately undertaking this kind of education is that those who will have the tasks of planning and leading must have a far deeper feel for and understanding of themselves as selves and as a part of other persons, other selves, than they usually do today ...without such educated, sensitized, emotional resources, leaders will continue to be too rigid, too defensive, too remote from themselves and thereby from others to have the flexible and bold state of mind that will be needed to cope humanely and imaginatively with plans and turmoil, order and disorder. It will take special efforts indeed to enlarge the emotional underpinning of those who recruit themselves to use the social technologies needed to run a complex society.

Unfortunately, significant changes in education do not come as direct consequences of such rational arguments. Only when the whole society shifts, for whatever subterranean reasons, toward a less economic and more humanistic orientation, are we likely to see much shift in education toward the goals described in Michael's plea.

These pleas are in line with, and an elaboration of, our suggestion in the concluding remarks of Chapter X, to the effect that educational policy goals should put relatively less emphasis on the economic and social efficacy of the educational enterprise, and relatively more on educating the individual person to assess, to critically evaluate, his environment. As a corollary to this we also suggested that relatively less resources should be allocated in favour of the continuous and sequential quantitative expansion of education in terms of years of schooling.

This last aspect may seem easier to realise than the first which, by definition, is concerned with beliefs and values. However, even the second aspect implies a revolution in educational thinking, because it is our view that such an important policy change only makes sense if education at the post-compulsory level is organised on a recurring basis instead of in sequential order. Section 4 will be devoted to an elaboration of this idea of recurrent education. But there is an obvious interaction between goals and resources and so we turn first to a discussion about resources for and financing of education.

3. Educational Costs, Expenditures and Finance

We have shown in Chapter III that the annual rate of increase in educational expenditure during the period 1950—1970 has been over 10%, at constant prices, in more than half of the industrialised countries, and more than 7% in practically all of them. Expenditures on higher education have increased most rapidly. We also indicated that during that same period educational expenditure increased at a rate nearly twice as fast as compared to the rate of increase of national income.

If these rates of increase are projected until 1980, the proportion of the national product devoted to education would be more than 10% in eight industrialised countries and would lie between 6 and 10% in the bulk of the other industrialised countries. The figures refer to public educational expenditure only. These are large figures, and, particularly when expressed in terms of public budgets, there are grounds for doubting whether they can, in fact, be achieved. Little wonder, therefore, that there are growing concerns over the volume of resources for education implied by present policies. The issues on which we will touch in this section are the following: (i) are we likely to reach soon a ceiling to the proportion of national income which can be devoted to education? (ii) is there scope for reducing costs, quite apart from whether any limit to available resources is being reached? This is, therefore, the issue of the technological and economic efficiency of the use of educational resources; and (iii) methods of educational finance.

Let us start off by saying a few words about *real* resources before we go on discussing the money measures of the value of these resources. The most important real resources used by the educational system are human: students and teachers. There is an interesting paradox here which arises from conventional national income accounting practices. Students are treated as if they had no opportunity costs and are, therefore, a free input, whereas teachers are treated as an input with a cost to the economy equivalent to the value of their salaries. Thus, an educational system which is relatively extravagant in its use of students (high wastage rates, long courses, low quality graduates) and sparing in its use of teachers (low student—teacher ratios, poorly paid, low quality teachers) can *appear* to be economically efficient. Of course, this says more about the inadequacy of the national accounting framework for educational policy purposes than it does about the real situation. However, it could be illuminating, for illustrative purposes, to push the paradox even further by relating the problem to the objectives of educational policy.

Imagine an educational policy based purely on social and cultural considerations. In such a situation, having students in the schools is an end in itself, education is being treated primarily as a consumption good, and the more students there are, the greater the output of the educational system. In this extreme case, output lost as a result of these students not working, would not be taken into consideration. At the other extreme, education might be treated entirely as an investment in human capital, the objective being to maximise either the level of national output at some specific future date, or to maximise the growth rate through time. In this case, any time spent in school would be treated as a loss of production and could be justified only if it were compensated for by an appropriate increase in future production.

Obviously, the real situation is somewhere between these two extremes. However, the important point is that if, in the future, the social and cultural aspects are to be relatively more emphasised, the resource utilisation policy is likely to move nearer the first alternative because of the emphasis on the more "qualitative" objectives. If investment aspects are to be emphasised, the second is the more appropriate way of looking at the resource inputs. Behind this admittedly caricatural way of presenting the issue lies a policy question of fundamental importance: are educational systems to develop in such a way that *inputs of students' time are considered a cost or not?*

Apart from students, by far the most important real resource input into the educational process is represented by teachers. It seems that in real terms, the teaching staff requirements of education during the 1970s are unlikely to be a serious burden on the economies of most industrialised nations. A doubling of enrolments with constant staff - student ratios would result in between 3 and 5% of the labour force as teachers in most countries. The considerable expansion of higher education means that the proportion of highly qualified manpower required by the educational system would not increase for any likely expansion. This general conclusion may, of course, not apply in the short run in particular sectors. There may be no overall problem, but a shortage of science teachers, for example. Some countries have an extreme shortage of mathematics teachers, brought about in part by the high demand of mathematics graduates in a technologically oriented society. There is a real danger of a downward spiral — too few teachers leading to too few students, resulting in an even greater shortage of teachers later. In such circumstances, the aim must be to convert this downward spiral into an upward one by emergency measures. The dynamics of the process are complicated, but in overall terms, it can be demonstrated that quite a small shift in the proportion of mathematics graduates who enter teaching could bring about the desired change within a few years. An important policy issue in some countries is how this small but vital change can be brought about.

When concern is expressed about a possible restriction on the resources available for educational expansion, it is, in fact, very often a concern with the financial resources that is being meant. The quantitative expansion of education does not show any sign of lessening. There is an increasingly important shift within total enrolments towards higher levels of education which have higher unit costs. The internal dynamics of educational expansion itself, therefore, imply growing outlays of financial resources. But this is not all. It is felt that within education, pre-primary, primary and lower secondary education should get more attention and higher priority relative to the higher levels than they have had in the past. This tendency is related, among others, to the objective of equality of educational opportunity. Thus, not only will a larger proportion of pupils be in the higher and more expensive levels of education, but the unit costs of the lower levels may increase, because of a trend towards more intensive and individualised teaching techniques.

Next to these pressures which will make for increasing financial outlays, there is also a fear that we are embarking on a period of increasing constraints. The past decade has seen a more rapid rise in educational expenditures than any other period in history. There is a fear that the good times cannot last. These fears are reinforced by the growing preoccupation of governments with the persisting inflationary tendencies in their economies. In addition, other social sectors are pressing for attention such as environmental problems, health, public transport, inner city problems, etc. Increasing proportions of educational expenditures have come from public budgets. Further increases on the scale of the past decade can only come from increased taxation, or a relative reduction in expenditures in other parts of the public sector, or from considerably increased private participation in the financing of education.

The wide variation in relative educational expenditures between countries make it clear that very much depends on priorities in policy goals and in the allocation of resources. The real problem seems to lie in the fact that goals have not been made sufficiently explicit and that we do not know how to be effective in pursuing the "new" goals because (as we demonstrated in earlier chapters and particularly in Chapter IX), our knowledge of the relationships between inputs and educational outputs is meagre. It is this simple truth which lies behind the emerging conviction that education will have to invest much more effort into development, the effective diffusion of innovations throughout the system, and the creation of a professionalised, and therefore more highly remunerated, teaching force which accepts responsibility for the continuing search for educational efficiency and effectiveness.

Given explicit educational policy goals and priorities, a "ceiling" to educational growth is more likely to be the consequence of a failure to promote the continuing improvements in the efficiency with which resources are used. It is this situation which accounts for the growing demands for "efficiency," "competition" and "management" in education. Such demands are usually seen as in conflict with the real purposes of education: quality and efficiency are seen as cat and dog. But this results, at least partly, from the fact that "quality" has been measured in terms of more expensive *inputs*. In the future the quality of education must be seen as an *output* which reflects the achievement of goals in terms of all the complexities with which society defines them. In this connection, it must be noted that present methods of educational finance usually offer very little incentive for efficiency, either in an economic or in a technological sense. During the recent very rapid expansion, educational technology has changed little, possibly less than any other economic sector. Methods of finance should offer greater incentives to technological and economic efficiency. For instance, there are few, if any, examples of a method of financing that provides any incentive whatsoever for a school or university to reduce the numbers of staff per student by, for example, substituting capital inputs for labour.

Increased participation of private financing could take two forms: a greater contribution by students and their families towards the real cost of their own education, and a greater contribution by the industrial sector to financing in education. Both these possibilities are often viewed with some scepticism. Reasons for this scepticism are grounded in the fact that for several decades the main increases in educational expenditure have come from public budgets and that this has been a clearly desired trend obtained in some countries after a long struggle. Moreover, there are few reasons to suppose that the private sector would, in the future, spontaneously be willing to make resources available on anything like the necessary scale, or with anything like the necessary regularity and security, to be other than a small addition to public expenditures. Any large-scale increase in contributions from industry might be made available that are unacceptable to educationists, to students and their families, or to the national political authorities. Present concern about the degree of industrial influence in university affairs is indicative of a wider unease. It is also unlikely that industry will offer very much support to the lower levels of education. The picture may change radically if a complete restructuring of post-compulsory schooling were to be introduced, along the lines of recurrent education, for example. This might create a very different relationship between industry and education than exists at present, which might also lead to mutually acceptable alternative financial arrangements.

We must add that there are many people, particularly in universities, who are equally alarmed by the dominant role of public finance in the educational and research sectors. They consider that such a reliance by universities on a single source of finance can pose a threat to academic freedom and independence without which no university can function properly. One of the big resource issues in some countries will be to devise systems of financing in which academic freedom is maintained, but in which there are safeguards on the use of public funds *and* incentives to increase efficiency.

The other possible source of private finance is a greater contribution from students and their families. It is generally, though not universally, admitted that such a policy is practicable only at the higher levels of education. The most convincing argument in favour of a larger share of the cost being borne by individuals is that, whatever the externalities of education, a large part of the benefits accrue to the individual. As we have amply demonstrated, there is a social class bias in educational opportunities in favour of upper socio-economic groups. Public expenditure thus represents a transfer of benefits, in effect very often a transfer from relatively poorer sections of society to richer, or potentially richer, people. This is, therefore, essentially an equity argument rather than an efficiency one, though it is often related to economic efficiency arguments on the grounds that it would give greater freedom of choice to students, and competition between the institutions for students would improve economic efficiency. Schemes that have been proposed and much debated include the "graduate tax" by which student loans are repaid over a graduate's working life that are either proportionate to or a definite percentage of personal income. Another interesting idea is the concept of a "voucher", a coupon with a prescribed purchasing power over a specified service. The key to the educational vouchers scheme is the distribution to all parents of vouchers exchangeable for education in any school, whether state or private, that satisfies minimum educational standards, the value of the voucher being related to some notion of the average costs of education of children of different ages. We shall have to refer to the specialised literature for a discussion of the pros and cons of these schemes. What should be said at this point is that, in spite of a considerable number of question marks that can and have been put forward both from the efficiency and equity points of view, these schemes have had at least the merit to look afresh at questions which will become more and more urgent in the years to come.

We must bring this brief discussion about resources for and financing of education to a close. We can summarise the main arguments as follows. There can be no conclusive evidence that ceilings are being reached with respect to the proportion of national income or total public expenditure devoted to education, because this depends clearly on the priorities within the societal goal structure and thus, in the final analysis, on the belief and value structure of our societies. However, what can be said is that, if rates of increase in educational expenditures continue at the pace observed during the past decade, alternative ways of finance may become a necessity in several countries. It would be wrong to discuss alternative educational financing schemes in isolation from societal and educational goals, and alternative educational strategies to reach these goals. There will undoubtedly be a strong tendency for the "quality versus efficieny" debate to gain in strength during coming years. At present, a rise in the "quality" of education is usually, in effect, equated with increased inputs. This unfortunately is usually the same as the definition of a decline in "efficiency". However, extreme care must be taken to engage in the right debate, concentrating on the right issues. This, once again, will depend on the goals society and education are moving towards. If countries wish, in the future, to put relatively more stress on social objectives, the criteria used in allocating resources and in measuring the *effectiveness* of education need to be adjusted accordingly. Obviously, whatever the goals of education, the economic and technological *efficiency* of the resources should be maximised. If it is recognised that the purpose of good management is to achieve objectives and not only to save resources, there is no reason why efficiency maximisation should be in conflict with the "real" goals of education.

In the above perspective the question of increased participation in educational financing of the private sector must also be viewed. This will probably only be possible and acceptable for all parties concerned if and when drastic changes are introduced in the relationship between educational span and active life, and between education and other sectors of society.

4. The Idea of Recurrent Education

If in this book we have presented a thesis, it is that the sequential process of quantitative educational growth cannot possibly continue indefinitely. We have shown that the principle of zero-correlation coupled with the belief in the economic and social efficacy of education results in a Sisyphean process of successive cycles of frustration at ever higher levels of educational attainment, reached after ever longer years of study. It is our contention that in many developed nations a point will soon be reached where this thesis will be felt and recognised, both by the individual and by governments. We have also asked ourselves the question whether educational policy goals should not put relatively less emphasis on the economic and social efficacy of education and relatively more on the critical and evaluative dimensions which it can convey to the individual. In short, less emphasis on "earning power" and more on "reasoning power." Although we have not advanced this proposition in mutually exclusive terms but rather in terms of relativities, it remains that such a shift in emphasis pre-supposes a change in the belief and value structure of society along the lines set out in section 2 above, and thus it assumes the problem solved. A chicken and egg problem — the interdependency between education and society — about which we have given our views in Chapter IV and in Chapter X.

Moreover, and we have also stressed that point in previous chapters, it remains true that for the time being more education increases the probability of the individual to benefit from upward social mobility. But it is our contention that this risks to be less and less the case while the sequential rat race continues its upward spiral. In the meantime the law of last entry only operates for the younger generations (those that are of school age), of the lower social classes, with the consequences as outlined in Chapters IX and X. However, the older generations do not even have this possibility — they have missed the boat and cannot hope to enter at all any more. This is, therefore, in the present circumstances an even more dramatic situation than for those who have at least the consolation that they will make it after all, education-wise that is.

Because we cannot hope to change the world overnight, but for all the above reasons at least, the only intermediate solution is to restructure post-compulsory education along recurrent lines, an idea we presented briefly in Chapter X. Let us set out the reasons for this proposition.

Before embarking on such a discussion, we must stress again not to confuse recurrent education with existing adult education schemes. Adult education, in the traditional sense, is a type of *informal* education embracing *any* kind of training, retraining, refresher course, etc. given in a variety of ways, such as evening classes, correspondence courses, on and off-the-job training, people's universities, etc. and usually of a *part-time* nature. Recurrent education is a fully integrated combination of formal and non-formal education for the juvenile as well as for adults who want to resume their education, interrupted earlier for a variety of reasons. It follows that, whereas adult education is an addition to the present educational structure without in any way changing it, recurrent education consistutes a break with the institutional and pedagogical structures of present education. However, if these two types of education differ greatly from one another, they are by no means mutually exclusive. The introduction of recurrent education would not in any way detract from the value of adult education schemes. Indeed, the two should and could be linked and even, as much as possible, merged into one consistent and complementary system.

In its purely educational objectives, recurrent education does not necessarily differ much from present forms of formal education. Where it does differ is in its primary social objectives which, broadly speaking, are equity, occupational flexibility, and integration of education with active life. We maintain that recurrent education is more likely to attain these three objectives than the present educational structure. The arguments against recurrent education could be based either on the belief that these objectives are already being satisfactorily achieved with present educational facilities, or on the conviction that these objectives will never be achieved, whatever the system of education.

With regard to the objective of *equity*, recurrent education has a dual role to play — first, to compensate for the deficiencies of past education, and second, to give the individual a further chance to take advantage of educational opportunities. The accelerated expansion of education over the last 15 years has resulted in greatly widening the gap between successive generations, even between those who are now in their late twenties or early thirties on the one hand, and the younger generation on the other. The first role of recurrent education, a temporary one, would be to narrow this gap by offering the older generation the educational opportunity it did not have earlier. The other role is of a permanent nature and constitutes the very essence of the new scheme. It has to do with the fact that motivation for study does not always coincide with the present age-span for schooling. Such motivation may come later in life and may result from different causes, such as the challenges and demands of the working environment, the realisation of the handicap which a poor education puts in the way of building up a career, a desire to develop a hitherto unexploited intellectual potential, or simply a thirst for knowledge as a means of self-fulfilment. It is not unreasonable to assume that more mature people may develop a motivation for education which they did not have at a young age. A system of recurrent education would enable them to resume education at the point at which it was interrupted. It remains to be seen whether priority should be given to the first or the second of these two functions, and how such priority would affect the programmes and recruitment. These may be quite different for each of the two functions. Spreading educational opportunity over a longer age-span would diminish the pressure on the traditional school system, particularly on higher education, without diminishing educational opportunity. No doubt the risk that, given the chance of returning to school at some future date, too many pupils would leave earlier than they otherwise might, and that those early leavers would later feel least motivated to resume their education, cannot be disregarded. This risk may diminish once recurrent education has become the general educational strategy, in particular, once the structures and programmes of secondary and higher education are suitably adapted to it, and an active recruitment policy is in operation.

The second major objective of recurrent education is to ensure effective interaction between education and the socio-economic sector. Education leads to a certificate or a diploma which serves as an entrance ticket to the labour market, but the present educational system is not very flexible, i.e., sensitive to changes occurring in the labour market, at least not in the short run. But these changes are bound to become more marked and more frequent with the acceleration of technological progress. As a result, there will be an even greater need than at present for a flexible educational system capable of adapting itself at short notice to the exigencies of technological change and of offering the right kind of training at the right time to the right people. Though the remedy may lie, partly, in a rethinking of the content and objectives of present forms of education, it lies mainly in a flexible system of recurrent education, aimed not only at training people in new techniques, but also at retraining those whose skills become inadequate to cope with constantly changing techniques.

Let us finally turn to the objective of integration. With the steep increase in enrolments and the prolongation of compulsory schooling and voluntary staying on, the dichotomy between the educational sector and other sectors of human activity, and between the educational span and the active working life of the individual has become so marked as to raise serious social problems. Education is becoming a powerful quasi-autonomous force of social and cultural criticism and is building up a claim for an active say in the shaping of society. But we are not concerned here with the conflict which this evolution creates between those who are clamouring for change and those who have an interest in maintaining a socio-economic structure safeguarded by an educational system which respects established values and cherishes the socio-cultural traditions on which their acceptance by society rests. Rather are we concerned with the values of the young generation as opposed to those which it finds on entering active working life. Because of the increasing length of schooling, most young people have developed their personality and acquired a set of values by the time they leave the educational system. The values they find when entering "active life" are very different from those they have formed during their educational period. The former are most concretely embodied in the socio-economic institutions within which they have to exert their activity. The danger resulting from this dichotomy is perhaps not so much the clash between these two sets of values — though the events of the past few years may give rise to some preoccupations with regard to such a possibility — as the growing irrelevance of one system to the other and, eventually, a growing gap between the younger and older generations, and between those who administer and those who are being administered.

In a different context, there is the problem of the desirability of further expanding the traditional system of education. At present, the arguments against extending the educational period for an ever-growing proportion of the school-age population centre largely around the material possibilities of a further expansion of the educational system. The pressure, notably on higher education, has become so great that, even in countries where access to higher education was traditionally opened to all those who had successfully completed the appropriate secondary level, restrictive policies, such as *numerus fixus or numerus clausus*, had to be introduced or are being seriously considered. However, even if resources would be virtually unlimited, it may be seriously doubted whether full enrolment of the population in, say, the 4-24 age-group would be desirable. It is this question of desirability — related to our discussion on the two sets of values and particularly of course to our thesis of the Sisyphean process of successive cycles of frustration implicit in a sequential educational structure — which is likely to become the main issue in future discussions on the expansion of education.

The most immediate and tangible effect of recurrent education would lie in the domain of occupational structures and career perspectives. The overall influence of education on the life pattern and career prospects of the individual could be profoundly altered by the combination of job experience and later education which recurrent education provides. But in all respects, recurrent education appears to be the only educational strategy which offers real possibilities of solving the dilemmas and paradoxes which we have touched upon in the previous chapters. There are obviously a certain number of serious problems which must be faced when one starts to take the idea of recurrent education seriously. We will review some of them.

There is first of all the question of "late" versus "early" education. It will be clear that a necessary precondition for recurrent education to be at all successful is that the necessary achievement level has been reached for take-off into higher levels of education. Without such an essential basis the individual simply could not benefit from further education. This implies that, *for certain social groups*, pre-school education programmes and compensatory education (as described in Chapter X) are a prerequisite for recurrent education and not a substitute. This also implies that the arguments in favour of postponing further education (after the basic period of 10 to 12 years) to a later age do not necessarily plead against "early learning." In this connection, we must turn again to the problem of the relative influence on educational achievement of home and social environment, on the one hand, and of "school factors" on the other. Evidence has shown that the former looses in relative influence as children grow up, but hardly any research has as yet been done on the effect of these two sets of factors upon the educational performance of adults. However, we know that a strong motivation for learning can arise at a later age, especially in cases where the traditional kind of education limits the career prospects of the individual. Observations made on current adult education schemes have shown the strong influence of the peer group, in this case primarily the occupational milieu, on motivations and expectations of adults. Thus, the crucial role of *home environment* in the case of "early" education is assumed in "late" education of the adult by his broader *social environment*, especially his *work environment*. This shift may very well plead in favour of recurrent education, although it is only fair to admit that little is known about the implied inter-relationships.

A second problem is related to the institutional and pedagogical structures of education. Because of its objectives and its clientele, recurrent education cannot be organised on the models of existing secondary, higher or adult education schemes. Its organisation must respond to the needs of a clientele whose initial motivation to resume education is high, but whose demands and expectations are of many different kinds; whose former learning experience will vary within a wide range; and whose home and neighbourhood environments, also very diverse, will affect their learning achievement in a way which is very different from what we now know about the impact of this factor on learning. What is clear is that recurrent education cannot be organised on a strict year and grade basis; its recipients must be able to take up and to leave studies whenever their situation allows or demands it. They must also be able to progress at different rates in different subjects, and to choose their subjects according to their needs and their tastes. This probably implies dropping the stringent condition of full-time courses. The programmes offered should *also* include part-time variants in order to increase the flexibility of the proposed scheme and to serve as a first step towards transforming existing adult educational programmes for integration into recurrent education. These various requirements have led to the idea of "capitalisable units of education," the *unités capitalisables*, which have been tried out on a limited scale in France. In this system, students acquire credit points for every "unit" of education which they have acquired, and combinations of such units may entitle them to admission to other educational institutions at a higher level. The system allows students to interrupt their education and resume it at some later date in accordance with their particular situation. There must, of course, be a minimum of organisational coherence, and the knowledge acquired by unit credits a long time ago may have to be "refreshed" before the student can resume his education at the point at which he interrupted it.

The introduction of "learning blocks" of this nature becomes even more important when a close relationship with adult education schemes is to be established. The idea of recurrent education is not in conflict with that of adult education; indeed, the two should and could be linked together and complement each other to fulfil a similar role. The end objective would be to conceive both as *one system* differing only in the way in which education is given — full-time courses on the one hand, part-time courses during the day or evening, during the weekend, during the vacation, etc. on the other. This reinforces the necessity to switch over to the concept of "capitalisable units" for an integrated system of full-time and part-time education.

The introduction of recurrent education may require new types of organisation of employment allowing for periods of work to alternate with periods of study. No adult education scheme has, as yet, and to that degree, had to face the problem of such institutionalised alternating periods. The organisational, legal and social problems created by such institutionalised alternating periods will have to be examined carefully.

Finally, as far as financing is concerned, the question that comes immediately to mind is whether recurrent education would be more costly than traditional education. There is, of course, no simple answer to this question. The cost of traditional education is bound to increase in the future, and in this respect, recurrent education would at least reduce the waste of time and resources in that it would enable those with low motivation or those who, for whatever reason, perform badly to leave the educational system with the idea at the back of their minds that they could always return to it when they are more strongly motivated . On the other hand, it should be borne in mind that the earnings foregone by adults returning to education are higher than those of young people and that adults can rarely count on any financial help from their family; on the contrary, most of them will have to support a family and will have contracted obligations and adopted a way of life which cannot be easily changed. These considerations would make for increased costs.

The financial aspects become still more complex when the concept of educational units is brought into the picture, because this concept calls for a possibly costly reorganisation of secondary, higher and adult education. The balance between these various factors will have to be established for each specific case in terms of probabilities. What will be needed is cost - effectiveness analyses of the various alternatives taking account of their impact both on education as a whole and on economic and social activity. A particular aspect which needs to be studied in this context is the unit cost of recurrent education as compared to that of traditional education. Another important question is whether, and if so to what extent, the recipient of recurrent education should contribute to its cost. Such contributions might be facilitated by loans or insurance schemes. Any financial help might vary in accordance with the age, family responsibilities and income of the recipient. And if we accept the principle that everyone has a right to, say, 16 years of full-time education, 10 or 12 of them to be taken between the ages of 6 and 16-18, and the rest later, and that this amount of education should be subsidised fully or partly, it is clear that those who have exhausted the ration of 16 years and who want to continue their education would have to pay their own way. In their case, part-time education may prove a suitable solution. This is one more reason why recurrent education should comprise a judicious mixture of part-time and full-time courses.

5. Plenty of Room at the Top?

When changing priorities in educational policy goal structures are discussed, many existing educational practices are questioned. However, the sequential nature of the educational process is hardly ever put into question. A typical example is the current debate about equality of educational opportunity and the envisaged educational changes in view of its realisation. The goal of equality of educational opportunity is of course a noble goal to be pursued. And even if it were not noble, this would not change its priority status, because the bulk of the population wants it for its children. But once again, this perfectly legitimate desire to give to all children their fair share of the educational cake is combined with the belief that education and education alone is the key to upward social mobility. This has never been entirely the case and will become less and less true in the future. But in as far as education does play a perceived role in the individual's economic and social status, this results in a rat race which we have explained through the principle of zero-correlation and the law of last entry.

Why is this so? The frustrations in job expectations can be explained by the fact that the occupational structure of the labour force changes in function of economic and technological forces much more than by what happens in the educational system, and also by the fact that there exists a built-in discrimination in our societies, which is reflected in hiring and firing practices on the labour market according to criteria which are not purely educational...! Of these two, the more important constraint is of course the existence of an occupational structure, whether we like it or not. There simply is not enough room at the top for the people that come streaming out of the educational pipeline in increasing numbers and with increasingly high educational qualifications. This in turn induces them to maintain an "educational differential" and to continue their studies for longer and longer periods.

The only way to bring this rat race to a halt, while increasing educational opportunities in line with the motivation of the individual, and in line with job opportunities, is recurrent education. This will not give us the best of times and it will not be the spring of hope. It simply is the best solution in the circumstances. But this solution is already quite revolutionary. All we can say in the end is that countries have the educational system they deserve. It is about time people realise the implications of this truism.

References

Chapter I

Anderson, C. Arnold (1961), "A Skeptical Note on Education and Mobility," in Halsey, Floud and Anderson, *Education, Economy and Society*, The Free Press of Glencoe, New York.

Coleman, J. *et al.* (1966), *Equality of Educational Opportunity*, U.S. Office of Education, Washington.

Emmerij, L. and Jallade, J.P. (1970), *Occupational and Educational Structures of the Labour Force and Levels of Economic Development*, OECD, Paris.

Halsey, A.H. (1961), *Ability and Educational Opportunity*, OECD, Paris.

Hansen, W.L. and Weisbrod, B.A. (1969), *Benefits, Costs and Finance of Public Higher Education*, Markham Publishing Company, Chicago.

Meade, J.E., (1964), *Efficiency, Equality and the Ownership of Property*, Allen and Unwin, London.

Nam, C. (1971), *Group Disparities in Educational Participation*, OECD, Paris.

Reder, M.W. (1969), "A Partial Survey of the Theory of Income Size Distribution," in L. Soltow (ed.), *Six Papers on the Size Distribution of Wealth and Income, Studies in Income and Wealth, No. 33*, National Bureau of Economic Research, New York.

Svennilson, I., Edding, F. and Elvin, L. (1962), *Targets for Education in Europe in 1970*, OECD, Paris.

Williams, G. (1971), "Educational Policies, Plans and Forecasts during the Nineteen-Sixties and -Seventies," in *The Development of Educational Planning*, OECD, Paris.

Chapter II

Callahan, R.E. (1962), *Education and the Cult of Efficiency*, University of Chicago Press, Chicago and London.

Cousin, V. (1837), *De l'Instruction Publique en Hollande*, F.G. Levrault, Librairie-Editeur, Paris, Strasbourg.

Denison, E.F. (1962), *The Sources of Economic Growth in the United States and the Alternatives Before Us*, Committee for Economic Development, Washington, D.C.

Emmerij, L. (1969), "Effects of Examinations on the Economy," in *The World Yearbook of Education 1969, Examinations*, Evans Brothers, London.

Ivey, D.G. (1968), "The Nonscience of Education," *The Science Teacher*, Vol. 35, March 1968.
Kristensen, T. (1962), in *Policy Conference on Economic Growth and Investment in Education*, OECD, Paris.
Vaizey, J. (1963), "The Role of Education in Economic Development," in *Planning Education for Economic and Social Development*, OECD, Paris.

Chapter III

Dubin, R. (1967), *The Teaching-Learning Paradox*, University of Oregon. Centre for the Advanced Study of Educational Administration, Eugene, Oregon.
Dubin, R. (1968), *The Medium May Be Related to the Message*, University of Oregon, Centre for the Advanced Study of Educational Administration, Eugene, Oregon.
Nam, C. (1971), *Group Disparities in Educational Participation*, OECD, Paris.

Chapter IV

Myrdal, G. (1968), *Asian Drama — An Enquiry into the Poverty of Nations*, Penguin Books, Harmondsworth, Middx.

Chapter V

Blaug, M. (1967), "Approaches to Educational Planning," *Economic Journal*, July.
OECD (1967), *Educational Policy and Planning: Netherlands*, Paris.
Parnes, H.S. (1963), "Manpower Analysis in Educational Planning," in *Planning Education for Economic and Social Development*, OECD, Paris.
Robbins Report on Higher Education (1963), HMSO, London.
UNESCO (1967), *Educational Planning in the U.S.S.R.*, Paris.
The World Year Book of Education 1967 — Educational Planning (1967), Evans Brothers, London.

Chapter VI

Hollister, R. (1966), *A Technical Evaluation of the First Phase of the Mediterranean Regional Project*, OECD, Paris.
OECD (1967), *Methods and Statistical Needs for Educational Planning*, Paris.
Parnes, H.S. (1962), *Forecasting Educational Needs for Economic and Social Development*, OECD, Paris.
Svennilson, I., Edding, F. and Elvin, L. (1962), *Targets for Education in Europe in 1970*, OECD, Paris.

Chapter VII

Armitage, P., Smith, C. and Alper, P. (1969), *Decision Models for Educational Planning* Allen Lane The Penguin Press, London.

Williams, G. (1971), "Educational Policies, Plans and Forecasts During the Nineteen-Sixties and -Seventies," in *The Development of Educational Planning*, OECD, Paris.

Chapter VIII

Adelman, I. (1966), "A Linear Programming Model of Educational Planning: A Case Study of Argentina," in I. Adelman and E. Thorbecke (eds.), *The Theory and Design of Economic Development*, Johns Hopkins Press, Baltimore.

Bénard, J. (1966), "Un Modèle d'Affectation Optimale des Ressources entre l'Economie et le Système Educatif," in Bulletin du CEPREL, No. 6, Paris, July 1966. An English summary of this model was published in *Mathematical Models in Educational Planning*, OECD, Paris.

Benveniste, G. (1968), "Towards a Sociology of National Development Planning," *Journal of Developing Areas*, Vol. 3, 1.

Bombach, G. (1964), "Long-term Requirements for Qualified Manpower in Relation to Economic Growth," in S.E. Harris (ed.), *Economic Aspects of Higher Education*, OECD, Paris.

Bowles, S. (1967), "The Efficient Allocation of Resources in Education," *Quarterly Journal of Economics*, May.

Churchman, X. and Schainblatt, X. (1965), "The Researcher and the Manager: A Dialectic of Implementation, " *Management Science*, Vol. II, 4, February.

Coombs, P.H. (1968), *What is Educational Planning*, UNESCO, Paris.

Habermas, J. (1966), "Verwissenschaftliche Politik in demokratischer Gesellschaft," in H. Krauch *et al.* (eds.), *Forschungsplanung*, Munich/Vienna.

Moser, C. and Redfern, P. (1965), "Education and Manpower: Some Current Research," in D.M. Berners Lee (ed.), *Models for Decision*, English Universities Press, London.

Thonstad, T. (1967), "A Mathematical Model of the Norwegian Educational System," in *Mathematical Models in Educational Planning*, OECD, Paris.

Tinbergen, J. (1967), *Development Planning*, World University Library, Weidenfeld and Nicolson, London.

Chapter IX

Bloom, B.S. (1970), "Learning for Mastery," in Bloom, Hastings and Madaus (eds.), *Formative and Summative Evaluation of Student Learning*, McGraw-Hill, New York.

Bourdieu, P. and Passeron, J.C. (1964), *Les Héritiers, Les Etudiants et la Culture*, Editions de Minuit, Paris.

Douglas, J.W.B. (1968), *All Our Future*, MacGibbon, London.

Girard, A. and Bastide, H. (1969), "Orientation et Sélection Scolaires: Cinq Années d'une Promotion," *Population*, Jan.-Feb. and March-April 1969.

Girod, R. and Tofigh, F. (1965), "Family Background and Incomes, School Career and Social Mobility of Young Males of Working Class Origin," *Acta Sociologica*, Vol. 9, fasc. 1-2.

Hansen, W.L., Weisbrod, B.A. and Scanlon, (1970), Does Schooling Really Count?," *American Economic Review*, March.
Himmelweit, H. and Swift, B. (1969), "A Model for the Understanding of School as a Socializing Agent," in Mussen (ed.), *New Directions in Developmental Psychology*, New York.
Husén, T. (1967), *International Study of Achievement in Mathematics*, John Wiley, New York.
Husén, T. (1969), *Talent, Opportunity and Career*, Almqvist and Wiksell, Stockholm.
Jensen, A. (1969), "How Much Can We Boost I.Q. and Scholastic Achievement?," *Harvard Educational Review*, Winter.
Plowden Report (1967), *Children and their Primary Schools*, A Report of the Central Advisory Council for Education (England), HMSO, London.
Weiss, R. (1969), "The Effect of Education on the Earnings of Blacks and Whites," Discussion Paper 14, Program of Regional and Urban Economics, Harvard University.
Wiseman, S. (1964), *Education and Environment*, University Press, Manchester.

Chapter X

Bourdieu, P. and Passeron, J.C. (1970), *La Reproduction, Elements pour une Théorie du Système d'Enseignement*, Editions de Minuit, Paris.
Cohen, D.K. (1969), "Policy for the Public Schools: Compensation and Integration," in *Equal Educational Opportunity, Harvard Educational Review*, Harvard University Press, Cambridge, Mass.
Fantini, M. and Weinstein, G. (1968), *The Disadvantaged: Challenge to Education*, Harper and Row, New York.
Froomkin, J. and Dugan, D. (eds.), (1969), "Inequality: Studies in Elementary and Secondary Education," *Planning Paper 69.2*, U.S. Office of Education, Washington D.C. See papers by Froomkin and Piccariello.
Little, A. and Smith, G. (1971), *Strategies of Compensation: A Review of Educational Projects for the Disadvantaged in the United States*, OECD, Paris.
Marklund, S. (1969), "School Organisation, School Location and Student Achievement," *International Review of Education*, 15, pp. 295—320.

Chapter XI

Schwarz, B. (1970), *SOM — A Simulation Model of the Educational System*, OECD, Paris.
OECD (1971), *The Use of Simulation Models in Educational Planning, A Critical Evaluation of SOM*, Paris.

Chapter XII

Blaug, M. (1970), *An Introduction to the Economics of Education*, Allen Lane The Penguin Press, London.

Harman, W. (1972), "Changing United States Society: Implications for Schools," in *Alternative Educational Futures in the United States and in Europe: Methods, Issues and Policy Relevance*, OECD, Paris.
Hutchins, R.M. (1968), *The Learning Society*, Praeger, New York.
Michael, D.N. (1968), *The Unprepared Society*, Basic Books, New York.
Mumford, L. (1965), "Technics and the Nature of Man," *Nature*, December 4, pp. 923—928.

Subject Index

Author Index